Routledge Revivals

UK Banking Supervision

UK Banking Supervision (1986) draws attention to some of the main problems, theoretical and practical, associated with banking supervision in the UK. It sets out to introduce and analyse the UK bank supervisory process, and it raises some important questions. The main emphasis is on the process and historical context of supervisory development and some of the most pressing problems engendered by supervision.

UK Banking Supervision

Evolution, Practice and Issues

Edited by

Edward P.M. Gardener

Routledge
Taylor & Francis Group
Routledge Revivals

First published in 1986
by Allen & Unwin (Publishers) Ltd

This edition first published in 2026 by Routledge
4 Park Square, Milton Park, Abingdon, Oxon, OX14 4RN

and by Routledge
605 Third Avenue, New York, NY 10017

Routledge is an imprint of the Taylor & Francis Group, an informa business

Publisher's Note
The publisher has gone to great lengths to ensure the quality of this reprint but points out that some imperfections in the original copies may be apparent.

Disclaimer
The publisher has made every effort to trace copyright holders and welcomes correspondence from those they have been unable to contact.

A Library of Congress record exists under LCCN: 85015717

ISBN: 978-1-041-34278-6 (hbk)
ISBN: 978-1-003-79196-6 (ebk)
ISBN: 978-1-041-34280-9 (pbk)

Book DOI 10.4324/9781003791966

UK Banking Supervision

Evolution, Practice and Issues

Edited by

Edward P. M. Gardener

University College of North Wales

London
ALLEN & UNWIN
Boston Sydney

Allen & Unwin (Publishers) Ltd,
40 Museum Street, London WC1A 1LU, UK

Allen & Unwin (Publishers) Ltd,
Park Lane, Hemel Hempstead, Herts HP2 4TE, UK

Allen & Unwin, Inc.,
8 Winchester Place, Winchester, Mass. 01890, USA

Allen & Unwin (Australia) Ltd,
8 Napier Street, North Sydney, NSW 2060, Australia

First published in 1986

British Library Cataloguing in Publication Data

Gardener, Edward P. M.
UK banking supervision : evolution, practice
and issues.— (Studies in financial institutions
and markets; 2)
1. Banks and banking – Great Britain – State supervision
I. Title II. Series
332.1'0941 HG1778.G7
ISBN 0-04-332102-X

Library of Congress Cataloging-in-Publication Data

UK banking supervision.
(Studies in financial institutions and markets ; 2)
Includes index.
1. Banks and banking – Great Britain – State supervision
Addresses, essays, lectures. I. Gardener,
Edward P. M. II. Series.
HG1778.G7U37 1986 332.1'0941 85-15717
ISBN 0-04-332102-X (alk. paper)

Set in 10 on 11 point Plantin by Grove Graphics, Tring
and printed in Great Britain by Billing and Son Ltd, London and Worcester

Contents

D Capital Adequacy

E Deposit Insurance

Preface

The 1970s marked a watershed for British banks and their regulatory authorities, particularly the Bank of England. Rapidly escalating inflation, high and volatile interest rates, fierce competition, and growing risks and crises were among the factors which evidenced the growing fragility of the financial system. This environment of risks and risk-taking was not unique to Britain's financial institutions and markets. Many other developed banking systems, including the international banking system, had started to come under severe pressure. The world was changing. Comparative stability had given way to a new era of turbulence in world banking and financial systems.

In late 1973, the British banking system faced its severest test in modern history – the so-called fringe (or secondary) banking crisis. The Bank of England and the core banks responded quickly to contain the crisis. One immediate result of these experiences was the realization that more comprehensive prudential regulation and bank supervision were necessary consequences of the new and evolving bank markets. Regulation covers legal and administrative measures which apply to all banks. Supervision is a process of monitoring individual banks to ensure that they obey regulations and do not behave imprudently. Important new supervisory measures were initiated in 1974. Throughout the 1970s, increasing concern and resources were directed towards bank supervision in the UK. The Johnson Matthey affair in the Autumn of 1984 and the bank's 'rescue' by the Bank of England were a timely reminder of the challenges faced by modern supervisors.

Alongside the new risks and the trauma of crisis, other forces were also operating to help shape the rapid growth of UK bank supervision. These included the EEC movement towards the harmonization of bank regulation and a growing acceptance by governments of the consumerism philosophy. As the bank supervisory function has grown, however, economists have continued to argue generally for less regulation. Market discipline, the 'unseen hand' of the market, is favoured by many economists as a more efficient regulator of bank resource decisions than legal prescriptions. Little wonder, then, that bank supervision has already produced a host of theoretical and practical problems. These problems are compounded in that supervision is often the partial product of political and social forces, besides economic and legal influences. In the UK, the more institutional problems of banking supervision have been largely ignored by mainstream economists.

This book draws attention to some of the main problems – theoretical and practical – associated with banking supervision in the UK. It sets out to introduce and analyse the UK bank supervisory process, and it raises some important questions. The main emphasis is on the process and historical context of supervisory development, and some of the most pressing problems engendered by supervision. One question addressed early on in the book is whether supervision is necessary; much of the supervisory debate has tended to accept supervision as a necessary fact of life. Attention is then directed at methods and styles of supervision. At the same time, several associated issues are raised.

Besides documenting related developments, this book attempts to identify and explore some of the fundamental questions about supervision. Nevertheless, the book is still very much selective, rather than comprehensive. Areas like international banking supervision, capital adequacy and competition could never be covered comprehensively in one volume. With these constraints in mind, the emphasis of the book is on domestic banking supervision. The objective is to explain and consider some of the distinguishing features of UK bank supervision. This also provides the background for a more detailed study of selected aspects of important problems, like capital adequacy and deposit insurance.

This text is not intended to be any kind of reference book or supervisory manual. It does not attempt to detail the minutiae of the UK supervisory process. An excellent account of the purely institutional structure and development of the UK supervisory system is contained in *The Management and Regulation of Banks* by John Cooper referred to on several occasions in Part A. In one sense, this collection may be seen as a complement to John Cooper's study. It has a different objective, and this is reflected in the scope of the collection of readings. Nevertheless, some background to the UK system and the general process of supervision is provided in Part A. These four opening papers by the editor are designed to set the scene for the later readings, besides raising and discussing some matters not covered elsewhere in the book.

The selection of readings in this book was made on the basis of several criteria. One rather obvious criterion was that the contributors should either be distinguished practitioners or serious students of supervision. Some emerging UK supervisory problems also occur in other countries, and they are much better documented and more rigorously debated in these countries. This has led to a number of papers in the book from contributors abroad. Although the book is designed to have a UK bias, it seemed unwise to ignore the realities of the market. Marco Onado was invited to write Chapter 9, and the whole of Section E is contributed by distinguished US scholars.

Another criterion was that the contributions should be current and topical. Again, this requirement is obvious enough. A final criterion was to introduce ideas and perspectives which may not be generally available to the wider audience sought by this collection. On the one hand, this has led to several especially commissioned papers, and some papers not previously published. On the other hand, it has led to invited papers which introduce perspectives from other economic fields and different branches of social science. Examples include Jane Sargent's paper in Chapter 7 and Les Metcalfe's contribution in Chapter 8.

This book is intended for a wide audience. At the most general level, the interested layman and social scientists from other disciplines should find it of some interest. British banks, banks operating in the UK and bank supervisors generally will find the collection both informative and, hopefully, provoking. Bankers in countries other than the UK should also find the book of interest. With the growing internationalization of banks and the increasing globalization of many banking markets, knowledge of the practice and issues associated with supervision in different countries becomes more relevant. Students of banking, monetary theory and financial economics will find that the book gives some new perspectives and offers avenues for further research. There has been a marked tendency to segment academic sub-disciplines in recent years. This has been one result of increased specialization. Banking supervision and regulation generally are areas which benefit from a greater cross-fertilization of ideas. Students of applied economics in banking and finance should find that this book improves their understanding of the regulatory forces that help shape financial systems.

The book is divided into five main sections as follows:

Part A Supervision – a Perspective
Part B Evolution and Practice
Part C Related Issues
Part D Capital Adequacy
Part E Deposit Insurance

Part A by the editor provides a general background to regulation in general and UK bank supervision in particular. It sets the scene for the rest of the book. Part B comprises four invited papers on different aspects of the growth and operation of supervision in the UK. The remaining three sections contain three papers apiece. Part C looks generally at selected areas, like competition and the problems associated with setting supervisory objectives. Parts D and E are devoted to specialist considerations of two fundamental areas of supervision, capital adequacy and deposit insurance. A great deal of US academic literature has grown around these areas, but they have not been so rigorously debated in the UK. Nevertheless, they are matters of topical concern, and they have stimulated increasing interest and debate.

Several acknowledgements are in order. First, to all the contributors who allowed me to present their views. All the copyright holders must also be thanked for allowing the reprint of these articles. It should be added that there is no implication that a contributor necessarily supports or opposes the views of another in this volume. In this sense, each paper is mutually exclusive of the others in the book. I am grateful to Jack Revell who stayed with the idea of this book and encouraged its completion. His contribution to this whole academic area is particularly great. At the same time I thank the publishers George Allen & Unwin who both fostered the project and provided a strong 'devil's advocate' role. I must also thank my secretary, Sue Potter, who toiled through the many drafts of the manuscripts. Jill Anker also provided considerable help in the typing. Finally, I must thank my wife, Anne Christine, and our children – Michael, Emma and John – for their continual support. Any errors or omissions are assumed, of course, by the editor.

Institute of European Finance
University College of North Wales
November 1984

Edward P. M. Gardener

PART A

Supervision – a Perspective

This opening collection of four papers sets out to provide a perspective on bank supervision in general, and UK supervision in particular. The starting point is a survey of some of the major structural changes and banking risks which emerged in the 1960s and 1970s. These were part of the general chain of events that helped lead up to the celebrated fringe (or secondary) banking crisis in Britain. It was these experiences which exposed the inadequacy of the 'old-style' Bank of England supervision, and thereby helped to shape the current UK approach. Chapters 2 and 3 examine supervision in the context of regulation generally, and explore some major supervisory conflicts and issues. Many of these areas are developed further in the specialist contributions which begin in Chapter 5. Chapter 4 finally sets the scene by outlining the evolution and structure of banking supervision in the UK.

1 Banking Crises and Risks

Some time during the 1970s the longest period of continuity in economic history came to an end. At some time during the last ten years we moved into turbulence.
Peter F. Drucker (1980), *Management in Turbulent Times* (London: Heinemann).

Introduction

A marked and disturbing feature of the 1970s and early 1980s has been the periodic emergence of problems, failures and crises in many different banking systems worldwide. The world banking system as well has experienced severe and continuing tests of its resilience. British bankers at the start of the 1970s found themselves at the dawn of a new epoch characterized ominously by increasing risks and uncertainties. Instability had replaced the previous ordered pattern of events. The banking crises and new banking risks that were spawned stimulated – and in many instances demanded – growing interest in banking prudence and its supervision.

Subsequent UK supervisory developments were in large measure a reaction to such pressures. Later contributions will explore these developments, together with their historical context and associated issues, in some detail. Our first task, however, must be to set the scene for a study of the supervisory function in general, and UK supervision in particular. To this end, our journey starts off with a consideration of those developments which helped lead up to the phenomenon of modern banking crises and the emergence of potentially greater risk exposures for banks. Although there were certainly other important forces at work in the development of UK supervision, increasing risk in the system was probably the single most important influence.

Background to Crises

Changes in the banking system during the 1960s

The British banking system is currently living through a period of marked, some would emphasize dramatic, change. Over the past twenty years or so many important developments emerged which radically transformed UK and world banking markets. The process continues today, and no one knows where it will end. Faced with keener competition, increased opportunities and threats, and growing uncertainty, British banks have responded in many ways. New products and more complex forms of banking organization have appeared. Sophisticated management skills and new technology are currently being harnessed. Theories that did not recognize banks as individual, adaptive firms in their own right, and the shorter-term, often harsh realities of the market, illustrated the widening gap between academics and practitioners. At the same time, some traditional banking and regulatory policies became increasingly suspect under the pressures of innovation, rapid change and growth.

The more stable and protected pre-1960 days of British banking are probably now gone forever. From the late 1950s in the UK, the political and economic climate was more encouraging towards new financial enterprises. The Conservative government of the day sought to restore the economy towards normality after the pressures of wartime and postwar restrictions. Credit controls were eased, for example, and borrowing regulation through the Capital Issues Committee finished. Dismantling these kinds of barriers, coupled with a rising standard of living, opened up the way for new and more aggressive profit-seeking enterprises in the UK financial sector. Competition began to increase and some of the newer, smaller financial operators failed; others did not remain very long in business. The new face of British banking had started to emerge. Subsequent events virtually transformed the traditional and cosy UK banking market.

The 1960s developed as a period of major structural innovations in the UK banking and financial system. These brought with them new opportunities and risks. One of the most significant structural developments was the growth of the so-called secondary banking system, together with its associated money markets, or parallel money markets. A part of this new secondary banking system – the so-called fringe – later became a source of the biggest upheaval in modern British banking. Although it is very difficult to classify them neatly because of their wide-ranging activities, the rapidly growing secondary banks had several distinguishing features. One common element was that they did not compete directly with the clearing banks – the deposit or primary banks – for payments transmission business. The secondary banks dealt mainly in the wholesale side of banking where the deposits and loans are typically for large amounts. Most of their deposit and lending business was for a fixed maturity (term deposits and term lending) and in foreign currencies. Agreements on rates between secondary banks were rare. Competition for business was fierce and this part of the banking sector grew rapidly.

In the present context, potential confusion has arisen over the term 'secondary banking', which is still widely used in the UK banking literature. For example, the expression secondary banking crisis is often used to describe the 1973–5 crisis sparked off by the troubles of the fringe banks. The fringe banks, however, were only a small part of the secondary banking system. In order to avoid this confusion, Revell (1975, p. 7) prefers to drop the use of the term secondary banking. He refers to the fringe banking crisis in order to describe the troubles of 1973–5. In this more specific use of terms, a fringe operator is one who engages in more risky business within any sector of the financial system. The original sense of the term secondary banking is rendered by terms like 'wholesale banking' or 'non-deposit banking'. We shall adopt this convention, and the term wholesale banking is now a common one in the UK banking literature. In adopting this convention, however, it would be as well to emphasize that fringe banks and the predominantly wholesale banking sector also engaged in some retail banking activities.

The phenomenal growth of the wholesale banks and their new mix of business militated against the development of suitable guidelines for prudential management. A new and virtually unexperienced risk : return trade-off problem had arisen for bankers and nobody knew the rules. Although more prudent bankers accepted that the maturity matching of deposit and loan maturities was the basic principle of wholesale banking, the extent of permissible maturity unmatching, the usual banking practice, was not obvious or well researched. The rules of traditional, fractional-reserve banking had developed through many decades of trial and error. Wholesale banking reached early maturity without the benefits of any such tested rules. In retrospect, there had to be a price paid for such a meteoric and largely unimpeded growth.

The parallel – now also more usually called wholesale – money markets evolved alongside the new wholesale banking system and contributed in large measure to its growth. Just as the discount market was the traditional money market of the primary banks, so the parallel markets emerged as the money markets of the fast-growing wholesale banks. The birth of these new markets can be traced back to 1955 when UK local authorities were no longer able to borrow at will from the Public Works Loan Board. At a time of apparent high interest rates, local authority treasurers went out to secure short-term, or temporary, money in the market. Banks began to bid for deposits to on-lend to local authorities, and the market in local authority deposits had begun. In 1957 we saw the emergence of the eurodollar market. The 1960s witnessed the start in London of several new important markets, including the inter-bank and certificates of deposits (CDs) markets in dollars and sterling. Some idea of the broad composition and structure of the main parallel markets at the end of 1970 is given in Table 1.1.

These new markets brought with them the innovatory banking technique of liability management, or endogenous deposit determination, first developed in the US during the early 1960s. A bank short of funds could simply go out on to these new wholesale money markets and bid for deposits. No longer did banks have to wait for deposits to flow in before they could

Table 1.1 *Parallel Markets' Resources*

		End 1970 *(£ million)*
Eurocurrency, etc. deposits		5,400
Local authority deposits		1,800
Inter-bank sterling deposits		1,700
Dollar CDs		1,600
Sterling CDs		1,100
Finance-house deposits		700
	Total	12,300

Source: Adapted from Revell, 1973, p. 270.

expand their lending volume. The banks that employed liability management effectively threw off the liquidity shackles of traditional deposit banking. They became potentially 'advances driven', rather than 'deposits driven'. Loans could be made in anticipation of the bank being able to go out and buy in the necessary supporting deposits on the inter-bank or CD markets. Later experience in the 1970s, however, demonstrated that banks driven through liability management could be exposed to significant dangers – particularly funding and interest rate risk exposures – where they grossly unmatched the maturities of their assets and liabilities. The wholesale markets are still predominantly short term with the majority of deposits being under six months maturity. Unlike the traditional discount market, the wholesale money markets have no lender of last resort, there is no direct intervention by the authorities, and all loans are unsecured.

The UK clearing banks, therefore, found themselves having to face up to a new competitive, aggressive and innovative operating environment during the decade of the 1960s. The distorting effects of being virtually the sole recipient sector of monetary controls made themselves felt on the clearing banks during this period. The recurring sterling crises over this time resulted in the reimposition of controls and the use of direct lending ceilings. Because they (and not the wholesale banks) were subject to cash and liquid assets ratios, for example, a direct participation in the parallel money markets by the clearing banks was less profitable for them. They were also subject to long-standing operating conventions, like the interest rate cartel, which constrained their direct activities in the new money markets. Nevertheless, they operated indirectly in wholesale banking, at least in a limited fashion, through subsidiaries and associate companies – the so-called 'clearers' cheaters'.

In the retail sterling market, the clearing banks also faced major competitive threats. Other financial institutions, especially the building societies, with apparent operating privileges (like tax concessions and freedom from monetary controls) and a new competitive fervour were making dramatic inroads into the traditional dominance of the clearing banks. All of these forces combined to reduce the clearing banks' share of the market. No longer were they an island surrounded by a sea of tranquillity. They soon saw the need to harness their considerable resources to meet the new threats and challenges.

Competition and Credit Control

The late 1960s witnessed several mergers amongst the clearing banks following the 1967 National Board for Prices and Incomes report on bank charges. In 1969 the clearing banks agreed to provide full disclosure of their profits. During the same period the authorities were seriously reconsidering their method of monetary control. This culminated in Competition and Credit Control (CCC) in September 1971, which set out to bring in a fairer and more market-orientated system. It had as a prime objective that the allocation of credit would be determined primarily by cost.

Lending ceilings were scrapped and ratio controls applied to all banks, including the wholesale banks. Many of the clearing banks' long-standing agreements (like that on interest rates) were also abandoned. The notion of a separate wholesale (or secondary) banking system began to weaken as the clearing banks started to operate directly in the wholesale markets. At the same time, the earlier idea of parallel money markets became blurred as the discount and wholesale markets became more operationally related. The Heath Conservative government followed the CCC measures with an expansionary monetary policy as part of its economic growth strategy.

Competition and Credit Control was designed to give greater scope for competition and innovation in the financial system. The Bank of England's corresponding benign attitude to the establishment of new banks resulted in a growing influx of banks to London. Table 1.2 provides an insight into the combined effects of the movement of banks to London and the changing nature of its financial activities over 1965 to 1971. The environment of the day stimulated inflation which became a more significant and growing problem. The rapid growth in the money supply during 1971–3 – the period of the so-called 'Barber boom' – helped to inflate dramatically the wholesale banking and property sectors.

From October 1971 to December 1973 the compound per annum growth rate of M3 reached 27.46 per cent. The compound growth in total banking sector advances (at 47.76 per cent) and assets (41.42 per cent) was even more dramatic over this same period. Total bank loans to the UK financial sector (excluding banks) grew from £779 million in 1967 to £5,512 million in 1973, a sevenfold growth. Banking, property and the stock market were in a boom phase: optimism and euphoria were the order of the day. All

Table 1.2 *UK Bank Deposits (£,000 million)*

		Comprising	
End of:	*Total deposits*	*UK residents*	*Overseas residents*
1965	14.7	10.8	3.9
1971	37.9	17.6	20.3

Source: Financial Statistics, Table 36, No. 99, July 1970, and Table 39, No. 121, May 1972.

of these developments, however, had operated to make the UK financial system increasingly fragile. It only needed a trigger to expose the financial weaknesses and risky banking which unfettered expansion and the quest for profit had helped to breed.

Crises in the 1970s and 1980s

The fringe banking crisis

The stimulus to competition precipitated by CCC helped to encourage a further surging growth of wholesale (especially fringe) banking institutions. Examining in Table 1.3 the progress of a small sample of the larger fringe bank groups that later faced troubles illustrates clearly the environment of the day. These institutions were effectively outside official prudential control. Paradoxically, these were the banks most in need of effective supervision by the authorities, but they had a virtual free hand to do as they pleased. They were subject to market constraints, but the markets themselves had become caught up in the inflationary and speculative fervour of the day. Innovation, excessive optimism, a competitive scramble for funds, and apparently easy profit opportunities are the traditional ingredients of speculative bubbles. The bubble was about to burst.

The fringe was largely funded through wholesale deposits bought on the new money markets, and their balance sheets were grossly unmatched by maturity. Short-term deposits (the bulk being under three months maturity) were typically being rolled over to fund loan and investment books with average maturities of the order of five years and beyond. Diversification in asset portfolios was also minimal at a time when many fringe banks were heavily involved in property development and its finance. Several of the established banks were also into property-related lending and associated financing. The seeds for potential disaster had been sown. All banking systems rest ultimately on confidence. Once confidence is lost or threatened,

Table 1.3 *Selected trend analysis of some larger secondary bank groups*

	Pre-tax profit (£m)			*Gross assets (£m)*		
	1965	*1971*	*1973*	*1965*	*1971*	*1973*
Cannon Street Investments	0.01	0.40	3.50	0.40	3.00	122.00
Cedar Holdings	0.02	0.90	1.90	8.00	18.00	128.00
Mercantile credit	2.50	8.20	12.80	12.00	243.00	377.00
Slater Walker Securities	0.80	16.30	23.40	20.00	280.00	588.00

Note: Gross assets figures over £10 million rounded to nearest £1 million. Year is that in which financial year ends. Gross assets at end of year or period of accounts.

Source: Reid, 1982, pp. 40 and 41.

the system may quickly face widespread pressure and collapse. Banking history reminds us repeatedly of this phenomenon.

Into the second half of 1973, UK interest rates finally passed the psychological barrier of double digits. They started to reach new peaks and exhibit marked volatility. Deposit maturities shortened for fringe operators in the wholesale markets and their differential above prime inter-bank rates widened. Fringe bank profit margins began to be squeezed drastically. The UK balance of payments came under growing pressure over 1973 and bank lending guidelines were effectively reintroduced. The severe mini budget of December 1973 brought in the 'corset' and the government set out finally to curb property speculation. For a time at least, the authorities eschewed the competitive freedom envisaged in the original CCC measures. The storm clouds were now gathering at a rapid pace.

A unique feature of the UK fringe banking crisis was that it was triggered in large part by a new kind of run which resulted from a loss of confidence – a run by wholesale depositors. It reflected a loss of confidence, nevertheless, and a reminder that some traditional banking precepts should never be forgotten. The crisis really started in November 1973 with the collapse of London and County Securities. This collapse was precipitated through the inability of London and County to roll over its money market deposits to fund its lending book. The bubble had finally begun to burst on the heady financing encouraged in part by the monetary and banking environment of the day.

Bad banking and sheer imprudence by the fringe came home to roost with a vengeance. The contagion spread rapidly and a number of fringe banks were soon known to be in serious difficulties. Even more established operators who might be regarded as clearly prudent under normal operating conditions came under the threat of panic withdrawal of deposits. In 1974 we saw the virtual collapse of the UK property and stock markets. The boom was over and growing fears replaced the euphoric build-up to the crisis.

Fortunately, the Bank of England and the core institutions acted promptly. The famous 'Lifeboat' operation was launched by the bank to recycle funds to those fringe banks facing liquidity (as opposed to solvency) difficulties. The Lifeboat was essentially a new form of lender of last resort action. It was also the largest, most complex bank rescue operation ever launched. It evidenced the flexibility and speedy response capabilities to crises inherent in the British banking system. Later on it became clear that some institutions with solvency problems had also been helped by the Lifeboat.

The fringe banking crisis served as a sharp reminder that the British banking system was not immune from crises and failures in the modern banking climate. It confirmed that British banking had entered a new and hostile operating environment. The British system was not to be alone in facing crises during the 1970s. Nor was the fringe banking crisis the only threat to be faced by British banks. Crises, banking difficulties and bank failures throughout the world distinguished the period as one of marked financial fragility. Banking systems and the international banking system entered an era of periodic and growing turbulence.

United States experiences

The US banking and financial system in particular found itself under considerable pressure as the 1970s developed. A growing dissatisfaction with banking controls devised initially in the aftermath of Depression experiences had already prompted an extensive rethink of the system of bank prudential regulation. Up to the mid 1970s, the US system experienced in recent times three periods of severe financial pressure. These were the credit crunches of 1966 and 1969–70, and the 1974–5 crisis. All of these crises were of increasing severity, although none of them approached the scale of the experiences of the 1920s and early 1930s. One noteworthy feature of these modern US crises is that no important financial market ceased to function, although foreign exchange markets were closed periodically during the last of them to allow for currency realignments. Interest rates reached successively higher peaks in each of these crises, and liability management remained a significant funding source for at least the established institutions.

Banking trends over this period included declining bank capital : risk asset ratios, a running down of secondary liquid assets, increasing reliance on funding through liability management sources, and a movement towards greater maturity intermediation. Many of these trends were particularly marked in larger US banks (with total assets over $500 million). The 1974–5 crisis also occurred at the end of an era of significant innovations in banking and bank-related finance. These trends operated to produce *de facto* deregulation in a period of marked competition. Traditional conservatism was abandoned or at least compromised by many banks in a bid to achieve more rapid balance sheet and profit growth. At the same time, US financial markets became increasingly volatile and more competitive. During 1973–5, inflation and high interest rates combined to produce a decline in the amount of real estate demanded. The Real Estate Investment Trust (REIT) crisis ensued and many banks that had invested in REITs incurred losses. At the end of 1974, reports were that no fewer than 150 banks were under close surveillance by the Comptroller.

One disturbing trend for US (and indeed world) bankers was the heralding of the era in the US of the large-bank failure. Table 1.4 provides testimony to this new phenomenon. US bank prudential regulation had been geared primarily to small bank problems; large banks were generally thought to be immune from failure. Between 1935 and 1970 no large US bank failed. A large bank failure was unthinkable, but the unthinkable happened: not just once, but again and again. The swelling list included the US National Bank of San Diego and Franklin National of New York. After 1970, the size of US banks requiring help grew and more than twenty banks with assets exceeding $50 million failed. The Federal Deposit Insurance Corporation bailout of First Pennsylvania Bank in 1980 raised the total assets of banks requiring assistance to over $20 billion. As the 1980s developed, it became clear that the large problem bank was not a passing 1970s phenomenon. In May 1984, Continental Illinois, the eighth-largest US bank, had to be bailed out twice in one week.

This change in US bank failure experience was in significant part bound up with the aggressive and competitive banking environment of the day. Bankers became more willing to take on the risks necessary to achieve their ambitious growth and profit targets. The monetary and financial climate helped to sustain this aggression and optimism. Eventually for many banks it brought home to roost the risky financing it had helped spawn. High volatility in money supply growth rates, rapid inflation and high interest rates were symptomatic of the times.

Although monetary and financial conditions helped breed (and themselves were partly bred by) the environment of risks and risk-taking, most failures that did occur up to the mid 1970s were apparently not the direct result of adverse economic conditions. Several studies suggest that the main causes of modern US large-bank failures were incompetent management practices, sometimes fraud, and, for several, over-extended real estate loan portfolios.

Table 1.4 *US Bank Failures, 1964–74*

Year	*No. of banks closed because of financial difficulties*	*Total deposits of closed banks ($ m)*	*Largest bank failure ($ m)*
1964	8	24	7.0
1965	9	45	40.2
1966	8	106	93.0
1967	4	11	3.9
1968	3	23	11.8
1969	9	40	10.5
1970	8	53	15.9
1971	6	132	66.8
1972[1]	4	1,092	992.0
1973	6	971	932.0
1974	4	1,571	1,440.5

Source: Fraser & Rose, 1980, p. 106.

Note: 1. Includes data for Bank of Commonwealth which received FDIC assistance but did not close.

A recent important study by Maisel (1981) argued strongly, however, that the most common cause of banking insolvencies and losses was the failure to plan adequately for events that may occur but are not expected.

Failures in the US drew attention to two other important operational features. First, financial deterioration in a bank typically takes time – it is not an overnight phenomenon. Secondly, the prevailing economic conditions usually provided the trigger mechanism for exposing problems and accelerating financial deterioration. Gambs (1977, p. 14) noted in this connection:

> Extremely bad management may not prove fatal to a bank until adverse economic conditions lead to unexpected deposit outflows or loan losses. Thus, even if every bank which fails is judged to have suffered from mismanagement or fraud, or operated in an overpopulated banking market, it may well be the case that adverse economic conditions will be the proximate cause of many bank failures.

It is interesting to note that UK experiences up to the fringe banking crisis contained many similarities to those in the US. Inflation, high interest rates, innovation, aggressive competition and property were among the common elements.

In the second half of the 1970s, serious inflation led to a rise in real estate values and this improved the position of many REITs. But high and volatile interest rates remained a problem for bankers. Several contemporary scholars of US banking risk during the 1970s assert that interest rate risk was the single most important problem facing the US banking industry. As the latter half of the 1970s developed, the US savings and loans (S & L) industry entered a crisis period. Significant maturity intermediation used to finance fixed-rate mortgages produced high interest rate risk exposure. With interest rates rising to high levels, the S & L industry came under pressure. By 1980, the net worth of many S & Ls had fallen to less than 2½ per cent of total savings accounts held – a potential failure position for a few. The 1970s moved into the 1980s accompanied by a sharply rising trend of US bank failures, especially in 1981 and 1982. Several well-known banks appeared on the problem lists of regulatory agencies, many banks lost the prime risk status of agencies like Moodys, and the international banking system came under renewed pressure.

International banking crises

Although the failures of even large domestic banks in the US have not stimulated the spectre of massive deposit runs, the failures of some international banks have made this threat a distinct possibility for other banks involved in international currency transactions. One important operational difference between domestic systems and the international banking system is that the latter does not have an international lender of last resort. Another important source of pressure for the international banking system was the March 1973 introduction of floating exchange rates with limited interventions.

The old fixed exchange rate system had given currency realignments significant predictability. This put dealers in a good position to take views or speculate on currency movements. Banks had begun to get used to the practically assured profit flow at low risk from their dealing rooms. Floating markedly increased risk since currencies could now go up as well as down. The new state of affairs put the speculators at risk and increased uncertainty. Banks faced the immediate need to renew and control carefully their exposure limits on foreign exchange positions, and their mismatch positions in the forward and eurocurrency markets. Subsequent events soon confirmed this operational priority.

The first casualty was the failure of the West German Bankhaus Herstatt in June 1974. Herstatt was the largest private bank in West Germany and its failure resulted from enormous foreign exchange losses. It was reported to have lost around $200 million from 'unauthorized' foreign exchange transactions. To put these losses in perspective, at the end of 1973 Herstatt had an equity base of only $31 million. Many criticisms were levelled at the way this failure was handled and its damaging repercussions on confidence in the international system. Herstatt closed its doors at the end of its business day. Due to differences in time zones, many banks were caught in the middle of spot transactions. These banks had delivered the foreign currency but had not yet been paid by Herstatt.

The Herstatt affair was quickly followed by reports of large losses from foreign currency operations by other European banks. These included the Union Bank of Switzerland, Lloyds (losses through fraud in a Swiss branch), the Westdeutsche Landesbank and Banque de Bruxelles. Outside Europe, the US giant Franklin National was another early casualty. Several European banks had also been caught earlier holding $85 million of standby letters of credit issued by the US National Bank which failed. On top of these mounting shocks to the system, the major oil price rises in 1973 (and later 1979 and 1980) added another source of growing pressure.

The institutional machinery of international banking – the international market for eurocurrency deposits and foreign exchange – became to a large extent the vehicle for recycling the new wealth of the oil-producing countries. This new wealth increasingly took the form of highly volatile and short-term deposits with international banks that had their counterpart in the mounting balance of payments deficits of the non oil-producing countries. The size of these new funds flows carried with it the potential for severe pressure on the international banking and financial system. These trends combined to increase concern about the solvency of major international banks. Growing anxiety was felt about the ability of the international system to withstand additional shocks. Early reports that quickly followed the 1974 events confirmed that some international deposits had already been moved for safety reasons from lesser known banks to larger, better known ones.

The large volume of international bank lending to lesser developed countries (LDCs) during the 1970s was bound up with the recycling problem engendered by the massive 1973 oil price rise. International banks found themselves practically awash with funds to lend. Central banks encouraged banks to on-lend these funds in order to alleviate the growing deficits on their balance of payments. Part of these deposits were directly on-lent to LDCs whilst others, for prudential reasons, were re-deposited in the London eurocurrency deposit market (as 'petro-funds') and on-lent again by the acquiring banks to LDCs. International bank lending to LDCs correspondingly soared, but effective bank risk analysis of sovereign borrowers was often lacking and margins were invariably narrow. The result was that bank capital ratios came under pressure. Banks entered the 1980s to face the mounting international debt crisis with their capital bases inadequately fuelled through the low-risk premiums embodied in earlier profit margins earned on their international lending.

The high world price inflation of the late 1970s and early 1980s contributed to this state of affairs. Accelerating inflation eroded the real values of the deposits being recycled and helped induce a corresponding element of complacency in both borrowers and lenders. But this treadmill of inflation required that the accelerator be kept down in order to maintain the illusion that repayment would not be over-burdensome. The growing world recession and the accompanying mounting threat of hyperinflation, however, stimulated drastic braking action. The restrictive monetary policies pursued by many of the larger developed countries (like the US and UK) which followed pushed up interest rates at a time of deep world recession. As a result, several major groups of borrowers were hit. The international debt crisis quickly followed. The early 1980s saw the launch of international Lifeboats for many sovereign borrowers in difficulties.

The late 1970s and early 1980s had already seen the emergence of servicing problems associated with the growing debt burdens of many countries like Brazil, Argentina, Mexico and Poland. In the eighteen months up to February following the international debt crisis which erupted in August 1982, around thirty countries interrupted full service on roughly $120 billion of external debt. The simultaneous and severe plight of major LDC trading and borrowing countries has helped endanger the recovery of the world economy on which their own return to full debt service status depends. International banks found themselves in a fragile position and exposed to mounting levels of risk and uncertainty.

The early 1980s produced more shocks for bankers worldwide. The collapse in the US in May 1982 of Drysdale Government Securities, for example, quickly spread problems to Chase Manhattan which reported its first-ever quarterly loss. The Penn Square failure followed and Continental Illinois Bank (one of the top ten largest US banks) reported shortly the biggest ever quarterly loss made by a US bank. In July 1982, the Canadian Bank of Nova Scotia (fiftieth largest bank in the world) felt it necessary to dismiss rumours regarding its stability. West Germany's bank für Gemeinwirtschaft (seventy-third in world size rankings) also sought in 1982 to repudiate adverse rumours on its strength.

In all these countries, however, banking problems have been contained within national boundaries. But the potential for these problems to spread outside national boundaries has grown with the rapid development of the international banking and financial system. It was estimated in the early 1980s by the Group of 30 that over 40 per cent of large banks' international deposits are redeposited with other international banks. The much publicized difficulties of Banco Ambrosiano in Italy threatened to affect many other banks and several banking systems. The Continental Illinois Bank difficulties in 1984 also had international repercussions. For a short time on 17 May following the problems of Continental Illinois, the world banking system hovered on the edge of its worst-ever crisis.

Banking Risks

As later chapters will show, the banking problems of the 1970s and 1980s helped to expose operational defects in existing supervisory systems, techniques and philosophies. The foregoing catalogue of 'doom and disaster' must not, of course, be viewed in isolation. Both the authorities and bankers themselves reacted positively to events, and the system has both survived and learnt from its experiences. Innovatory techniques and new banking markets have been a source of new strength as well as providing scope for sometimes novel difficulties.

Nevertheless, recent experiences have stimulated increasing concern with the risks of banking. Banking cannot be divorced from risk-taking: in an operational sense the main business of banking is the taking on of risks. In channelling funds from savers to borrowers, together with their other main lines of business, banks face many risks. The ultimate responsibility for identifying, measuring and controlling these risks must, of course, lie with bank management. Nevertheless, we shall see later that the supervisory function has assumed a growing and more direct interest in this important side of banking. It will be useful at this point to stop a while and consider the main traditional and newer risks faced by the modern banking firm.

General risks

A fundamental risk faced by all banks is liquidity or funding risk. This is the risk that a bank will not be able to meet legitimate demands for funds by depositors or by existing or potential borrowers. It also includes the funding risk that a bank will not be able to roll over or renew deposits. This risk was emphasized yet again with the experiences of Continental Illinois in May 1984. In theory, banks could eliminate this funding risk by matching exactly the maturities of their assets and liabilities. In practice, however, the bulk of a bank's deposits and loans are maturity unmatched. A primary and indeed growing banking function today is to engage in maturity transformation. Depositors' preferences and borrowers' needs currently emphasize the importance of this key banking function. At the same time, banks face the problem of estimating withdrawal patterns on their potentially short-term deposits, like current accounts, and the essentially uncertain drawdown patterns on overdrafts, still a significant lending vehicle in the UK. As a result, funding risk is an important operational problem for modern banking firms and supervisors.

The traditional liquidity reservoir of banks has been in their cash and liquid (or reserve) assets. These sources remain important, but the problem of banking liquidity is now much more complex. This is because banking liquidity has become an altogether more dynamic concept with the evolution of liability management sources and other developments. Banks can now buy-in liquidity when needed from the wholesale money markets. The amount of potential funding from this new liquidity pool is not shown in conventional accounting statements. A bank liquidity analysis today, therefore, requires some estimate of the funds that will be available to banks under various scenarios. In short, some form of simulated funds projection or cash flow analysis is required. Balancing existing and potential liquidity demands against a bank's liquidity resources is a task of great complexity where little precision is possible. Faced with this kind of task, an efficient framework of analysis is more appropriate than an allegedly scientific guideline. Many such frameworks or techniques have been developed within the area of balance sheet management.

Related to funding risk and maturity mismatch is another important banking risk which has been labelled interest rate mismatch risk. It is really a form of profit risk, and it is bound up with a bank's funding posture, its portfolio of liabilities in relation to its corresponding assets structure. In theory, a bank could be exactly maturity matched, and still be exposed to interest rate mismatch risk. For instance, six-month variable rate deposits may be funding six-month fixed rate loans. This interest rate mismatch risk is seen if interest rates start to climb – the original margin is squeezed and might even become negative.

With the rising and volatile interest rate environment of the early 1970s, interest rate mismatch risk became a more serious problem. One result has been that the technique of variable rate lending has grown in recent years. This technique has transferred the risk on to the borrowers, though, and led to other banking problems in the high interest environment of the late 1970s and early 1980s. As the early 1980s developed, bank spreads and margins came under growing pressure with increasing competition and projected longer-term falls in interest rates. A higher proportion of bank deposits are now linked to market interest rates, thereby reducing the endowment element in bank profits.

Maturity ladders have been developed to monitor funding risk (for all currencies combined) and interest rate mismatch risk over different currencies. Swap positions also need to be monitored. Banks may mismatch in swap positions in each currency or between currency pairings. The new London International Financial Futures Exchange (LIFFE) offers an additional mechanism to deposit and swap markets for banks to reduce their interest rate mismatch risk. It seems likely from LIFFE's progress to date and US experience with financial futures that LIFFE may become a much more important vehicle in the future for banks to hedge and take interest rate positions. A considerable body of modern balance sheet management, incorporating techniques like gap analysis and spread management, have been devoted to handling bank funding and interest rate risk management.

Although liquidity risk has been a central element in bank management and banking theory, credit risk remains another major risk exposure for modern banks. It refers to the risk that a borrower may default or alter a repayment schedule – i.e. reschedule. Various kinds of security arrangements have been devised and sophisticated credit-screening schemes have emerged. With the recent world recession, industrial depression and general uncertainty, British banks have faced a rising trend in their loan losses. Often the real losses in that part of a loan book built up during a depression period are not realized until well into the following upswing of the business cycle. The early 1980s in the UK witnessed another 'Lifeboat model'. Lifeboats were launched for domestic industrial borrowers whose creditworthiness was in question by their bankers.

In managing credit risk exposure, diversification of the loan book is an important desideratum. As was mentioned earlier, this was a major operational weakness of many of the fringe wholesale banks up to the crisis of 1973–5. Diversification also implies that a bank should avoid too many large single loans. Otherwise, the failure of one large borrower may seriously affect the bank's stability and strength, at least for a time.

International Risks

One of the major potential problems faced by international banks today is the growing volume of sovereign risks. A sovereign risk is a kind of credit risk where the borrower is an overseas country or the loan is effectively guaranteed by a foreign government. It has already been emphasized that bank sovereign lending increased markedly following the oil price rises of 1973 and 1979–80. The bulk of this lending has been unsecured, and it has involved a wide group of banks. As with other forms of bank lending, sovereign lending is subject to a prior credit risk analysis, but the rules are not so clear. Personal and corporate credit risk analysis was an evolutionary process. A kind of 'consensus model' eventually developed within the banking system from which operational rules and guidelines were devised. Sovereign risk analysis has developed much more quickly and in a rather haphazard, *ad hoc* sort of manner. So far, this can only have helped exacerbate the state of affairs which culminated in the sovereign debt problems of the late 1970s and early 1980s.

Sovereign lending is distinguished from other main forms of bank lending by several features. The belief by international bankers that a sovereign borrower could never fail apparently made bankers less prudent, both in their risk assessment and in the size of loan extended. Another noteworthy feature of sovereign lending is the concomitant political dimensions of the loan. Sharp restrictive domestic measures in order to help create the resources needed to repay a foreign loan may have far-reaching political repercussions.

A third major risk category for banks is foreign currency risks. As we have already seen, the years after 1973 witnessed many banking problems directly related to this phenomenon. Foreign currency risk exposure can be sub-divided into two components – the dealing and structural positions. The dealing risk arises from a bank's day-to-day operating, spot and forward, in the foreign exchange markets. Structural risk refers to exposures of a longer-term nature, like those arising from banks' fixed and long-term assets and liabilities.

Several other important risks are encountered by banks. These are usually not mutually exclusive from other main categories of risk. For example, profit risk may be formally identified as arising from inadequate earnings, earnings variability, inflation and growth. Earnings variability, of course, may often be a product of other risk exposures, like interest rate mismatch risk, examined earlier. Another risk category is investment risk – the risks involved in changes in the value of assets like marketable investments and fixed assets. Banks also face risks from contingent liabilities, operating risks, fraud risks, fiduciary and exceptional risks. Many risk classification schemes are possible, but the main risks have been identified – except one.

Solvency Risk

The missing risk in our list so far is solvency risk – the risk that a bank may become insolvent – and it is really synonymous with the bank capital-adequacy question. It is ultimately concerned with a bank's overall portfolio, or mix of risks, both within and outside the balance sheet. A bank's capital cushion is viewed operationally as a kind of internal insurance fund against uncertainty, a last line of defence. This does not imply abrogation of the central bank lender of last resort function, or that banks must be hedged against every possible disaster. What it does imply is that a bank's total risk exposure should be identified, measured in some useful operational way, and evaluated in the light of the bank's capital cushion. As the main continuous flow into the reservoir of bank capital is profits, a capital adequacy analysis is not far removed from an appraisal of bank profit adequacy. Indeed, the two cannot really be divorced.

Solvency risk has been and remains a major problem in several banking systems. Consequently, capital adequacy (or solvency) assessments have received growing emphasis. In one sense capital adequacy is an illusory and paradoxical concept. This is because an adequate capital base – however defined – is one that effectively helps to forestall the ultimate event(s) it is designed to meet. Adequate capital so defined is an important element in preserving confidence in the banking system. Once confidence is lost, however, no viable amount of capital alone can save a bank. A similar paradox surrounds bank deposit insurance schemes – they are primarily designed to prevent the event insured against. In an operational context, however, capital adequacy is now a vital supervisory area. This is because an efficient capital adequacy analysis focuses attention on a bank's overall risk exposure, it may draw out important risk relationships, and it probes into a bank's capacity to carry its current and projected risk exposures.

The process of capital adequacy analysis, therefore, itself helps reduce solvency risk. It is not surprising that capital adequacy analysis is a focal element in many bank supervisory systems. Practically all supervisory rules have either some direct or indirect bearing on a bank's capital resources. Capital ratios may assume an even greater importance in the future if the trend towards more market orientated methods of monetary control continues. We shall return to this problem and associated issues on several occasions later. Part D of this book is devoted to the area. Capital adequacy is a complex problem, which is bound up with several important banking issues. For the present we need only note its importance and broader implications for banking risk. Adequate capital in this context is synonymous with an acceptable level of bank risk exposure. Adequate and acceptable are, of course, qualitative terms. This suggests that alleged precision in the capital adequacy area is illusory and probably misleading.

Are Crises Endemic?

A noteworthy trend in most developed banking systems has been declining bank capital ratios. This is a secular phenomenon. Although there have been periods of improvement and stability, the secular drift downwards in bank capital ratios is clear and unmistakable. There is no doubt that there have been developments which have reduced the need for bank capital. But the nagging question remains. Have bank capital ratios been declining towards dangerous levels? Were 1970s and 1980s experiences in part a product of this phenomenon? A more fundamental question encompasses this concern and raises others. Are periodic banking and financial crises endemic to modern free enterprise economies? As we shall see later, one primary function of modern banking supervision is to help reduce the probability of financial crises.

Minsky (1975) was an early and important student of financial crises. He argues that fragility has been a major feature of the US economy since the mid 1960s. The core of his argument is that periodic financial crises result from the normal functioning of a mature economy like that of the US. Financial instability and crises are facts of economic life. Financial instability can be viewed analytically as a process in which rapid and accelerating changes in asset (both financial and capital) prices occur relative to the prices of current output. Analytical precision is difficult in this area, but it is not necessary anyway for present purposes. Periods of instability and crises are clearly evident, they are positive facts of economic life, and students like Kindleberger (1978) have documented them in some detail.

Minsky posits that the standard body of today's economic theory implies that financial instability is an impossibility, a non-event. In Kindleberger and Laffargue (1982, p. 13) he suggests in typical iconoclastic vein:

> The floundering of the capitalist economies in the 1970s reflects the irrelevance of the theoretical framework that the economists of the policy establishments apply when they advise and instruct political leaders. In part, the malaise of capitalist countries is iatrogenic – the disease has been induced in the patient by the physicians.

and later (p. 14) adds:

> Before theory became a victim of mathematics and observations were replaced by printouts, economists recognized that financial crises occurred and set their minds to explaining why they took place and their effects on system performance.

Minsky developed an interesting model of financial crises based on observed events.

A robust financial system is defined as one where modest changes in cash flows, payment commitments and capitalization rates do not affect the debt repayment ability of private economic units. Fragility is the opposite state of affairs. The Minsky financial-instability hypothesis argues that changes in cash flow relations over a period of good years transforms robust systems into fragile financial systems. In short, the internal dynamics of capitalist systems lead to financial structures which are conducive to financial crises. The central bank's responsibility as lender of last resort is to prevent the generalized fall in asset values occasioned by the position-making actions of private economic units who have become increasingly dominated by units with more risky financing policies.

Another important role of the central bank is seen as guiding the evolution of financial systems so that the plight of more risky financing forms – which Minsky labels speculative and Ponzi, as opposed to safer hedge financing – is kept at a safe (robust) level. A proposition that flows from Minsky's financial – instability hypothesis is that a quick abortion – via the deficits of big government and lender of last resort intervention – of the debt-deflation interactive process that leads to deep depression has a cost in the form of an inflationary recession. Despite their persuasiveness, Minsky's theories have not yet been popularly accepted.

A recent (1977) book edited by Altman and Sametz, for example, contained several studies of recent US financial crises. The discussants on this collection of papers showed a preference for an eclectic crises theory, and they stressed the problem of unanticipated inflation and risky corporate financial policies in fuelling financial crises. Altman (Altman & Sametz, 1977, p. 137) concluded:

> My own impression of these papers is that a consensus is developed that the concept of 'crisis inevitability' has few supporters either in theory or in practice. In contrast to the Minsky approach, the other papers stress the 'therapeutic' effects of learning by experience: the development of 'conservative' financial policies in the *private* sector, and the evolution towards 'correct' *public* monetary and fiscal policies.

Other students in the UK, however, have also attempted to explain financial crises and their likely consequences.

Barclay (Barclay, Gardener & Revell, 1978) studied the UK fringe banking crisis in some detail and compared it to the celebrated financial crises which occurred periodically until the last quarter of the nineteenth century. From this study the hypothesis developed that the process leading towards financial crises is started through surplus profits in banking and bank-related finance tempting a growing number of new operators into these activities. Two important factors leading to these pockets of surplus profit appear to be financial innovation and government regulation. Barclay and Revell (Barclay, Gardener & Revell, 1978) go on to propose that a cyclical pattern in bank risk assumption is observable. As the fringe institutions increasingly exploit these pockets of surplus profit, so the more established institutions are tempted to get involved. Eventually competition and the promise of apparent easy profit bring in the more prudent and established units.

But this profitable activity is inherently risky and problems arise when events later take a turn for the worse. The eventual downturn produces the phenomenon of 'loss bunching' and penalties for over-committed banks may now be severe. Revell proposed in his evidence to the Wilson Committee (reprinted in Barclay, Gardener & Revell, 1978) that conventions and agreement between banks are implicit forms of self-regulation designed to prevent banks getting tempted into these more risky forms of activity.

Up until the early 1970s, financial crises and banking difficulties were comparatively rare events. Experience has shown, however, that as the most recent financial crisis fades into history, its impact on current decisions lessens. More innovatory forms of finance appear and soon new limits of prudence are approached. Even the more conservative may start to forget the lessons from history. The seeds become sown for the next bout of more risky and speculative financing. In essence a kind of 'Gresham's law' in financing policies operates – more risky financing begins to assume greater importance over safer and proven prudential financing forms. It gives support to the philosophical stance that the only thing we can learn from history is that men learn nothing from history.

But where has this excursion taken us on our present course? Well, it is already clear that no theory of financial crises has yet been developed which is widely accepted. These considerations are not meant to downgrade the path-breaking work of Minsky and similar students. Their efforts have provided much greater insight into how modern financial crises have developed. Later on we shall return to reconsider in other settings the operational implications of the modern market economists who might dispute the Minsky view. But for present purposes the relevant question that introduced this section may now be reformulated. Are modern banking crises possible and potentially damaging to economic welfare? The short answer must be an emphatic yes.

It is this potential market failure which has provided one of the strongest justifications for the prudential regulation of banks. One of the main tasks of bank prudential regulation is to prevent disturbances in the financial sector from destabilizing activity in other economic sectors. Before we tackle this specific task of banking supervision, however, we must explore the broader nature and context of bank regulation. A useful starting point is to consider the economic nature of regulation in general. The following chapter takes up this thread.

References and Bibliography

Altman, E. I. & A. W. Sametz (ed.) (1977), *Financial Crises: Institutions and Markets in a Fragile Environment* (New York: Wiley Interscience).

Bank of England Quarterly Bulletin (1978), 'The secondary banking crisis and the Bank of England's support operations', vol. 8, no. 9 (June), pp. 230–9.

Barclay, C., E. P. M. Gardener & J. Revell (1978), *Competition and Regulation of Banks*, Bangor Occasional Papers in Economics No. 14 (Cardiff: University of Wales Press).

Brick, John R. (ed.) (1980), *Bank Management: Concepts and Issues* (Richmond, Virginia: Robert F. Dame, Inc).

Drucker, P. F. (1980), *Managing in Turbulent Times* (London: William Heinemann).

Fraser, D. P. & P. S. Rose (1980), *Financial Institutions and Markets in a Changing World* (Dallas, Texas: Business Publications).

Gambs, C. M. (1977), 'Bank failures – an historical perspective', Federal Reserve Bank of Kansas City, *Monthly Review* (June), pp. 10–20.

Gardener, E. P. M. (1983), 'Balance sheet management – new tool for an old problem?' *Bankers Magazine* (USA), vol. 166, no. 4 (July–Aug.), pp. 58–62.

Gardener, E. P. M. (1983), 'A balance sheet approach to bank risk management', *European Management Journal*, vol. 2, no. 1 (Summer), pp. 84–93.

Grant, A. T. K. (1977), *Economic Uncertainty and Financial Structure* (London: Macmillan).

Kindleberger, C. P. (1978), *Manias, Panics, and Crashes: A History of Financial Crises* (London: Macmillan).

Kindleberger, C. P. & J. P. Laffargue (1982), *Financial Crises: Theory, History and Policy* (London: Cambridge University Press).

Maisel, S. J. (ed.) (1981), *Risk and Capital Adequacy in Commercial Banks* (New York: National Bureau of Economic Research).

Minsky, H. (1975), 'Financial resources in a fragile financial environment', *Challenge*, vol. 18, no. 3 (Aug.), pp. 6–13.
Reid, M. (1982), *The Secondary Banking Crisis, 1973–75* (London: Macmillan).
Revell, J. R. S. (1973), *The British Financial System* (London: Macmillan).
Revell, J. R. S. (1975), *Solvency and Regulation of Banks*, Bangor Occasional Papers in Economics, No. 5 (Cardiff: University of Wales Press).
Yeager, Frederick and Neil Seitz (1982), *Financial Institution Management: Text and Cases* (Reston, Virginia: Reston Publishing).

2 A General Perspective of Banking Prudential Regulation

. . . the principles of both bankers and supervisors have been hammered out on the anvil of practical experience rather than produced as intellectually elegant blueprints drawn up in ivory towers.
John Cooper (1984) *The Management and Regulation of Banks* (London: Macmillan)

The Debate on Regulation in General

Background
This main section is concerned with all forms of regulation as a prelude to the consideration of those specific forms of regulation that are applied to banks. A general perspective of regulation is a useful background for helping to understand the evolution and nature of bank regulation. It will be emphasized, however, that because of their unique economic roles, banks are subject to special considerations, and these help shape their respective regulatory systems. The realities of the market also tend to dominate some important theoretical prescriptions in the area.

Regulation pervades Western economies and it takes many different forms. Over the past twenty years or so regulation has everywhere developed as a significant growth industry. Regulations and regulators have proliferated. Alongside these trends, however, there is mounting popular feeling that there is too much government regulation. 'Competition and innovation are being stifled' and 'Let the market do its job' exemplify some of these contemporary themes. Apparent support for these views might indicate that the pendulum of history is poised again to swing back through into a period of renewed *laissez faire*. Substantial deregulation of financial institutions would very likely soon result.

In the present banking climate of potential high risk, however, we should consider these views carefully. We need to examine first the case for at least some bank regulation, and this will be one of the main objectives of the present chapter. Attention may then be focused on alternatives to prudential regulation. The case for regulation does not justify, and may not even suggest, the corresponding best technique for regulating. Selecting, evaluating, implementing and monitoring supervisory techniques have tended to dominate the supervisory literature. One reason is perhaps obvious. Inappropriate regulations may sometimes be more dangerous than no regulations at all. Recognizing and proving the dangers of regulations, and subsequently dismantling them, however, may cloud the fact that some regulation is always necessary. In rebuilding the house, we must be careful not to damage the essential foundations.

A great deal of recent US research has been conducted into regulation and much of it suggests that regulation in that country is often inefficient. The bulk of the traditional economics literature on regulation emanates from the United States, and it is based naturally on US data and experiences. Many US regulatory schemes apparently fail the cost : benefit test. There is also growing evidence that extant government regulations may often have the perverse effect of exacerbating, rather than solving, a problem. This evidence from the United States is particularly persuasive in the case of competitive and quasi-competitive industries. Although there are well-known dangers and limitations in translating one country's experiences to another, many US views are gaining a growing popularity in other developed countries.

Concern with regulation

These trends and mounting evidence have, therefore, stimulated a growing concern with regulation and its effects. The direct effects of regulation can be substantial, but the indirect effects may sometimes be even more significant and difficult to quantify. Many economists have argued strongly that regulation has generally failed by placing too much emphasis on command and control, and not enough on decentralised economic incentives. From the early 1970s, much more insight into the regulatory process has been gained through the work of economists, lawyers and political scientists. One result of this movement in the United States, for example, has been a change in emphasis towards a greater reliance on market forces in industry-specific regulations. At the same time, other forces (like consumerism) have in their turn stimulated a marked growth in non-industry-specific regulation. This latter form of regulation occurs even when the regulated markets are functioning efficiently, and it is directed at various social goals like discrimination, privacy, consumer protection and disclosure requirements. The signs are that this sector of the regulatory business is liable to grow fastest over the next decade. Certainly consumer (especially depositor) protection is one important rationale for banking supervision.

Several different levels of analysis surround regulation and associated issues. At a fundamental level, of course, we may ask whether regulation in any form is necessary. Can the 'unseen hand' of the market be relied upon to attain maximum social welfare from its resource allocation? At a more operational level, attention is commonly focused on selecting the best methods of regulation, given that regulation exists. Another problem is that conflicts may sometimes arise between different regulatory policies. We need to be aware of these potential conflicts so that they can be avoided. For example, an ambitious monetary policy may be counter-productive (and impossible anyway) when a significant part of the banking sector is prudentially weak. At another level, a growing body of work has appeared recently on the economic interests served by regulation. Returning again to more fundamental issues, we might consider whether economic theory needs to be modified in view of widespread regulation. Certainly we cannot hope to resolve all of these questions and issues, but we can at least examine generally the rationale and methods of bank regulation.

It is a fact that banks are regulated by different bodies and for a variety of reasons. Banking regulation has also been a growth industry, and banks have traditionally been highly regulated firms. As a result, much effort has been directed into evaluating and comparing various systems and techniques of bank regulation. Positive analysis of regulation – measuring its actual as opposed to intended effects – has become increasingly popular. These studies often embody normative prescriptions. Strong arguments may be developed which support one form of regulation over another. It may be argued that it is better to regulate one area of activity rather than another to achieve a given objective. Nevertheless, it is undeniable that many students and practitioners accept that banking regulation is a fact of life, a necessary burden. They may be correct, but we should explore this position carefully.

Another school of thought has begun to argue convincingly that regulation generally has costs which may often exceed the alleged benefits. They favour a greater reliance on the role of the market in banking decisions. This line of argument embodies a more fundamental normative prescription. How should bank resource allocation decisions be made? In its more extreme versions it questions the very need for contemporary prudential regulatory systems. Passive acceptance of the need for formal prudential regulation and the iconoclastic prescription that it is unnecessary, perverse in its effects and counter-productive can be viewed as two polar extremes within a spectrum of different (often conflicting) views which surround bank prudential regulation. To begin an exploration of these issues we need to examine first some basic principles. A logical starting point is to consider the fundamental nature of regulation.

What is regulation?

Regulation generally suggests the intervention of government or some such authoritative body. More often than not the legal framework is employed. Legislation is enacted to achieve an objective so that some form of command and control process is invariably involved. Nevertheless, regulation in the economic sphere may sometimes be more subtle. The Bank of England's traditional use of moral suasion is an example. Another example from the banking arena is the employment of cartels and agreements. These are essentially forms of self-regulation, *inter alia*, although they become imbued with greater formality when condoned or encouraged by a higher authority. In a more general context, regulation is also performed, of course, by the market, the unseen hand. An efficient market regulates through penalizing institutions which adopt inappropriate risk : return positions. A higher risk position invariably requires a higher compensating return. Excessive risk, the inability to achieve this return, may be penalized ultimately by failure precipitated through the operation of market forces.

It is already clear that regulation is not an easy concept to pin down outside a specific context. For present purposes, however, regulation may be identified broadly through its employment of some form of central planning as opposed to the use of the unfettered market mechanism. Regulation is often characterized by the use of an agency which may be created especially to achieve and monitor the regulatory process.

In practice, regulation and the market mechanism interact and cannot often be viewed independently. A centrally regulated enterprise, for example, may often operate in (or be influenced by) some almost unregulated markets. The regulations to which such an enterprise is subject may also seek to replicate certain market mechanisms, either to aid resource allocation or to retain competitive position. Such a case might be a nationalized industry which is set centrally a target rate of return derived in part from market data. It is difficult to find in practice a completely unregulated sphere of economic activity. As we have already seen, regulation has grown markedly in all countries.

Regulation, therefore, is a pervasive force in modern economies. It operates throughout most levels of the economy, and its influence is wide-ranging – often extending far beyond its direct or immediate effects. Consequently, defining regulation is usually dependent upon the context of the analysis or discussion. Although the term regulation is often used in different settings, it generally refers to the replacement of market economic incentives by the edicts of government. In a narrower definition it comprises policies whose main aim is to correct for what economists label market failures. These policies comprise rules which restrict or direct action by participants. The list of potential market failures includes natural monopoly, incomplete information and restricted entry to the market.

Regulation is often imposed in a free enterprise economy, therefore, to supplant and sometimes encourage the competitive market. As we all know, the economist's ideal market is perfectly competitive. Social scientists have concluded that the political and social consequences of less-than-free markets are inferior as well. Under perfect market conditions, marginal costs are equated to marginal revenue at a point where social welfare is maximized. Market failure exists where this ideal cannot be attained. At one extreme, market failure occurs when the market ceases to function at all. It also happens when the market cannot operate in a competitive manner. Natural monopoly, it will be recalled, is one standard textbook example of this latter kind of market failure.

The economics literature does not contain a universal and widely accepted definition of regulation. At one extreme is the strict definition of regulation, like governing in accordance with the law. At an operational level, regulation refers to control over what individual economic units may do and sometimes how they can perform these activities. Beyond these more restrictive definitions, regulation may be said to smooth over or regularize markets and activities. In a Stiglerian context, regulation may be viewed as any policy which alters market outcomes through the exercise of some coercive government power. At this definitional level, regulation is a wide, practically limitless force.

Sometimes a superficial and circular approach is adopted – regulation is what regulators do. But regulation is not just what regulators do; it is how they do it. Regulation, for instance, may be tight or lax; it may be paternalistic or dictatorial; and regulation may be limited or all-embracing. In this setting, regulation may be characterized more efficiently by its effect on the economic efficiency of the units or market under regulation.

In setting out to correct a market failure, regulation imposes costs. Up until the early 1960s it was generally believed (or at least implied) that government regulation was somehow costless. It is now accepted that all types of regulations have some effect on costs. These costs include the provision of data and information to regulators, and the maintenance of internal information systems by those regulated to ensure that regulations are being met. Another potential cost in the banking context includes reduced competition: the potential wastes of non-price competition may proliferate. Some regulations may have significant hidden costs, like reducing the flexibility and reactive capabilities of the regulated institutions to change and opportunities.

Regulations may also affect management style. Managements, for instance, may become more orientated towards satisfying the regulators than meeting their proper business demands and objectives. Inappropriate regulations may themselves prompt the wrong kind of innovation during periods of growing competition. Institutions subject to regulation may innovate to avoid the burdens imposed by regulation. In short, regulation may reduce bank productivity and raise the costs of borrowing and lending. Defining regulation in a universal sense may thus prove less useful than appraising its costs and benefits. We need to examine generally why regulation arises.

Justifications for regulation

Regulation, then, appears to be supplied whenever relief is desirable from the deficiencies and weaknesses of an unfettered market. This is the conventional view of regulation. Up until the late 1950s it was generally felt that economic markets were inherently fragile. The public interest explanation for regulation lays down that regulation is supplied in response to the public's demand for relief from inequitable or inefficient market practices. It focuses attention on consumers' interests. For example, the welfare maximum from competitive markets may not be attained when technology facilitates natural monopoly or where externalities are present. The public interest hypothesis implies that government will intervene in these kinds of situation. Regulation is viewed strictly as a remedial activity. It is undertaken primarily to eliminate or reduce the costs associated with some market failure.

Despite its intuitive appeal, the public interest explanation is often not consistent with the facts. Regulation may sometimes be undertaken to fulfil objectives which lie outside the strict public interest. Recent US research has indicated, for instance, that regulation is not positively correlated with monopolistic market structure or the presence of external economies or diseconomies. The public interest approach also appears to have embodied the belief that government regulation is practically costless. This view has been subject to increasing criticism. Another significant problem with the public interest explanation is the lack of a clear mechanism by which the alleged and defined public interest is translated into the required legislative action. Although the public interest (or consumer protection) hypothesis is not generally robust, it has by no means been shelved. It will become clear later that it is an important argument for regulating banks.

Another significant explanation for regulation may be labelled the capture hypotheses. These assert in one form or another that regulation is demanded by interest groups that are attempting to promote their own private interests. There are several different versions of the capture explanation, and not all of them are consistent. Indeed, significant differences of opinion still exist between many capture theorists. Like the public interest explanation, the so-called capture hypotheses frequently do not stand up to close examination. For example, the capture (or producer protection) hypotheses generally emphasize that producers gain through regulation. The fact that customer groups often benefit from regulation as well is generally ignored.

A pathbreaking attempt to formulate an economic theory of regulation was embodied in a famous study of Professor Stigler. Posner and Peltzman were among the writers who also developed and contributed to this new approach. As with the political scientists' version of the capture hypothesis, Stigler admitted the capture by interest groups other than the regulated firms. But Stigler's theory was much more than another version of capture theories. He set out to recast the process and dynamics of regulation using conventional tools of economic analysis. Supply and demand reasoning were applied to the problem. The result was a more clearly defined and robust theory – one more easily testable with facts and data. This formulation has been labelled the new economic theory of regulation. In Stigler's own words (1978, p. 3):

> The central tasks of the theory of economic regulation are to explain who will receive the benefits or burdens of regulation, what form regulation will take, and the effects of regulation upon the allocation of resources.

The theory asserts that people seek to advance their own self-interest in a rational manner.

The new economic theory contends that the item being traded under regulation is the right to tax the wealth of everyone in the non-regulated group. This rarely takes the form of an explicit cash transfer. More usually it is reflected in indirect benefits, like restricted entry and price legislation. The demanders of regulation are groups seeking to increase their wealth. Suppliers are those who have the power to prescribe market rules. In essence, the theory argues that politicians provide regulatory benefits in order to obtain more political support.

Winning bidders in this market are typically groups that are small in relation to the total market. It is easier to coordinate activity and take effective action in a smaller group. A smaller group also makes it easier to exclude others outside the group receiving regulatory benefits, thereby avoiding the so-called free rider problem. Applying this theory, politicians – the ultimate suppliers of regulations – impose or reduce regulations only when this action gives them more net votes than alternative actions. The economic theory of regulation is a significant step forward from earlier explanations of regulation. Nevertheless, a great deal of theoretical and empirical work remains to be done. It is still early days to label this new economic theory of regulation a general and definitive one.

Many versions of contemporary theories of regulation are specific to particular countries and systems. Because regulation is fundamentally a politically induced process, the ability to generalize any theory across country boundaries is often inappropriate and misleading. Values, institutions, and political and social cultures differ greatly between countries. Even within a single country and for similar reasons, generalizing a theory to different stages of its development may be just as difficult. In short, the search for a general theory of regulation has not proved easy. But our particular search objectives must now become more specific. Having briefly set the scene, we may focus our attention towards the regulation of banks. First of all, we need to be clear on the nature of bank regulation.

Regulation Applied to Banks

Kinds of bank regulation

An important body of regulations has been applied traditionally to banks for reasons of general financial and economic policy. Sometimes these regulations are labelled 'macro-economic controls'. They can also be labelled 'economic controls', or 'monetary and credit controls'. In all systems banks are subject to regulation for monetary control purposes. This kind of regulation has several broad objectives which all students of economics have bred into them from numerous standard textbooks. These objectives include contributing towards preserving overall balance in the economy, helping to sustain competition, and facilitating the most appropriate allocation of resources to important economic sectors. The basic objective is to ensure that the banking system makes its proper contribution towards the government's macro-economic objectives, or at the very least that the banking system does not pull in the opposite direction. The controls used in this area have included cash and liquid assets ratios, open market operations, interest rate mechanisms, and central bank lending ceilings, directions and discount rate facilities.

Government also controls the activities of financial markets and financial institutions for a variety of other apparently sound reasons. These regulations, or controls, have several broad aims. Examples include the encouragement of fair dealings, the provision of more information, prevention of fraudulent dealings and ensuring safety. Collectively, these kinds of regulations are labelled 'prudential regulations'. Some economists refer to them generally as micro-economic controls. Prudential regulation covers those legal and administrative measures applying to all banks. Supervision is the process directed primarily at monitoring and sometimes directing individual banks in order to ensure that they obey regulations and do not behave imprudently. Some writers, however, have used the terms 'prudential regulation' and 'supervision' interchangeably. The context of the following discussion should help to clarify any possible confusion in this area.

Banking supervision is concerned fundamentally with the financial health or safety of individual banks. It is ultimately concerned with monitoring and helping to preserve the soundness of the banking system, and promoting a continued high degree of public confidence in banks. Operationally, it seeks to ensure that banks are run in a prudent manner. The fundamental aim is to protect depositors and avoid confidence crises and major funds movements. Proposals to remove or even reduce supervision are often viewed with alarm as a possible recipe for financial crises. After all, many supervisory systems developed as reactions to crises. It seems to follow that if you take away or significantly amend the supervisory system, the doors may be re-opened for another crisis to develop.

Supervision is invariably given the ultimate force of law. Banks in Britain, for example, are subject to the 1979 Banking Act. Under this statutory umbrella, a variety of instruments and techniques are used to help supervise banks. These typically include licensing, specification of allowable business, and, in some cases, balance sheet ratio controls. Although the traditional emphasis is on the prudential health of the individual bank, Les Metcalfe (see Chapter 8) draws attention towards the need for a wider, more macro view of the banking system in supervision. Further insight into this macro perspective of supervision may be seen in Cooper (1984, p. 223):

> As one British banker put it when discussing the new principles of supervision with an official of the Bank of England, 'if you look after the liquidity of the market as a whole, we can look after the liquidity of our individual banks'.

Supervision, therefore, has both micro- and macro-economic dimensions.

The micro dimension of banking supervision has traditionally been its main emphasis. It is concerned with the individual bank, and its asset, liability and capital mix. The micro dimension is concerned with important operational areas like liquidity, capital adequacy, and foreign exchange exposure. On a broader level, it is also concerned with important associated areas like operating efficiency, the range of financial instruments available, and the rates of interest charged by banks. An immediate problem in studying supervisory methods is that all these areas may also be subjected to and affected by other kinds of regulation.

On the macro level, supervision is concerned with areas like the risk of the system as a whole, its stability, and the depth and strength of the main markets dealt in by banks. Another contemporary problem for supervisors at this level is assessing the prudential implications of banks moving into new markets and territories. Already it is clear that a neat segmentation of the micro and macro aspects of supervision may not always be possible or desirable. New instruments (like Certificates of Deposits (CDs) in the 1960s, for example) belong to the micro sphere of banking supervision. But the depth, stability and resilience of the markets in which they are traded are an obvious macro concern in the sense that we have defined it.

It is clear that all forms of bank regulation carry the potential for influencing the kind of business undertaken by the regulated banks. This is because regulations, when effective, can alter the risks and corresponding returns faced by banks. Consider the case, for instance, where prudential regulations are effective and banks have to be licensed. A licensing system implies that the licensed operators may be able to extract a regulatory rent in the form of growing and protected profit margins. This might happen through the restrictions on competition (both existing and potential) brought about by regulations restricting the numbers of institutions that can perform banking business. On the other hand, economic controls may correspondingly impede the competitive abilities of regulated institutions. Bank regulations, therefore, usually have significant implications for competition. Although too much competition has its dangers for prudential safety, excessive restrictions may strifle innovations and the ability to meet legitimate demands on the system. Jack Revell takes up these issues in Chapter 10.

Although at an expository level we can neatly distinguish between monetary regulation and supervision, in practice the two areas may often overlap. Indeed, the supervisory function is invariably exercised in the knowledge of a responsible monetary authority. At another level, the main purpose of the lender of last resort function is usually seen as protecting aggregate bank deposits. It is not designed to protect all banks and all depositors. In this role, though, it may also protect individual banks and depositors. Even this apparently neat distinction, however, has become blurred. The US Federal Reserve Board, for example, has provided last resort facilities to individual large banks in recent years. The Bank of England's Lifeboat also evidences a more specific, less system-orientated, lender of last resort function. In the next chapter we shall explore in a little more detail the relationship between monetary policy and prudential regulation. For the present, we can now consider more directly why banks are supervised.

Rationale for supervision

According to the Stiglerian model of regulation introduced earlier, no matter what the original aim of a regulatory agency, the agency is eventually co-opted by the industry. The regulations imposed become those demanded by the private interests of those regulated. This model applied to UK banking implies that the supervisory framework may eventually develop towards a form demanded by the industry. We shall remain neutral on this hypothesis, although I suspect that some bankers reading this paragraph might find it difficult to contain their neutrality! However, the study by Jane Sargent (in Chapter 7) does remind us of the role of politics and pressure groups in shaping bank supervisory legislation.

A primary aim of supervision is to help ensure that soundness or financial health is maintained in the banking system. In Minsky's terms (from the preceding chapter), this implies that 'Ponzi' financing in particular does not begin to figure significantly in bank financial structures. This kind of financing by economic units is one of the most risky forms identified by Minsky. Sound, or prudentially safe, banking systems are generally believed to be essential for economic stability. After all, a threat to the banking system is a threat to an economy's whole system for the exchange of goods and services.

One important rationale for supervision, then, is to ensure that there exists a high degree of public confidence in banks. The operational objective is to protect depositors and avoid major disturbances in confidence and funds movements. A fundamental rationale for supervision in this setting, therefore, is to help protect the solvency of individual banks. It attempts to do this by monitoring and helping to ensure that banks are prudently run. This depositor-protection rationale when translated operationally into rules for helping to preserve bank solvency has both economic and social aspects.

Protecting bank depositors may be more justified on social grounds than economic ones. It may be socially unacceptable that the savings of small depositors may be lost to them by the imprudent actions of banks.

There is no necessary presumption in this rationale that supervision alone can do the job of preserving bank solvency. Supervision does imply, however, that in its absence imprudent banking practices might eventually develop in some banks. It also suggests that these practices, if left unchecked, carry within them the seeds of problems whose potential consequences cannot be left to the sole control of an unfettered market. There is no denying that production of unequivocal 'scientific evidence' in the modern economic vein to validate these views is difficult, probably impossible, and unnecessary anyway. Both early and modern banking history have generated persuasive supporting evidence. Very few students of banking who have examined this evidence would argue that there is no strong, pragmatic case for at least some prudential regulation. In a recent scholarly study, for example, Maisel (1981, p. 5) stated:

> Yet the need for some regulation is widely recognized. Without regulation, an undue percentage of financial institutions are likely to take excessive risks.

Of course, acceptance of this view does not by itself tackle the critical questions of how much regulation and supervision and of what kind.

In a free-enterprise economy, the economic rationale for regulation is sometimes to encourage the competitive market, and in other cases to replace or modify it. When the market cannot do its job properly, taking into account all the associated costs and benefits, a market failure is said to occur. Market failure may take several forms in the case of financial markets and financial institutions, and these failures or their respective potential provide the main economic rationales for regulation. The need to restrict monopoly power and promote competition exemplify such rationales. Rules may be developed to prevent monopolistic practices like cartel behaviour. Regulations developed to promote competition may sometimes conflict with those enacted to preserve banking safety. A trade-off may need to be made between the benefits of more competition and the advantages of greater banking safety and stability. We shall explore this problem in the next chapter.

Information and confidence

Several important rationales for regulation reflect informational deficiencies. A difference in information between contract parties, for example, may open up the possibility for one party to expropriate wealth at the expense of the less well-informed parties. The latter are generally unsophisticated, like most consumers, and the corrective rules may curtail allowable contracts and require fuller disclosure of information. Other informational weaknesses in the market may open up the possibility for agents to act against the interests of their employers. An example of this situation would be where agents had access to special information which could be used to secure personal profit at the expense of their employers. Corrective rules for this kind of problem include restrictions on the potential for insider trading and, once again, fuller disclosure of information to all interested parties. All of these rationales can be used to help support the case for prudentially regulating financial institutions.

Nevertheless, the primary economic and historical rationale for bank supervision is the avoidance of market failure caused by asymmetric information. The problem arises because of differences in information between those owning and managing banks and their depositors. This problem is best seen when financial institutions are unregulated. In this case depositors attempt periodically to withdraw funds if they are fearful for the safety of their funds. The UK fringe banking crisis, for instance, has reminded us forcefully that the threat of this kind of market failure is a real and dangerous one in an unsupervised banking system. Banking supervision and associated solvency regulations are directed towards monitoring the prudential soundness of banks. In the majority of banks, of course, prudential rules would be stringently observed and developed in the absence of any formal supervision. It may take imprudence in just one or two small and otherwise insignificant institutions, however, to cause problems for all banks.

The essence of fractional reserve banking has always been confidence. As long as banks engage in maturity transformation and take on risks, public confidence will remain an essential foundation stone for banking stability, growth and development. Confidence is an intangible concept, but it is the basis of all Western banking systems and the international banking system. Supervision alone, of course, could not guarantee bank soundness and the maintenance of public confidence in banks. A responsible monetary authority, a reasonably stable political, economic and social environment, and a professional and competent bank management are necessary (and arguably much more important) ingredients. None of these desirable attributes, however, corrects the kind of deficiencies and weaknesses that modern supervision is designed to tackle. What evidence have we that stability of the overall monetary environment, for example, and even generally competent bank management are guarantees that every individual bank will behave prudently? They may be necessary conditions, but they are clearly not sufficient ones for preserving banking stability and confidence. It takes problems in only a very small sector of the industry to stimulate broader questions of confidence.

An important rationale for supervision, therefore, rests primarily on the existence or potential of certain market weaknesses, particularly market failure precipitated through asymmetric information. In this kind of situation, supervision may (at least in principle) increase somebody's economic lot without making anybody else worse off. In this general context, the public interest explanation of regulation is traditionally appropriate to banks. Bank prudential regulations are often justified as promoting the public interest. In this setting they can provide significant public and private benefits. At a macro level, instability may be reduced through the aid of supervision. On a micro plane, individual depositors are protected. But could the information deficiencies which provide a primary rationale for regulation be corrected in a better way? How exactly do they justify at least some supervision?

Where information costs are high, supervision may be a more economically productive way of preserving bank soundness. Information costs may themselves be either quantifiable or intangible. Quantifiable (or direct) information costs include the production and publication in suitable form of relevant banking data. These data include key trends and developments, especially those carrying risk implications, in markets and countries dealt in by banks. In principle at least, these data could be provided by some neutral agency to the banking public at large. So this informational aspect alone may not provide a rationale for supervision. It is in the intangible cost sphere that a much stronger supporting rationale is seen for supervision.

One immediate intangible (or indirect) cost of information is how individual bank lenders and borrowers, both existing and potential, can interpret these data and supporting information. Considerable expertise is needed and undoubted economies of scale exist in processing and interpretation. Economies of scale are obtained most efficiently in this area through the economic exploitation of a body of skilled personnel dealing with a large number of banks over a considerable period of time. Awareness needs to be fostered of potentially risky developments in different parts of the banking system. Sophisticated tools of analysis may need to be applied and continual awareness is required of developments in other banking and supervisory systems. Often, the ability to judge bank management capabilities and integrity may be required. This kind of qualitative evaluation can only be undertaken through personal contacts and frequent exchanges over a period of time.

Another of the essential tasks of modern supervision is to look ahead and try to foresee significant changes in bank risk exposures, and the emergence of new ones. What hope, incentive or need is there for individual depositors and lenders to acquire such skills? The economic law of the division of labour helps support the case for a separate and specialized supervisory function. Adam Smith in his day (and I stress in his day) would probably not support bank supervision in preference to the unfettered market, but he identified a key economic law that we may employ. Increasing returns from specialization and the division of labour may be obtained in the process of assessing bank risks for prudential purposes through employing bank supervisors.

Another intangible information cost of relevance is the potential adverse effects on depositor, lender and market psychology of information needed to assess bank riskiness. The risk implications of rescheduled international loans in the current banking environment are just one example. Even sophisticated banking students do not know what the full implications of such exposures will be in time. Nevertheless, they are much less likely to 'lose their nerve' or be subject to sudden attacks of irrationality. For example, they are more likely to understand the role of international liquidity in buying time for banks to work out potential bad loans. Full disclosure and total reliance on the free market imply the need for full information and processing capabilities and for rationality. But these are not characteristics of bank consumers in the real world in which banks operate. Supervision allows borrowers and lenders to deal with banks of all sizes without the need to attempt a formal and costly risk analysis. This is an important component of the bundle of utilities, the economic good, produced by supervision.

Another component of this bundle of utilities is perhaps more macro orientated. United States banking experiences during the Great Depression and subsequent events (like the UK 1973–5 crisis) exemplified the importance of a responsible monetary authority. Specifically, this is the key role of the central bank's lender of last resort function. As we mentioned earlier, the main role of this support function is to protect aggregate bank deposits. It is a liquidity support for the system as a whole, and it is a last-resort facility. Supervision is needed to ensure that it does not become a first-resort facility. Otherwise, the public at large bear banking risks which should properly fall on the bank's shareholders. Thus, supervision avoids the subsidizing by the public of excessive risk leveraging by bank shareholders. This kind of risk is referred to generally as 'moral hazard'. Later on we shall encounter other instances of potential moral hazard risk which bear on banking supervision.

Supervision of Banks

Supervisory methods

For present purposes, we can identify generally three broad channels through which the authorities intervene in banking markets to bolster confidence. These are through the central bank lender of last resort action, deposit insurance, and the supervisory process embodying detailed solvency regulations. It has already been explained that the lender of last resort function is designed primarily to protect aggregate bank deposits. Although it has indirect (and latterly sometimes direct) implications for bank supervision, the lender of last resort function is not conventionally regarded as a supervisory method *per se*. The core of modern banking supervision is based on deposit insurance and detailed solvency regulations.

Deposit insurance is essentially an insurance scheme through which banks subscribe to a common fund in order to protect certain classes of depositors. It was introduced successfully into the US banking system following the famous 1933 'bank holiday'. Since that time it has become widely regarded as one of the most important single factors in helping to preserve US banking stability. Commonly produced evidence to support this view is the marked absence of retail depositor runs in the US since the Great Depression. Other factors are certainly in part responsible for this same phenomenon, but US bankers and banking students generally ascribe high relative weighting to the contribution of deposit insurance towards maintaining overall banking stability.

Deposit insurance is designed primarily to reduce the probability of bank runs. In essence, it is designed to prevent the event (bank runs) insured against. It does this simply by bolstering confidence in the system. Protected depositors do not need to worry if a bank fails because their deposits are covered under the insurance scheme. At the same time, deposit insurance exists to reimburse the depositors of those banks that do fail. One problem with contemporary deposit insurance schemes is that the insurance premiums do not generally reflect bank riskiness. An established, low-risk operator pays the same premiums as a new, higher-risk bank. Many economists and bankers have criticized this aspect of deposit insurance, and these issues are taken up by Mark Flannery, Paul Horvitz and Paul Peterson in Part E of this book.

At this time, much US research in particular is being concentrated on how risk-related deposit insurance premiums might be derived operationally. This is a complex issue, and it is related to the thorny problem of bank capital adequacy. Because of qualitative factors and various cross-subsidization features of banking risk, it seems likely that the search for a generally acceptable risk-related insurance scheme will be a difficult one. It is the existence of contemporary flat-rate deposit insurance schemes which helps support the co-existence of detailed solvency regulations, the core of supervisory methods. This is because flat-rate deposit insurance and the lender of last resort function give rise to the phenomenon of moral hazard in banking.

The potential and nature of moral hazard can be seen by considering a banking world in which the lender of last resort function was exercised whenever the banking system came under pressure, and in which a flat-rate deposit insurance scheme co-existed. In this hypothetical world, there is also no supervision. The profit-seeking, innovative banker in this world would not be too long in realizing that substantial and comparatively safe risk leveraging is possible. Banks would naturally have a propensity to push their risk leveraging beyond those levels that would be dictated by the usual rules of prudence.

In contemporary banking systems, like that of the UK, the lender of last resort function, deposit insurance and detailed solvency regulations are interdependent in promoting confidence and curbing the moral hazard potential. It is in this context that many have argued, for example, that contemporary deposit insurance creates a need for bank regulation (see Mark Flannery's views in Chapter 15). The 1979 UK Banking Act established a Deposit Protection Scheme which became operational in the early 1980s. Any supervisory system in which the severity of the controls is independent of individual bank risk is exposed to this moral hazard risk. Such a system may contribute directly to increased risk levels in banks. Evidence of moral hazard potential in banking systems can be seen at one level when low-risk banks – often the core, or primary banks – demand the supervision of other, more risky operators.

Detailed solvency regulations are generally the most complex area of banking regulations. It is hardly surprising, therefore, that they are also a frequently misunderstood dimension of regulation. They include several categories of regulation which may affect bank solvency. Some of these, like pricing constraints and entry restrictions, are designed to protect banks against excessive competition. Examples include restrictions on the rates of interest payable on different kinds of deposits and licensing requirements. Other categories of solvency regulation are designed to constrain the freedom of management to hold risky portfolios. Under this heading come activity restrictions, balance sheet structure controls, and restrictions on insider conduct intended to curb self-dealing and conflicts of interest.

Supervisory techniques essentially seek to monitor and control capital, liquidity, diversification and risks. Simultaneously, they attempt to foster sound management. One immediate problem is that no objective measure has yet been developed which is generally accepted and which satisfies the above objectives. In practice, controls tend to be based on a mixture of historical precedent, subjective assessments, industry norms, intuition, and supervisory preferences. It is against this background that the major debates on bank supervision have tended to focus on the quantity and type of regulation, rather than questioning the need for at least some kind of regulation.

The complexity of the supervisory process is seen at one level in the range of different methods employed. These may cover techniques like ratio controls, licensing, bank examinations, deposit insurance and diversification restrictions. At another level, we have seen that the supervisory process is not the only regulatory action to which banks are exposed. Little wonder that one of the oldest debates in public policy concerns the best way to regulate banks. Increased safety has a cost in the form of reduced bank efficiency. How to achieve the correct trade-off between these two important goals, however, has not yet been resolved. Indeed, universal acceptance of views in this area is unlikely anyway because it implies broader political questions on the optimum banking system. Nevertheless, we shall return later on a number of occasions (see Chapter 3 and Jack Revell in Chapter 10, for instance) to the trade-off between supervision and competition.

Objectives and instruments

The general objectives of supervision seem clear enough. The preservation of confidence, monitoring and regulating banking solvency, curbing excessive risk in the system, and all the other important rationales and aims that we have already identified. These general objectives are widely accepted, although vigorous debate often arises on how much supervision and what form of supervision can best attain these ends. This leads on to a practical issue of some concern. How do we measure or appraise the specific efficiency and effectiveness of a supervisory instrument? Efficiency concerns the relative success of the instrument in cost : benefit terms of achieving a stated objective. Effectiveness bears directly on its ability to achieve the aims assigned to it. In these terms, an instrument may be effective, but inefficient; it cannot be efficient and ineffective. The basic problem, however, is the specification of the objective assigned to each instrument. Neither efficiency nor effectiveness can really be assessed without these data.

A single regulation, for example, may have different goals. We have also seen that several different regulations may seek collectively to achieve a common end, like preserving confidence in the banking system. For measurement purposes, two immediate problems arise. First, the objectives specified are often intangible and qualitative in nature. Secondly, it may be difficult or impossible to unbundle a regulation from several other regulations which bear directly or indirectly on the specified objective. It seems likely that considerable synergy exists between the collection of different regulations applied to banks, especially in key areas like banking confidence.

Some regulatory techniques may have more clearly specified objectives. For example, capital ratios may be designed to limit excessive risk exposure in banks, but even here we have to be very careful. This is because there are often significant risk and return interrelationships within the bank. By this is meant that liquidity, solvency and profit are often highly interdependent. Low solvency risk (stringent capital adequacy standards) is usually obtained at the cost of lower profit. Lower profit today may restrict the capacity to grow (because capital account growth is correspondingly reduced) tomorrow. It may also affect liquidity if a bank's borrowing capacity is reduced through poor profit performance. In short, trade-offs have to be made by banks between liquidity, solvency and profit. Often, the effects of a change in any one of these three elements is complex and dynamic, it may affect many other variables and risk exposures, and extend far into the future. This operational feature complicates measuring the effects of a specific regulation or regulatory change, although it does not preclude it.

One operational feature of banking which does create appraisal problems for a specific supervisory technique concerns the cross-subsidization of risk within the bank. Just as several banking regulations may be aimed, directly or indirectly, at the same target, so a bank's prudential resources of one kind may meet several demands. A good example is the capital adequacy position. Not only does it act as a general confidence cushion against uncertainty, it also helps to buttress the liquidity position. For instance, it may be used to absorb losses on securities sold to meet unexpected liquidity pressures. The capital adequacy position also facilitates the ability of a bank to generate profits. Capital adequacy also implies that the bank is reasonably profitable and prudently liquid. How much it contributes to profitability and liquidity, and vice versa, is a much more difficult question. Nevertheless, it is a fact of life that these three elements cross-subsidize each other. The relative importance of each also varies through time and under different circumstances.

Of course, many supervisory techniques are also assigned the qualitative function of preserving banking confidence, either singly or as part of the overall supervisory package. Another problem that we have already seen is that other regulations (like those designed to foster banking competition) may conflict with general supervisory objectives. All these features make a clear specification of the objective(s) of a particular supervisory instrument a difficult practical task. This present corresponding problems in assessing the efficiency of instruments. It also makes the matching of supervisory objectives and instruments a difficult job. Marco Onado tackles some aspects of this general problem in Chapter 9.

Supervisory style

Supervisory style is concerned with how the supervisory authorities employ the techniques at their disposal. In one sense, this style is part and parcel of supervisory method, but it will prove convenient and useful to examine it separately. Supervisory methods – like licensing, ratios and bank examinations – are the same in many banking systems, but supervisory style can differ markedly. Supervisory style is reflected in both the philosophy employed by the authorities and the way that supervision is implemented operationally. The style of supervision is probably the single most important factor bearing on both the efficiency and effectiveness of supervision.

In practice supervisors have tended to adopt various styles of supervision. Two supervisory authorities, for example, may employ the same technique, but adopt very different approaches to its implementation and interpretation. Let us take the example of a capital ratio, like the ratio capital : deposits. In the face of the complexity of the supervisory process, supervisors F may adopt a flexible approach. The ratio components (numerators and denominators) are clearly specified, but a mandatory ratio level – the minimum level required – is not prescribed for all banks. Supervisors L, on the other hand, may favour the legal prescription of mandatory levels for all banks. In an earlier paper (Gardener, 1978) I identified these two polar extremes, respectively, as 'government by men' and 'government by law'. The traditional UK approach of suasion comes close to the former (model F), and the Continental preference for 'transparency' the latter (model L). In practice, of course, these two extreme models are hardly ever found. But they provide a useful focal point for some further considerations. Both models have associated costs and benefits.

Model L is the one favoured perhaps by lawyers. It is clear in its prescriptions and therefore resolves considerable uncertainty. The mandatory rules themselves are often derived from historical (allegedly proven) experience. But there may be considerable costs. One of these encompasses another moral hazard danger. If the same ratio levels are prescribed for all banks without recognizing differences in their inherent riskiness, the higher-risk operators may effectively be subsidized by the more prudent and efficient managements. The latter may also be penalized more heavily in that they could, if left to their own devices, operate as prudently as other banks, but with lower-risk cushioning. In short, innovation may be restricted and progressive managements penalized.

The flexible supervisory system, model F, has the advantage that it is more responsive to change and innovations. Individual banks are not placed in the straitjacket of common, mandatory ratio levels. More risky banks are required to acquire higher levels of prudential cushioning, and vice versa. This is the model most favoured by the market economist who believes firmly in the unseen hand of the market. It is potentially a more market-orientated system. The cost is that the system may become too lax and permissive. At the extreme, it may become virtually free market regulation (see Chapter3). With the co-existence of flat-rate deposit insurance and an effective lender of last resort function, moral hazard becomes a danger.

This brief examination is a reminder again that banking safety is not a free good. It has an opportunity cost in the form of lower earnings. Measuring this cost is, as we have seen, a difficult task. Two interesting conflicts are now evident in the supervisory debate. From a macro point of view, supervision is a desirable economic good because it leads to a more stable banking system. On the other hand, the micro (efficiency) level may often support more deregulation on the grounds that regulation may lead to inefficient markets.

Regulations should only be imposed when their marginal benefits exceed their marginal costs. Within a particular supervisory system, banks may need to be regulated more strictly at times if the safety of the system is to be preserved. Conditions may be such that excessive risk-taking by some banks becomes a stronger possibility. This might seem to lend support to a general view that supervisors should be most conservative when banks want to be most liberal, and vice versa. Besides seeming contrary to human behaviour, the conditions might often be appropriate for banks to be more liberal. In practice, supervisory standards change over time as preferences, style and techniques change. Modern supervision has to assess altering conditions and adapt accordingly.

How supervise?

We have drawn out rationales for supervision and discussed associated areas, like supervisory objectives and instruments. But a much more fundamental issue concerns the abilities of supervisors to supervise and regulate. We need to draw a distinction between supervision and complete control. A clear line may need to be specified between supervisory aims and management tasks.

It is sometimes asserted that supervision implies that supervisors know better than management how to run banks. The very existence of supervision is almost taken to be an insult to bank management competence. This view reflects a fundamental misconception as to the role of supervisors. Although the preceding analysis should have answered much of this criticism, at least implicitly, we need to be a little more specific. The supervisory authorities cannot (and would not generally wish to) run banks, because that is simply not their job. After all, with complete internal authority and full access to the relevant information, management itself is faced with a full-time task. Even with these characteristics and data, control over all bank variables by management is never complete and always difficult.

An outside body, like the supervisory authorities, would be faced with a much more difficult task than management if it attempted to control each bank completely. Indeed, it would be an impossible task. Modern supervision attempts to make banks conform to a comparatively small number of prudential rules. Most banks conform to these or similar ones anyway. Other matters are left to the discretion of management. As we shall see, UK supervision may be likened to the role of a referee with the banks as players. Another analogy sees the supervisors as a kind of management consultancy service, but with clout. Chapter 4 will explain how the Bank of England has adopted a supervisory philosophy first referred to by Revell (1975) as 'vicarious participation' in bank management. Our next task in the following chapter will be to consider in more detail some of the problems and conflicts that can arise in the practical supervisory process.

References and Bibliography

Campbell, T. S. (1982), *Financial Institutions, Markets and Economic Activity* (New York: McGraw-Hill).

Cooper, John (1984), *The Management and Regulation of Banks* (London: Macmillan).

Edwards, F. R. (1979), *Issues in Financial Regulation* (New York: McGraw-Hill).

Fels, Allan (1981), *Theories of Economic Regulation and their Application to Australia*, Internal Discussion Paper (Clayton, Vic.: Monash University).

Gardener, E. P. M. (1978), 'Capital adequacy and bank prudential regulation', *Journal of Bank Research*, vol. 9, no. 3 (Autumn), pp. 173–80.

Kalish III, Lionel and R. Alton Gilbert (1973), 'The influence of bank regulation on the operating efficiency of commercial banks', *The Journal of Finance*, vol. XXVIII, no. 5 (Dec.), pp. 1287–301.

Maisel, Sherman, J. (ed.) (1981), *Risk and Capital Adequacy in Commercial Banks* (Chicago and London: University of Chicago Press).

Mullineaux, David J. (1978), 'Regulation: Whence it came and whether it's here to stay', *Business Review*, Federal Reserve Bank of Philadelphia (Sept.–Oct.), pp. 3–11.

Noll, Roger G. (1980), *What is regulation?* Social Science Working Paper 324, Division of the Humanities and Social Sciences, California Institute of Technology (Pasadena: California).

Peltzman, Sam (1976), 'Toward a more general theory of regulation', *The Journal of Law and Economics*, vol. XIX, no. 2 (Aug.), pp. 211–40.

Posner, Richard, A. (1974), 'Theories of economic regulation', *Bell Journal of Economics and Management Science*, vol. 5, no. 2 (Autumn), pp. 335–58.

Revell, J. R. S. (1975), *Solvency and Regulation of Banks*, Bangor Occasional Papers in Economics, No. 5 (Cardiff: University of Wales Press).

Stigler, George, J. (1978), 'The theory of economic regulation', *Bell Journal of Economics and Management Science*, vol. 2, no. 1 (Spring), pp. 3–21.

Wilson, George W. (1982), 'Regulating and deregulating business', *Business Horizons*, (July/Aug.).

3 Supervisory Issues

Perhaps more significant than the debate over the need for regulation is controversy over its form.
Sherman J. Maisel (1981), *Risk and Capital Adequacy in Commercial Banks* (Chicago and London: University of Chicago Press).

Introduction

Supervisors and bankers do not live in the economist's perfectly competitive world of longer-term equilibrium. All too often recently, shorter-term disequilibria have dominated both supervisory practices and philosophy. This has been a necessary reaction to immediate events. It would be disturbing, however, if the conditions under which UK supervision developed rapidly and the immediate problems it has had to tackle were to preclude the relevance now of fundamental questioning and critical appraisal. Some of these fundamental questions will now be explored.

The list of issues considered here is by no means complete. However, it does comprise a wide-ranging survey of some of the key problems and questions raised by the modern supervisory process. This survey provides additional necessary background to the specialist contributions which follow later in the collected readings section of this book; many of the areas introduced will be developed further in these chapters. In little over a decade, the banking supervisory process has grown in potential academic richness. The following discussion should help confirm the possibilities and need for continuing research into this important process. It also serves as a warning about the complexity of some fundamental supervisory issues.

The first major issue to be explored is the role of the market in bank supervision. By allowing the market to play a larger role in bank supervision, some of the costs associated with supervision may be avoided. Many proponents of bank deregulation in the US, for example, argue along these same lines.

Supervision and the Market

The market revisited

Supervision involves the replacement or modification of the unimpeded economic signals of the market by commands and controls. In recent years, prudential regulations have grown alongside the worldwide trend of proliferating regulation throughout most Western economies. One of the features of the twentieth century has been the declining proportion of resources whose use is determined by the market mechanism. A corresponding growth of central planning and control has resulted. This decline in the use of the unfettered market constitutes a real paradigm crisis for most market (non-Marxist) economists.

Interestingly enough, Evans (1981) reminds us that theoretical economics does not provide support for either regulation or deregulation. It is the perfect competition model from economics, though, which is often used to support deregulation. Under the perfect competition model, marginal cost is equated to marginal revenue at the point where social welfare is maximized. It is against this background that market economists generally favour resource allocation through impersonal market signals, rather than the prescriptions of regulatory agencies and other similar bodies. The most ardent supporters of free enterprise argue that the best regulator of profit-seeking enterprises is the 'unseen hand' which operates through free markets driven by all-out competition. Our first consideration, therefore, is whether we can leave banking supervision to this kind of free market? It will be useful to examine several relevant aspects of this question.

First of all, one might start off by developing a rather cynical line of argument. It commences by questioning the validity of the perfect competition model in practical banking operations and the related question of supervision. Eliminating supervision to secure the alleged benefits of perfect competition assumes, first, either that banks would be immediately subject to perfect competition, or that forces would be released which would stimulate a rapid evolution towards this hypothetical ideal state. A monetary economist might argue, however, that the main banking input, money, is always subject (at least potentially) to monopoly control. The government or central bank has the monopoly power to restrict nominal money output and raise interest rates. This economic state of affairs is not likely to be affected by eliminating supervision. Nor are all the other market imperfections which exist in banking and financial systems likely to disappear.

The fact is that the real banking world does not seem to conform even potentially to the perfect competition model. Nor is there any reason for supposing that the absence of supervision would alter this fact. It would be extremely hard to envisage a realistic state of affairs where most markets dealt in by banks were perfectly competitive. Indeed, a paradox quickly emerges. Banks operate by exploiting market imperfections. The intermediation process is itself largely dependent on market imperfections. If one of the ultimate benefits of perfect competition is to eliminate these market imperfections, the banking role of financial intermediation may correspondingly be threatened. But we are on conceptual and difficult ground. We are talking about a highly idealistic normative prescription, a theoretical construct. Let us examine more closely what perfect or near perfect competition might imply in a more practical, institutional light. In this setting, perfect competition is taken to be synonymous with the absence of any form of bank regulation.

A competitive industry is one where there are many firms selling their products at the lowest price so that they still find it profitable to remain in that sector. Under these conditions, no firm is extracting any monopoly rent, i.e. no firm earns any excess profit. Abusive and inefficient behaviour is corrected through the impersonal forces of the market. In this kind of competitive market, the weak and inefficient firms do not survive in the long run. In the unregulated banking industry, therefore, we could expect to see a close relationship between profit and competition. Rising profit would attract new entrants who would eventually tend to reduce profit. Insufficient profit, on the other hand, also leads to a corresponding withdrawal of banks or contraction of the industry. This may encompass voluntary withdrawal, reduction in the operations of banks remaining in the industry, and/or the failure of some banks. In the long run all would be well since the unseen hand secures the most efficient resource allocation.

The problem is that for the banking industry, the long run may be far too long. In the short run, even a single bank failure can have far-reaching and disproportionate consequences. The loss of wealth that may be occasioned through a bank failure is not the same as the loss of an equal amount of other kinds of wealth. Many theoretical economists fail to recognize this important operational fact. Bank failures may give rise to significant and far-reaching negative externalities.

The failure of one bank may immediately raise questions about the solvency of all other banks. Although deposit insurance may eradicate retail deposit runs of the US Great Depression variety, the modern wholesale money markets, for example, are not similarly protected. Indeed, because they are better informed, the sensitivity of wholesale markets to rumours is almost certainly higher than in less sophisticated retail markets. In practice, however, these markets appear sometimes to exhibit markedly unstable features following a crisis and rumours. The latter may eventually become self-fulfilling and a source of more instability. Systematic irrationality appears to be the paradoxical occasional product of apparently efficient markets. Stability and efficiency may exist in the long run. In the short run, however, instability and temporary inefficiencies can do great damage. We need to recognize institutional facts of life when examining the possible recasting of banking regulation to secure theoretical benefits.

Those who argue that the proven discipline of the market is the best regulator of banking behaviour seek to recast the banking market in their own image. Short of institutional failure and disruptions of the financial system, market forces provide no limitations on the innovations developed by bankers. During periods of virtual *laissez-faire* in banking supervision, banks innovated vigorously to gain additional profits through eliminating market imperfections. But these innovations themselves tended to decrease the stability of the financial system. In the US and other developed countries, many economists argue strongly for banking deregulation. Of course, deregulation may well increase the efficiency of the system, but we do not know this from historical or modern banking experience. In fact, the 'proven discipline' of the banking market in an historical setting supports at least some regulation.

Historical experience has been that the forces of banking competition, when given full sway, eventually have to be curbed. This is partly because the external effects of a single bank failure are felt not only by other financial institutions and business firms but also by depositors; they may be temporarily or permanently deprived of their wealth, together with their confidence in the banking system. Once confidence in the system is lost, output of the 'economic product' of intermediation is correspondingly reduced. This product encompasses all the utilities bundled into the claims produced through the financial intermediation process. Many of these arise through the exploitation of economies of scale and require the continual maintenance of confidence in the system.

The highly geared structure of the banking firm and the nature of the deposit instrument offer unique opportunities in an unregulated competitive environment for banks to expropriate (wittingly or unwittingly) depositors' wealth. The bank failures that have usually followed a period of *laissez-faire* have invariably prompted significant (sometimes overwhelming) regulatory reactions. Competition is then replaced by stability, and surviving institutions are often granted practical quasi monopolies. They are protected from competition (through licensing, for instance) and their risk-taking often subsidized (by flat-rate deposit insurance, for example). These reactionary, anti-competitive moves then breed inefficiencies and other costs. The arteries of banking begin to harden. For a time, however, the potential consequences of these developments are not exposed.

Role of the market

The kind of supervisory system instituted as a response to crises or other shorter-term pressures may soon acquire a virtual life of its own. Over a period of time it achieves 'success' in the sense that the crisis is not repeated. The fact that a renewed crisis does not develop is often ascribed to the new supervision, even though this may be only part of the story. More rigorous supervision may have been justified (at least for a time) by events of yesterday, but banks operate today and for tomorrow. Conditions alter and banks and their markets change. The 1960s and 1970s, for example, saw a marked change in the nature of banking business. Competition, inflation, innovation and rapid technological evolution produced different kinds of banks and banking markets from those of previous years. Supervisory rules and methods developed in earlier banking history became increasingly suspect. This trend has not diminished as we move further into the 1980s. It has been a particular source of attention in the US deregulation debate.

We can draw two initial conclusions from these considerations. First, prudential regulation once installed, especially following some banking crisis, may subsequently become difficult to remove. The underlying philosophy appears to be that if the medicine corrected the disease in the first place, continual dosing may be the best form of future protection. Indeed, more and more of the medicine may eliminate all prospects of ever getting the disease. We know that this treatment, despite its intuitive logic, does not usually work in the case of the human organism. US experience in particular suggests that it may also not work in the case of the banking system. The second conclusion we can draw is that supervisors cannot ignore the market.

Prudential regulations are ultimately subject to the forces of the market. The market pushes and pulls at regulatory constraints. Market forces eventually draw out opportunities to avoid restrictive and inappropriate regulations. Other financial institutions may see openings to exploit opportunities not available currently to regulated ones. The regulated institutions may then find themselves at a competitive disadvantage compared with their more liberated brethren. This state of affairs can help breed significant and dangerous inefficiencies. It may eventually threaten banking stability.

On the one hand, the regulated and correspondingly disadvantaged institutions may seek to innovate around the restrictive regulations. This economic response may produce avoidable instability in the system. Another aspect is that the market opportunities denied to the heavily regulated institutions may be fields in which they have more intrinsic expertise than the less regulated institutions. In short, heavily regulated institutions could perform those economic tasks more efficiently if given the opportunity. Society is the net loser if it has to pay more for the economic output of banks.

Another aspect of potential inefficiency is that the profits and other benefits extracted from the opportunities denied to the regulated institutions may in turn be used to help cross-subsidize other activities performed (or planned to be undertaken) by the less regulated institutions. These may be activities again more efficiently performed by the heavily regulated group of institutions. In short, supervision may breed and foster inefficiencies if it ignores the realities of the market. Inflation exacerbates this problem.

High and volatile inflation rates have been a major underlying cause of increased bank riskiness over recent years. Their influence has been felt throughout the banking firm. Record high and uncertain interest rates, operating cost pressures, and the risks and losses associated with the environment of uncertainty are a sample of the channels through which recent inflation experiences have worked through into the banking system. Another problem for banks in the UK and other countries has been that high inflation has accompanied severe economic depression. One result has been that high nominal (paper) profits have been earned during a period when potential bank losses have been building up for eventual realization at a later stage of the business cycle. Another problem has been that inflation coupled with technological developments, both real and financial, has stimulated banks to innovate around supervisory regulation.

As the burden of supervision increases, so the corresponding benefit for doing things differently rises. Greater efforts to alter market solutions through regulation are liable to induce a corresponding economic response in the form of bank innovations to avoid the regulation. Regulation-induced innovations are developed by banks. These may be product substitutions or completely new services. Inflation comes into the picture because by raising nominal interest rates, accelerating inflation increases the opportunity cost burdens of existing regulations. In short, it becomes more attractive to innovate around a regulation. This attraction is enhanced when exogenous technological change also lowers the marginal costs of avoiding regulatory burdens.

Given this scenario, the political process of prudential regulation is subject to reduced efficiency as banks undertake the economic process of regulatory avoidance. As innovations spread, other less competitive banks and financial institutions are stimulated to respond to the growing competitive pressures. Supervision may become increasingly less effective unless the supervisors respond quickly to close the loopholes created through bank innovations of the kind described.

But many supervisory systems react more slowly to change than the institutions they supervise. The political system is more forgiving of excessive delay than of hasty, but possibly inappropriate, responses. Eventually, though, a process of re-regulation takes place and the above cycle may start again when conditions are ripe. This is the kind of picture painted by Kane's (1981) informative bank model of the 'regulatory dialectic'. The practical implications for present purposes are again clear. Supervisors may ignore the market for a time, but eventually market forces make themselves felt on bank resource allocation decisions. Clearly, realistic supervision has to recognize and develop alongside these market forces. This is necessary in order to ensure that supervision remains effective, that possibly risky avoidance innovations do not become a problem, and that the benefits of competition are secured.

Towards resolving the dilemma

One possible solution to this dilemma is to ensure as far as possible that regulation involves minimum interference with the efficient operations of the regulated institutions and the markets in which they deal. Economic theory and recent US experiences support the view that banking efficiency may be increased if the price mechanism is given an important role to play in determining the types and amounts of bank loans, investments and deposits. It has been argued that some bank supervision is desirable. The political reality is also that no government would ever allow its banking system a completely free rein to engage in all-out competition, the law of the jungle. Although supervision is not likely to disappear completely in favour of an idealized economic model, the benefits from efficient competition must never be ignored or downgraded. Jack Revell examines later (in Chapter 10) why banking competition requires corresponding supervision to keep the system safe.

The practical problem is to develop a supervisory system which allows the market mechanism to work, and which keeps the system safe at the same time. This is a tall order and there are no easy answers. One avenue of research has been the application of modern finance tools to the problem (Maisel, 1981). A central issue is the amount of risk a banking firm can take on in relation to its own prudential resources. This bears on the much-vexed capital adequacy question. Modern finance tools, like portfolio theory, have been developed and proposed.

But these models themselves imply near-perfect markets and other similar conditions. A related difficulty is that the market has no incentive to take into account the wider social costs inherent in actual and potential bank failures. As we have seen, this is one important justification for supervision. Another operational problem is that the market does not have sufficient information to make efficient risk : return trade-offs. The market is not provided with anything like the detailed information currently supplied to supervisors. Information like detailed loan losses, large loan exposures, maturity and interest-rate mismatches exemplify the kinds of data denied to the market.

In recent years the emphasis has been on more disclosure to the market from banks. In 1969, for example, UK banks agreed to full disclosure of their profits. But bankers and their regulators have traditionally been reluctant to publish full and confidential information on banking condition and performance. We touched on this problem in the last chapter. Their argument is that the market may over-react to some of these disclosures under certain conditions. The short-term consequences and costs of this kind of over-reaction may be disproportionate to the alleged longer-term benefits secured from such full disclosure. Because of the unique role of banks in the economy, banking risks and profits are politically and socially sensitive issues. This line of argument has also appeared recently in the US debate on risk-related deposit insurance premiums. At a practical level, it is reflected in the banker's historical use of hidden or secret reserves to smooth published profits.

Against this background, it appears likely for at least the near term that no banking system will move rapidly towards fuller disclosure of banks' confidential risk positions along the lines discussed. Bank stability is largely about confidence, and this confidence philosophy is reflected also in banks' operations. Banking is traditionally a confidential business. On the other hand, recent experiences have shown clearly the dangers to banking stability of allowing some banks complete freedom to compete, do as they please, and not be answerable to a higher authority until it is too late and market forces eventually bring things to a head. In a normative setting, then, strong grounds exist for some form of risk disclosure to a higher authority.

Given this state of affairs and these normative desiderata, supervisory authorities have to fulfil the role of a perfectly informed market. In effect, they have to act as a kind of proxy for the kind of free market forces that would operate if the market were (or could be) fully informed. It is for this reason that supervisory authorities should pay close attention to banking performance. This is necessary if only to ensure that licensed operators are not extracting any significant monopoly rent. Of course, market forces do bear strongly on banking performance. The market makes risk : return trade-offs on individual banks and the banking sector as a whole, and these are reflected in market performance indicators like P/E ratios, beta coefficients and bond ratings. They also influence directly bank decision-making.

Although the market is not fully informed in the ideal sense we have specified, it is certainly not ignorant, and it is likely to become more and more knowledgeable in the future. Information is currently gathered from sources like published banking data, analysts' opinions and market rumours. Pettway (1980), for example, has demonstrated and proposed that supervisors might usefully employ market data as part of their early warning system. In a banking system like that of the US comprising over 14,000 banks this may prove a useful avenue for further development. In the UK Saunders and Ward (1976) also demonstrated the sensitivity of UK market data to bank riskiness using the capital-asset pricing model (CAPM).

It is in assessing the adequacy of banking performance in relation to corresponding risk exposure that market data are liable to be potentially important in UK supervision. This is because the market is an operational transmission mechanism between risk and return. Because banks operate in the market and respond to its forces, it is clearly important and cannot be ignored. There is scope for more detailed research into the exact role of the market in assessing bank performance and risk by banking supervisors. Widespread, inefficient banking might eventually be the cost of downgrading the market. This may be too high a cost for banking safety.

The market may also have a role to play in another problem liable to absorb significant supervisory resources. The 1970s and 1980s have witnessed a plethora of major structural developments in the banking and financial services industries. Large department stores are becoming significant financial services providers, other industrial companies are looking to the financial services sector for diversification possibilities, UK banks have moved into new fields like the home mortgage market, and building societies are correspondingly moving ever closer to traditional banking business and other new activities. This small sample of developments is just the tip of the current innovatory iceberg, which grows bigger almost by the month.

The new banking activities constantly being developed nowadays have direct supervisory implications. Deciding how far and to what extent individual banks can develop new lines of activity is liable to be another major supervisory challenge of the 1980s. The risk : return profiles for such activities need to be assessed in the light of the banks' existing portfolio of business. Once again, the potential scope for market data and tools suggests itself. These data may assist supervisors in appreciating the kinds of trade-offs which may need to be made between the risk and return associated with such developments. In this setting, a major supervisory function and rationale is that of 'honest broker'. Supervisors are in a unique position to process centrally information and opinions about new developments in order to arrive at a balanced view.

The reality of the banking market is such, however, that neither bankers nor supervisors would place their trust completely in a single market-based model, whether it is a formal model like the CAPM or a rather looser collection of pragmatic market measures. No model exists which can state unequivocally under all likely conditions whether banks are safe or risky. Nevertheless, these data may be formalized further and fed into a larger 'consensus model' of a bank's risk : return position. This consensus model comprises supervisors, bankers and the market. Supervisors need to retain the flexibility and open-mindedness to respond positively to bankers' arguments and market signals.

It is not a case of the market replacing supervisors, or vice versa. Both have a clear role. Essentially the supervisor's role is to let the market and bank managements operate with as much freedom as supervisors deem safe. A flexible system of supervision, which encourages dialogue between supervisors and management and responds when necessary, is perhaps the best operational way of achieving the benefits sought. At the end of the day, supervisors have the responsibility to say when enough is enough. They also have the concomitant responsibility to ensure that ingrained caution does not unnecessarily clog the engine of banking innovation and efficiency.

Coverage and Equity

Which institutions should be supervised?

Several supervisory issues are associated with the innovatory and rapid developments in banks and banking markets over recent years. One problem is whether particular kinds of financial institution should be regulated. Prudential regulation in practice usually involves identifying sectors of financial institutions and supervising them accordingly. But this sectoral approach may become increasingly difficult as the barriers between different kinds of financial institution continue to break down. If a bank merges with a building society and then purchases a major insurance company, is the resultant financial institution a bank? What kind of financial institution is it?

At an operational level, these considerations reflect the question of consolidation. This bears directly on how far up or down the ladder of consolidation supervisors may need to go when deciding their area of jurisdiction and concern. If a banking group is owned ultimately by a manufacturing concern, for example, does the supervisory consolidation process (consolidation upwards in this case) need to include the non-financial manufacturing concern? Although neat formulae and rules may not be possible in this area, one view is that consolidation upwards stops at the boundaries of the banking or financial group in the conglomerate. So long as the channels of finance, control and influence between the banking part and other members of the group are identified, clearly specified and monitored, this seems a practical and logical solution. But there may still be problems.

What happens if the much publicized difficulties or collapse of a non-financial company owning a bank threaten that bank? A possible reaction to such events would be for the bank concerned to experience growing problems in securing and rolling over wholesale deposits to fund its lending book. This scenario may be extended to consider the threats which such a chain of events might have for other similar banks. The banking system might eventually face a crisis of confidence.

Should the supervisory authorities be willing to stand behind the manufacturing company – to launch a lifeboat – in this kind of crisis? If the answer is yes, the authorities have a reciprocal obligation (and obvious interest) to supervise the manufacturing concern. Another related problem bears on how far the supervisory authorities can insulate the banking segment of the conglomerate from the kind of commercial response that a threat to the group's owning company (or other major units in the group) might precipitate. For example, if the group felt that the threatened company was a key component, the banking segment might be stripped of its assets, and its profits channelled off to help keep it afloat. How far should the authorities be prepared to interfere in this (albeit hypothetical) kind of free play of market forces?

It seems practical that the supervisory authorities should not be expected generally to consolidate upwards and encompass non-banking concerns within the supervisory process. Supervisory resources are a limited good. The benefits of specialization which are secured by concentrating on banks are also likely to be diminished if supervisors widen considerably their sphere of operation. It would be very difficult to find solid reasons for supervisory influence to extend significantly into the non-financial corporate sector. This does not lessen the need for the kind of more general monitoring process recommended earlier. Like much of supervision, this is simply applied common sense.

It seems clear, however, that the special characteristics and functions of banks dictate that they be treated differently in certain respects from other members of a group. The prospect of banks within larger corporate groups being set up primarily as cheap finance conduits, for example, would probably be unacceptable on wider grounds than supervision. Supervisors need to make it clear that banks acquired by companies or forming a non-controlling part of a larger corporate group are subject to special considerations. For these reasons, they need to be operated autonomously from the rest of the group. In the case of severe difficulties within the group, supervisory authorities may need to separate the bank out as a complete entity. Sometimes a supervised directed merger of the bank with another one might be necessary.

Related but different supervisory problems arise when 'consolidation downwards' is considered. If a bank acquires a controlling stake in a travel agency, for example, does this mean that this operation should be unsupervised? It is here that the supervisory principles outlined earlier in considering consolidation upwards may not apply. Supervisors may have no choice other than to maintain a more direct interest in these other lines of business. This is because losses or risks in these operations may directly affect a bank's overall risk position. Another reason is that leaving some activities unsupervised may encourage banks towards those same activities. For these reasons, a stronger case exists that consolidation downwards should encompass all activities under the control of the bank. Of course, this does not imply the same supervisory process or level of involvement. Supervisors cannot be expert in everything.

It is true that mainline supervision is not geared towards the wide range of activities that might come under this umbrella. Supervision, after all, is concerned primarily with conventional or traditional forms of banking activity. There is no reason to believe that traditional banking business will disappear in the near future. But the barriers of traditional banking are now becoming increasingly blurred. Modern supervision cannot ignore these trends and supervisors have to face up to the broader supervisory implications. It is in this area of supervision where expertise is naturally weak that more attention may be directed by supervisors to market data. As was suggested earlier, these may be used to help assess the risk-and-return implications of new lines of banking activity.

Ultimately, though, the consensus model of supervisors, bankers and the market will apply. Supervisors once again assume their underlying function as honest brokers, helping to delimit how far and to what extent different kinds of bank can engage in newer (previously unexperienced) activities. The problem of consolidation is likely to be a growing supervisory issue throughout the 1980s and beyond.

Competitive equality

In a normative setting, an equitable supervisory system should achieve competitive equality. Although competitive equality is often supported or implied in discussions, it is rarely defined. In practice, it is a difficult concept to translate into operational rules. Competitive equality in the present context simply means that the same financial institutions should be supervised in exactly the same way. A supervisory burden imposed on one of them should be imposed also on the other. Easy enough to say in the cramped theoretical world of our example. In practice, things are not so clear.

Competitive equality has much wider regulatory implications than supervision. It may arise, for example, in the context of taxation treatments for different kinds of financial institution. Our concern is primarily with its supervisory implications. An immediate problem drawn out earlier is that the barriers between different kinds of financial institution are constantly being eroded. This means that it may be increasingly difficult to talk of the competitive equality of different kinds of financial institution. For present purposes it emphasizes the operational difficulties in identifying the same or similar financial institutions.

This problem cannot really be avoided by specifying the same mandatory rules for everyone. Besides the moral hazard risk of such a system, equality of treatment is not secured by treating unequals equally. One way around this difficulty is to specify the same general supervisory framework for all institutions, but to adapt the rules to different sectors and institutions. This is close to the UK model. Although this is an operational compromise, we may still explore the concept a little further. Besides its economic logic if it can be applied in practice, competitive equality often underlies criticisms of various supervisory proposals.

Only in the very simplest cases can we tell whether one financial institution (or kind of financial institution) has greater supervisory privileges than another. The reason is simple. Financial institutions are becoming increasingly differentiated from each other as they diversify and grow. Increasingly we find ourselves comparing apples with oranges. But do we need to focus on or identify similar financial institutions in this way? Mayer for one has argued that we do not. He states in this respect (1980, p. 9):

> But unfortunately, the fact that one usually cannot determine what competitive equality for various financial institutions means does not matter, because even if it could be defined operationally, this criterion would be useless. The main message of this paper is that despite the fact that numerous appeals to competitive equality generally focus on equity to institutions, there is no reason why one should aim at equity between financial *institutions per se*. Equitable treatment *of institutions* has nothing to recommend it.

Sharpe and Hogan (1982) also employ Mayer's views in their criticism of the recent Australian Campbell Report.

Mayer argues that what really matters are two things. First, treating equitably the persons involved. For present purposes these are the owners of the bank and its customers. Secondly, regulatory burdens should be set so that they maximize efficiency. The three criteria for competitive equality, then, are fairness to owners, fairness to customers, and efficiency. But neither Mayer (1980) nor Sharpe and Hogan (1982) explain rigorously how this notion can be applied.

In the case of owners, for instance, Mayer admits that what is equitable treatment for them is unclear. One interpretation would be that fairness to the owners requires the fulfilment of the reasonable expectation held by them when they acquired their equity that the rules would not be changed arbitrarily. Arbitrarily might imply that they did not expect any changes in laws and regulations, so that the existing supervisory system should remain unaltered. Another interpretation might be that the authorities should maintain the status quo of existing institutions by preventing new institutions from entering the market under the influence of changing economic conditions or technological advances. Still another (probably less frequent) possibility is that the owners bought their equity stakes in the expectation that regulations would be changed in a certain way.

These are just a sample of the difficulties of applying this criterion. Another operational problem is that different shareholder groups or types (with different objectives) may hold a bank's equity. Deciding on the appropriate fairness-to-owners criteria in practice may be even more difficult than it appears in Mayer's analysis. But Mayer recognizes the fuzziness of this concept and still maintains that it is dangerous to ignore the criterion. He points out that a 'good society' is not generally considered one which rewards and punishes in a completely arbitrary way.

The equity-to-customer criterion is markedly different from that of equity to owners. Consumers have not generally made the kind of large investment that owners have in dealing with a particular financial institution. The equity problem here is that if any costs (like supervisory ones) are imposed arbitrarily on a product, this is inequitable. It correspondingly levies a completely arbitrary direct tax on the product's consumers. This criterion suggests that, assuming no externalities, the same burden should be imposed on every activity of every financial institution.

Once again, Mayer admits that it may be extremely difficult to measure the net burden or net benefit of regulations for customers of certain financial institutions. Another problem not discussed by Mayer again concerns the different kinds of customers who might deal with different financial institutions in the same kind of product. Can we justifiably assume that because they are all purchasing the same product their preferences are the same? The third Mayer criterion, economy efficiency, always gives the same answer as the fairness-to-customer criterion. It requires that the burdens placed on competing activities be equal, unless there are certain externalities.

This model of competitive equality is useful because it draws out the main parties affected by the competitive implications of supervisory regulation. It also illustrates the conceptual and practical problems faced by supervisors in tackling this issue. Even when the three component criteria of competitive equality can be isolated and appraised, how do we handle conflicts? If fairness to owners dictates that a measure be imposed, but economic efficiency dictates otherwise, how should supervisors decide? Competitive equality is a complex supervisory issue and there are no exact answers or neat formulae. In this connexion, Campbell (1982, p. 433) pointed out: 'Unfortunately, it is difficult if not impossible to accurately measure the amount of competition, or efficiency resulting from competition, that is sacrificed due to the regulatory system.' Little wonder, perhaps, that some economists have favoured more radical alternatives to contemporary supervision.

Supervisory Alternatives

The most radical economic alternative to contemporary supervision is simply to abandon it completely in favour of free market forces. However, we have examined many strong reasons why this may not be desirable in the case of banks. At a positive level we might argue that no government would allow banks a free rein to engage in *laissez-faire* banking. It is generally agreed that at least some prudential supervision is necessary. Given this regulatory scenario, we should concentrate on devising the best techniques of supervision. But the practice of supervision is inextricably bound up with the amount of supervision.

Rejecting the complete replacement of supervision by the free market is not a black and white decision. As we have seen, there are various shades of grey which bear on the amount of desirable supervision. In short, how big a role should the market be allowed to play in banking supervision? Edwards and Scott (in Edwards, 1979) examined the justifications for supervision in some detail. As we saw in the previous chapter, the economic justification stems primarily from the existence of certain market failures – like externalities and informational problems. In this general setting, Edwards and Scott see banks providing three major economic services or products. They are a source of liquidity for all sectors, they provide a payments mechanism, and they produce a low-risk, highly divisible investment asset (savings deposits). They label these respectively the liquidity rationale, the payments system rationale, and the savings asset rationale.

Analysing these rationales, Edwards and Scott conclude (and not all economists would agree with this) that the most compelling efficiency reason for government regulation is probably the liquidity rationale. Their general conclusion is that deposit insurance and lender of last resort facilities available for purposes of monetary policy are more than adequate to meet the main economic rationales for supervision. They added that some form of government involvement would be necessary to correct informational deficiencies, and solvency regulations (balance sheet controls only) may be necessary as part of the deposit insurance scheme. In analysing non-economic rationales for supervision, like protecting certain classes of consumers, they also felt that effective deposit insurance would be adequate to satisfy these social goals of fairness and equity.

Recent years have witnessed growing US research and interest in the deposit insurance alternative to contemporary supervision. We saw earlier that flat-rate deposit insurance produces the potential of moral hazard risk: low- and high-risk banks all pay the same percentage premium. It is for this reason that detailed solvency regulations are usually felt necessary to curb the resulting potential for banks to reduce their capital and increase risk. Mark Flannery examines these important issues in Chapter 15. Many economists now argue that a risk-related deposit insurance scheme would be a marked improvement on contemporary flat-rate schemes.

The UK clearing banks were critical of the deposit protection fund heralded in with the 1979 Banking Act. They argued that they were effectively subsidizing more risky operators in the system. A risk-related deposit insurance scheme would eliminate this feature of the banking market. Risk-related schemes, however, face considerable practical difficulties. The major one, of course, is how do you fix the premiums?

Some economists argue that premiums could be set by the market. Banks would then be required to purchase deposit insurance on the open market. The authorities would direct and monitor the deposit tranches requiring insurance. Even more radical schemes propose that banks themselves should be free to decide how much of their deposits to insure and where to insure them. These latter proposals, of course, open up 'free rider' problems. Allowing the market to insure deposits also gives rise to the practical problem of information disclosure. Current research, therefore, has tended to focus on how supervisors may go about fixing the premiums. Market data and finance tools have been investigated as supervisory aids in this area.

Risk-related deposit insurance is developing as one of the most important academic topics in US supervision. Economists (like Sharpe and Hogan, 1982) are also using this work to support more market-orientated regulatory systems in their own countries. Many economists feel that an operational risk-related deposit insurance scheme would practically eliminate the contemporary framework of bank prudential regulation and supervision. This debate is liable to grow, and some relevant issues are discussed in the papers by Paul Horvitz (Chapter 16) and Paul Peterson (Chapter 17). United States regulatory agencies like the Federal Deposit Insurance Corporation (FDIC) and the Federal Home Loan Bank Board (FHLBB) are currently investigating such systems. Risk-related deposit insurance could be one of the key supervisory debates of the second half of the 1980s.

Another radical alternative to contemporary supervision was proposed by Kareken (1983). He suggested that the banking industry might be freed from the threat of runs by requiring banks to value their assets at market prices – that is mark them to market. Banks would value all their assets continuously at current market value. This present-value approach is favoured by economists who operate in a world of real income and wealth where valuation results from discounting cash flows using rates that reflect existing interest rates in the market.

In this setting, banks would be seen as offering fixed monetary promises. What Kareken means by this is unclear. After all, bank deposits are fixed monetary obligations anyway. Many economists adopt the view that a loss is a loss, whether it is realized or not. Presumably, keeping the market and the public at large continuously informed of the pattern of bank losses (realized and unrealized) gives more accurate information on a bank's continuing solvency. What is not clear is whether accuracy in these terms is the same as reassurance to depositors and other interested parties. Given market rumours and their potential short-term consequences, one may suspect not.

Present-value accounting is a concept that is beginning to receive attention in banking circles. Certainly for supervisory and bank internal decision-making purposes, some form of present-value accounting may be desirable. But once again there are severe practical problems. What discount rate(s) should be employed? How should loans be valued in a present-value setting? Is present value relevant to, say, a government bond which has a high probability of being held to its maturity? Another problem bears on valuing deposits. These are legally fixed monetary obligations and have to be repaid in the same fixed nominal terms.

A major technical problem with present-value accounting is the choice of discount rate. This reflects directly on the risk-related deposit insurance debate and the capital adequacy question. It is bound up directly with how the riskiness of items within bank portfolios should be measured. Once this problem is solved, solutions start to present themselves to other key problems like risk-related deposit insurance.

A bank's present-value balance sheet would almost certainly be a markedly different statement from contemporary bank accounting presentations. This is not only because of the different valuation procedures applied to the same items included in both statements, but also because of the inclusion of other items not usually found in standard accounting balance sheets. These items would include, for example, the present value of the 'synthetic' assets and liabilities generated by banks in their off-balance-sheet transactions, like those in financial futures, swaps and options.

Publishing a present-value balance sheet along these lines is liable to fall foul of the informational problems discussed earlier. Besides the significant practical difficulties of producing the data, there may be severe interpretational difficulties. Such an economic statement of assets, liabilities and capital would be complex, and it would have real information content only for sophisticated operators. It may mean little and create uncertainties for the financially unsophisticated. At one level it is equivalent to the suggestion of giving the market full information and letting it do the job of supervisors. For reasons of this kind, a present-value balance sheet may not be a feasible or useful document for banks to publish. However, it may have significant practical utility for both management and supervisors.

Risk and Capital Adequacy

Changes in banking risk

One of the clear messages of the preceding analysis is that the banking industry has undergone almost revolutionary changes over the past two decades. The structure of the banking system has changed in several important respects. New banks have emerged and much more complex forms of banking organization developed. This process continues today. The 1970s saw an emphasis on international business. The signs are that retail banking and capital markets are likely to be a main area of banking development during the 1980s.

Competition in the banking and financial sectors has grown alongside these developments, and it is bound up with the concomitant process of innovation. Technology has further stimulated banking developments. At the same time, financial markets have become more risky and volatile. Inflation has also had important effects on banks and banking risks.

One important outcome from all these developmvnts has been that the volume and potential impact of risks facing banks have increased. At the same time, banking risk has become a much more complex concept. An important rationale for supervision is to appraise and monitor banking risks. A fundamental purpose of supervision is to help ensure the soundness and stability of the banking system. The evidence suggests clearly that banks have taken on greater risks over the past two decades. Supervisory expertise and effectiveness should keep pace with these developments.

Although one cannot dispute the relevance of the market in helping to determine the price of bank riskiness – that is, the risk : return trade-offs – the market unaided cannot do the job. The events of 1984 following the Continental Illinois difficulties remind us forcefully of the way markets may amplify rumours. There is always the danger that a mistaken rumour may become self-fulfilling through the market mechanism. Just in case, depositors take out funds from suspect banks. Under these conditions no bank is safe. Effective supervision is one institutional weapon that helps curb such tendencies.

In this environment, objective evaluations of banking risk are desirable. This process of risk appraisal should also improve knowledge about the kinds of trade-offs in banking risk management. For instance, the extent to which a bank may prudently take on more risk in relation to its expected profit return. Clear information is necessary on all risk exposures carried by a bank. This need became evident, for example, following the abandonment of the fixed exchange-rate system in the early 1970s. Banks needed to monitor and prescribe limits on their foreign exchange exposures. More recently, in the early 1980s, it was rumoured that some large banks had not always maintained a clear picture of their own international debt exposures on a consolidated basis. Identification, measurement and control are the canons of effective risk management.

Capital adequacy

The supervisory approach to the bank risk problem has traditionally been incorporated into the so-called capital adequacy debate, and we touched on this important function in Chapter 1. This debate has been an important part of the US banking literature following the Great Depression. Capital adequacy was hardly acknowledged, much less debated, in the UK until the fringe banking crisis. Capital adequacy has been and continues to be a contentious issue in banking circles. A later section of this book (Part D) explores some aspects of the subject, and it is now a very wide and topical area. Maisel's (1981) book, for example, is devoted to the problem.

A primary purpose of bank capital is to act as a kind of internal insurance fund against uncertainty within the banking firm. This implies that to appraise capital adequacy, detailed knowledge of banking risk exposure is needed. Risks and uncertainties have become more important in the modern banking firm. One important reason for banking problems has been the failure to plan for events that may occur although they are unexpected. Capital adequacy and the associated risk measurement, therefore, are important management and supervisory tasks.

Current developments constantly raise new questions. What a bank does or should do is becoming more fluid. What is a bank is now a much more difficult question. Even in the days of relative stability in banking, the capital adequacy question was complex and essentially unresolved. If the capital adequacy position is to guard against uncertainty, no final decision on the problem will ever be forthcoming. By definition, uncertainty defies exactitude. Against this background, a plethora of capital adequacy schemes has been developed and tested. These range from simple balance sheet ratios to more complex risk : assets formulae. Disaster tests, simulation exercises, statistical discriminant schemes, and market-based measures have also been developed. The list is long and likely to grow as fashions, prejudices and conditions alter. What all these schemes have in common, however, is that they attempt to appraise bank riskiness in relation to the corresponding capital base. Many supervisory authorities recognise the operational limitations of such schemes by using them as screening devices or trigger mechanisms.

Financial economists criticize many contemporary capital adequacy schemes because they are based on static data, like those from balance sheets. They argue that risk measurement necessitates considering the bank's economic income and economic balance sheet. This is the kind of reasoning that helps support the present-value approach to bank accounting. Examining current book values is not seen to be an adequate test of a bank's solvency. Contemporary accounting book values either understate or overstate real net worth. Supervisory decisions based on book rather than economic (or real) capital fail to utilize significant information available about expected earnings. Conventional accounting provisions do not fully reflect these alleged economic effects. Finance students argue, therefore, that the first stage in a capital adequacy analysis is to convert book values to economic values. This approach requires calculating the present value of the bank by discounting all future cash flows.

The economists' approach to capital adequacy analysis may be summarized as a three-stage process: measuring the bank's initial net worth, its expected net real return in the period, and the probability distribution or variance of the expected return. In this framework, portfolio theory and market-based models may be used to help locate the appropriate risk-and-return position for a bank. A detailed study of this approach by Maisel (1981) emphasized the importance of diversification policies. Many of these schemes have been developed to help support risk-related deposit insurance.

Despite their potential utility, these schemes are more revolutionary than evolutionary to contemporary supervisors. In terms of operational acceptability, they are well ahead of their time. There are also severe practical problems. We have already touched on some of these in the last section. The discount rate problem, for instance, or discounting for risk is a severe practical difficulty. Variance of expected returns, or any other statistical moment, may not be an appropriate operational measure alone of bank riskiness. Many of these models make assumptions like perfect information, zero transactions costs and efficient markets.

These are the kind of criticisms that may be levelled at any theory or model. We must be careful not to throw the baby out with the bath water. All theories and models require some abstraction. Simplifications and assumptions have to be made in order to see the wood for the trees. The tools now exist to explore some interesting aspects of banking risk. This is the research stage. We shall then have to assess the practical operational implications of these findings. The research by Maisel and his collaborators drew out several important practical findings for banking risk. These included the recent rise in US bank risks, possible inappropriate regulatory machinery, the role of diversification in bank balance sheets, and the need to plan for future unforeseen and unexpected events.

Practical supervisory systems for capital adequacy appraisal have tended to focus on balance sheet schemes. Using balance-sheet data, ratios like capital : deposits and capital : total assets are computed. More complex operational schemes place assets into different risk classes and assign corresponding capital coefficients to these risk classes. These capital covers are then summed and compared with the book capital. Many important aspects of banking risk can never be captured by such processes, and Gardener develops this point in Chapter 14.

Recently, other developments have weakened further the conventional balance-sheet approach to banking risk. A whole new financial technology for coping with some important banking risks has arisen in recent years. Two of the most important risks faced by banks over the past decade have been interest-rate risks and exchange-rate movements. New markets and instruments have developed to cope with these. They include new markets dealing in futures, swaps and options. Positions built up by a bank in using these new financial instruments give rise to manufactured or synthetic assets and liabilities not shown in conventional bank accounting balance sheets.

These new instruments and techniques may help to support another strong operational rationale for supervision in a climate of risk and innovation. An immediate problem for an individual bank exploiting these new developments is how far they can safely employ them. As honest brokers, the supervisory authorities can distil the experiences of all banks within the consensus model of supervision. By collecting and analysing data on the experiences of all banks, safer and more robust rules can be developed. Of course, this does not detract in any way from the management's responsibilities to make its own decisions.

Many supervisory authorities, like those in the UK, recognize the inherent limitations of the capital adequacy and related risk appraisal schemes they employ. These schemes are employed as frameworks for analysis, rather than as mandatory, minimum requirements for all banks. They are the focal point, the touchstone, of the kind of consensus model of supervision practised in the UK. This approach avoids the moral hazard dangers referred to earlier when the same solvency or other similar ratios are applied to all banks independently of individual bank risk. Ultimately, however, supervisors have the final say on the extent of permissible riskiness. In the UK, for example, they adopted the concept of free capital to avoid banks manufacturing capital adequacy out of accounting transactions like fixed-asset revaluations. More recently, they have prescribed rules on the amount of subordinated loan issues allowed in capital adequacy appraisals.

There are many issues tied up with capital adequacy analysis that will continue to tax the resources of bankers, supervisors and students of finance. Some bankers feel that the exclusion of a larger portion of their fixed capital, like branches and head offices, from capital ratios is inappropriate. They argue that these assets could be realized if necessary. The extent of allowable loan capital is debatable. Healthy and open debate on these kinds of issue should be encouraged in an evolutionary consensus model of bank supervision.

Capital adequacy analysis – incorporating a full-scale analysis of all banking risks – is a fundamental component of modern bank supervision. Capital adequacy rulings may bear directly on both the solvency and profitability of the banking firm. The required rate of return earned by banks has to incorporate a margin of retained profit to feed capital. This margin of retention should reflect bank riskiness. Excessive mandatory capital levels may restrict bank profitability and growth potential. In this setting, balance sheet management has begun to emerge as an important managerial and supervisory framework of analysis.

Balance sheet management emphasizes the trade-offs, the continual implicit bargaining, between the three major objectives of banking policy: profitability, liquidity and capital adequacy (or solvency). Profitability and liquidity risk considerations need to be incorporated into a realistic capital adequacy analysis. With the present movement again towards more market-orientated methods of monetary control, capital adequacy standards may assume growing importance as the effective constraints to bank expansion. This may result from the movement away from direct, or interventionist, systems of monetary control towards more market-orientated systems.

Monetary Policy and Supervision

A major supervisory area that has not been yet discussed concerns the relationship between monetary policy and supervision. Several issues are bound up with this question. These include whether the monetary policy and supervisory regulators should be separate agencies, and whether the same body can efficiently fulfil both functions. Other related issues concern the relative importance of monetary policy and supervision, and their possible interdependencies. Another important concern is the possibility of conflicts arising between these two forms of policy.

Monetary policy and supervision might conceivably conflict in several different ways. An obvious conflict would be where supervisory practice led to conflicts with a counter-cyclical monetary policy. A monetary policy could favour expansionary measures, for example, at a time when supervisory considerations required a sharp curbing of bank expansion. When supervision and monetary policy are carried out by the same agency, conflicts of interest might arise so that one function is dominated by the other. Another conflict arises in the sense that both functions compete for the scarce resources and time of regulatory policy-makers.

The central issue is whether and in what form monetary policy and supervision conflict. The other important questions are generally related in some way to this fundamental issue. The key question is whether the supervisory process has strong procyclical elements, thereby tending to frustrate, or at least lessen the impact of, countercyclical monetary policy. In the UK at least there does not appear to be any substantial evidence of such a policy clash. One should also add that there has also been hardly any open debate or academic research in this specific area. The US evidence is also apparently sparse and not convincing. This is an empirical matter which must remain open and unresolved. Nevertheless, we can explore it from another direction.

The potential relationship between supervision, competition and monetary policy was seen clearly in the UK during the period of the early 1970s leading up to the fringe-banking crisis. One lesson was that an expansionary monetary policy allowing much freer competition may be especially dangerous when supervision is inadequate. Inadequate supervision can help to frustrate a monetary policy. Recently in the US, questions have been raised whether the Continental Illinois experiences have diverted the course of monetary policy. The Federal Reserve Board denies it. Nevertheless, the practical implications of all these considerations are rather obvious. Banking instability and publicized banking difficulties can affect both the conduct and objectives of monetary policy.

One aim of supervision, therefore, is the preservation of a healthy banking system so as to increase the efficiency of monetary policy. It effectively oils the wheels of monetary policy. Supervision cannot achieve this aim unaided, and other important factors – like the quality of bank management and market forces – are also at play. Indeed, many of these factors may often be more significant than supervision alone. Despite this, the essential point remains. Efficient supervision may help foster the environment for effective monetary policy. In this context the body responsible for monetary policy has a direct interest in ensuring that supervision is efficient.

Supervisory objectives are different from those of monetary policy. This is clearly evident at the macro-economic level. Modern banking experience has also supported the view that supervision is not a minor, peripheral regulatory function. The traditional UK view has been that monetary policy considerations were more important than supervision. We shall see in the following chapter that this view was simply a natural product of the UK banking market and experiences: modern bank supervision was not felt necessary in the UK until the early 1970s. Since then supervision has grown rapidly in importance. It is probably true to suggest that it now has equivalent banking status to monetary policy.

But the fundamental point is that supervision and monetary policy are essentially dissimilar tasks. The goals of supervision are important enough in their own right. Any attempts to subvert them to other policy objectives would be inappropriate and probably dangerous. Serious conflicts and dangerous precedents might arise if politics, whether internal or external, compromised supervisory tasks and aims. This is not to deny that there will always be unavoidable and sometimes necessary relationships between the two sets of monetary policy and supervisory control measures. At the margin they might often shade into one another – for example, in the liquidity ratio field. Nevertheless, the objectives and tasks of supervision are sufficiently dissimilar to monetary policy as to warrant their pursuit free from other non-supervisory pressures.

Given this state of affairs, the best operational solution might be to specify clearly and publicly the supervisory (and monetary control) aims of the day. This should help lead to better policy. It should also facilitate the appraisal of the real costs and benefits of supervision. At the same time, recognition of this differentiation of supervision and monetary policy leads to acceptance of the view that there are economies of specialization in the two functions. The Bank of England recognizes this operational need by its Supervision Division, which is independent of monetary policy decision-making. Against this background, the time has now come to specify in more detail the development and structure of the UK supervisory system. The next chapter takes up this task.

References and Bibliography

Bank of England (1984), *The Development and Operation of Monetary Policy 1960–1983* (Oxford: Clarendon Press).

Campbell, T. S. (1982), *Financial Institutions, Markets and Economic Activity* (New York: McGraw-Hill).

Edwards, F. R. (1979), *Issues in Financial Regulation* (New York: McGraw-Hill).

Evans, R. G. (1981), *Slouching Toward Chicago: Regulatory Reform as Revealed Religion*, Department of Economics, University of British Columbia, Discussion Paper No. 81–42 (Dec.).

Gardener, E. P. M. (1981), *Capital Adequacy and Banking Supervision*, Bangor Occasional Papers in Economics, No. 19 (Cardiff: University of Wales Press).

Kane, Edward, J. (1981), 'Accelerating inflation, technological innovation, and the decreasing effectiveness of banking regulation', *Journal of Finance*, vol. XXXVI, no. 2 (May), pp. 355–67.

Kareken, John, H. (1983), 'Deposit insurance reform or deregulation is the cart not the horse', Federal Reserve Bank of Minneapolis, *Quarterly Review*, vol. 7, no. 2 (Spring), pp. 1–9.

Maisel, Sherman, J. (ed.) (1981), *Risk and Capital Adequacy in Commercial Banks* (Chicago and London: University of Chicago Press).

Mayer, Thomas (1980), 'Competitive equality as a criterion for financial reform', *Journal of Banking and Finance*, vol. 4, no. 1 (March), pp. 7–15.

Meyer, Jr, Robert A. (1980), 'The regulated financial firm', *Quarterly Review of Economics and Business*, vol. 20, no. 4 (Winter), pp. 44–57.

Pettway, Richard H. (1980), 'Potential insolvency, market efficiency, and bank regulation of large commercial banks', *Journal of Financial and Quantitative Analysis*, vol. XV, no. 1 (March), pp. 219–36.

Saunders, Anthony and Charles Ward, (1976), 'Regulation, risk and performance of UK clearing banks 1965–75', *The Journal of Industrial Economics*, vol. XXV, no. 2 (Dec.), pp. 143–59.

Sharpe, J. G. and W. P. Hogan (1982), *Regulation, Investor/Depositor Protection and the Campbell Report*, Research Report/Occasional Paper No. 75, The University of Newcastle, NSW, Australia (June).

Spellman, Lewis J. (1982), *The Depository Firm and Industry: Theory, History, and Regulation* (London: Academic Press).

Wilson, George W. (1982), 'Regulating and deregulating business', *Business Horizons*, vol. 25, no. 4 (July/Aug.), pp. 45–52.

4 Supervision in the United Kingdom

The political and economic forces that converge to make law and regulation are more often than not so complex as to be unfathomable.
Edwards and Scott in F. R. Edwards (1979), *Issues In Financial Regulation* (New York: McGraw-Hill)

Introduction

Alongside the dramatic institutional changes within the British banking and financial system over the past two decades, there has been a marked growth in the bank supervisory function. Prior to the early 1970s, supervisory issues like capital adequacy and balance-sheet management were not significant in UK banking circles. They were barely mentioned in the contemporary UK banking literature. What little formal supervision there was focused on the primary, or inner core, banks. This state of affairs simply reflected the comparatively long experience in the UK of a stable banking system dominated by a small number of first-class names. Crises, instability and bank failures of the 1970s variety were not really felt to be relevant to British banking.

In order to understand the current supervisory system, we need to appreciate the forces that have helped both to shape and to constrain its development. Part B of the book addresses this area, although it could never be all-embracing. The current chapter provides a further necessary background to Part B and the later papers. It does this by summarizing the historical context and current system of supervision in the UK. At the same time, it will attempt to fill in some gaps not covered elsewhere in the book. We shall start off with a general consideration of the UK system prior to the traumatic events of 1973–5.

Supervision Before the Fringe-Banking Crisis

Background to supervision

Up to the 1970s, there was effectively no formal system of bank supervision as we know it today. It was really during the early 1970s that British and worldwide concern with banking supervision grew. This concern reflected the increasing turbulence and risks in banking and financial systems throughout the world. In Britain, supervisory developments were also a reflection of a growing EEC commitment to the harmonization of banking regulations. These regulations included banking supervision, and a highly detailed system of controls was first mooted in 1972. Another powerful and related influence was a growing acceptance of the political philosophy that depositors should be protected against the loss of wealth occasioned by bank failures. This was part of the wider acceptance of the philosophy of consumerism.

Up until 1979 there was no formal bank regulatory – including monetary and credit control – legislation in the UK. The Bank of England traditionally enacted its policies through the use of 'moral suasion', a form of coercive persuasion. This approach was in sharp contrast to that in the US and many European countries. One immediate consequence of there being no formal system of bank licensing or chartering was that no generally accepted definition of a bank existed. Eventually this led to specific problems, but it was symptomatic of the highly flexible system of regulation in the UK.

In practice, UK banks were subject to various sections of many different laws. At the same time, there were several lists of firms regarded as banks for the purposes of different statutes. Acquiring the full status of a bank under this regime was a lengthy process. It involved progressing through a series of recognitions for particular purposes. The first step in this ladder was the use of the words 'bank', 'bankers' or 'banking' in the title of a company incorporated in the UK. This was regulated by the Department of Trade.

Prospective bankers also had to obtain a licence under the Moneylenders Acts unless they clearly met certain conditions, otherwise debtors had no legal obligation to repay advances made. A famous 1965 court case helped lead to the 'Section 123' certificate of banking status. The 1967 Companies Act gave the Department of Trade power to grant this certificate conferring banking status on a company if it met certain conditions. The relevance of Section 123 status disappeared with the enactment of the 1974 Consumer Credit Act.

Another important stage towards obtaining full banking status was recognition by the Treasury (on the Bank of England's advice) as an authorized dealer in foreign exchange under the Exchange Control Act 1947. This typically took an indigenous bank several years to acquire from the time of its first obtaining Section 123 status. A final important step towards full banking status was inclusion in the Schedule 8 list of the 1948 Companies Act. This enabled a bank to maintain hidden reserves in its balance sheet and to conceal its true profit and loss results.

The Protection of Depositors Act 1963 imposed conditions on the way banks (other than recognized banks) could advertise for deposits. Other recognitions (like inclusion on the Schedule 8 list and, latterly, authorized dealer status) exempted banks from these requirements. This arrangement was later amended in Section 127 of the 1967 Companies Act. This led to the creation of yet another list of banks called Section 127 banks. Another valued recognition was that granted by the Inland Revenue under Section 54 of the Income and Corporation Taxes Act 1970; this allowed banks to pay and receive interest gross of tax.

This ladder of recognitions was the forerunner of supervision as we know it today. The departments involved consulted the Bank of England in every case before banks could be added to the three main lists described above – the authorized banks list, the Schedule 8 list, and the Section 127 list. Each step up the ladder removed certain obstacles and conferred valued privileges. At the same time, they brought with them growing responsibilities.

Authorized dealer status admitted those recognized banks to the banking sector of the Bank of England's official statistics. In practice, only companies that appeared on one or more of the three main lists were included in the Bank's own list of 'statistical banks'. These statistical banks were virtually synonymous with the list of banks that were required to satisfy the Bank of England's monetary policy regulations. The business of these listed banks was subjected to comparatively close supervision by the Bank of England.

Despite its laborious appearance, this system of recognitions was flexible. The essence of it was that banks regarded the privileges obtained as sufficiently valuable to compensate for the concomitant obligations. One prized externality of the official recognitions was that they were seen as a major factor in the maintenance of public confidence. Banks regarded their hard-won recognitions as sufficiently valuable not to risk the displeasure of the Bank. Effectively, Bank of England control was exercised through the medium of 'gentlemen's agreements'. Self-regulation and self-discipline characterized the bank control philosophy of the day. It worked well enough until the late 1960s.

Genesis of modern supervision

As the 1960s developed, it started to become clear that the regulatory philosophy of self-regulation and self-discipline had some flaws. Despite the apparent attractions of official recognition, it carried with it sometimes onerous restrictions. During the 1960s, the recognized banks came under severe lending restrictions imposed by the authorities. At the same time, competition facing banks was increasing. Under these conditions, there was an undoubted incentive for new banks to acquire the bare minimum of recognitions in order to avoid the regulatory constraints imposed by the authorities. This state of affairs was the breeding ground for the development of the fringe banks.

In the absence of a legal framework, banking supervision was carried out informally by the Bank of England. This system emphasized periodic interviews between bank management and the Bank of England. Although the Bank monitored certain prudential ratios, no minimum ratio levels were prescribed. The ratios imposed by the Bank of England – the cash, liquidity, and, later, reserve assets ratios – were laid down for monetary policy reasons. Supervision was carried out by the Discount Office of the Bank of England until the summer of 1974. The main function of the Discount Office, however, was to influence short-term interest rates.

An account of the Discount Office's approach to supervision was documented by Revell (1975) in a study which was really the first significant academic survey of bank supervision and related issues in the UK. The Discount Office apparently monitored two ratios in particular, a solvency and a liquidity ratio. The solvency (or capital adequacy) ratio measured the ratio of free resources (shareholders' funds, less fixed and capital assets) to public liabilities (current plus contingent liabilities). In the liquidity ratio, a bank's 'quick assets' (all immediately liquefiable assets) were related to its deposits. A flexible approach was used in monitoring these ratios, and the individual circumstances of each bank were considered important. A band of acceptable ratio results was used in preference to mandatory minimum levels.

The main supervisory emphasis appeared to be on the informal meetings held between the Bank and the representatives belonging to each bank. These were based on the accounts which banks submitted regularly to the Bank of England. This flexible and largely informal system started to come under strain with the influx of new banks to London, the increase in the number of people directing bank business, and growing competition. Although the Competition and Credit Control (CCC) measures of September 1971 had sought to remove part of the segmented monetary and credit controls (concentrated on the clearing banks) of the 1960s, it was the fringe banking crisis that proved an important supervisory landmark. It led to a significant change in the administration (rather than philosophy) of UK bank supervision.

Revell (1975, p. 48) suggests that a strong case could be made that the major cause of the fringe crisis was not the Bank of England supervisory system itself, but the loophole in that supervision resulting from Section 123 status. Section 123 banks who were exempt from the provisions of the Protection of Depositors Act did not have to make returns to any official body, although they were required to publish half-yearly accounts. The Department of Trade could withdraw Section 123 status if a bank's circumstances had changed, but this was difficult to monitor. The Department had no continuing supervisory capability, and so the Section 123 banks were effectively free to pursue the banking policies which eventually helped lead up to the crisis of 1973–5.

It is perhaps significant that a number of banks fully recognized by the Bank of England were also found to have indulged in the same kind of bad banking practised by the fringe. The result of these experiences was to support further the growing realization that the Bank of England's supervisory system was not rigorous enough for the more demanding era heralded by the events of the early 1970s and confirmed by the trauma of the fringe banking crisis. The Bank of England responded promptly to these pressures with new measures in August 1974. These marked the emergence of the modern bank supervisory function in the UK. Although the administration and status of banking supervision altered, the Bank of England's underlying supervisory philosophy remained unchanged.

Supervision Since the Fringe Banking Crisis

The 1970s system and philosophy

A new Banking Supervision Division within the Chief Cashier's Department was set up by the Bank of England. This move considerably extended the supervisory responsibilities exercised previously by the Discount Office. The first task of the new Division was to obtain additional information from banks and interview their management representatives. These banks included most British registered banks and around fifty of the Section 123 banks. The latter were selected primarily because of their size and importance. Foreign banks and consortium banks were supervised in a separate way.

One immediate consequence of these new developments was a significant increase in the volume of the bank statistics required by the supervisory authorities. A maturity analysis of sterling deposits and assets was required, for example, broken down over specified categories. Much more detail on certain memorandum items (like standby facilities with listed banks) was also acquired. The existing and supplementary supervisory returns, therefore, provided the authorities with much more detail on banks' prudential positions. British registered banks now provide information covering both their domestic and international business.

Some of these data were required in future on a regular quarterly basis. Nevertheless, the most important part of the supervisory process remained the regular interviews with each bank's representatives. These interviews can lead to the Bank discussing a bank's cash budget and other plans. The move to more freely floating exchange rates in March 1973 helped reinforce the necessity of an effective bank supervisory system. The collapse of Bankhaus Herstatt in 1974 was a timely warning of the turbulence being experienced in the foreign exchange and eurocurrency markets. These events led to growing Bank of England concern with branches of foreign banks, foreign exchange dealings, and consortium banks.

The Bank of England's general philosophy on supervision was explained in a 1975 paper by George Blunden. This underlying philosophy has helped shape both the evolution and form of UK supervision by the Bank. The four elemental characteristics of the philosophy were summarized as flexibility, personal, progressive, and participative. The essence of flexibility is that the Bank has never attempted to make banks conform to rigid guidelines. This contrasts with the preference for legal codification of supervisory rules and the general 'transparency' of Continental European systems of bank prudential regulation. Emphasis is placed on the differences that may exist between banks and the need to adapt to changing circumstances.

Following from the Bank's concern with flexibility, its approach is also personal. Great store is placed in supervision on the quality and reputation of bank management. One result of this Bank of England concern has been to keep the number of its supervisory staff small and involved long-term. The progressive aspect signifies the Bank's belief that it takes time for a bank to acquire the highest standing. This is reflected operationally in banks being required to pass through a series of recognitions. The final aspect of participation confirms the Bank's regard for the opinions of the market and experiences with other banks supervised when appraising a bank's prudential soundness.

The clearing banks in their evidence to the Wilson Committee emphasized that the most important prudential constraints on banks were those which were self-imposed. In this general context, Cooper (1984, p. 257) suggests that: 'Most, if not all, British banks would warmly endorse this concept of the Bank as referee with a full player's knowledge of the game.' As we have explained, the core of the Bank of England's supervisory approach is the process of dialogue with management. Revell (1975) first coined the expression 'vicarious participation' in bank management to summarize this distinguishing aspect of the Bank's approach. It recognizes that management's job is to manage, and the task of supervision is to monitor that this has been done prudently in co-operation with management. This is a practical example of the kind of consensus model of supervision referred to in the last chapter.

Two important features of the Bank of England approach to supervision, therefore, are its participative character and the discretion given to the supervisors. These are regulatory features not particularly favoured by what may be labelled the 'legal school' of regulation: supervisory model L of Chapter 2. Lawyers regard this approach as almost a kind of uncontrolled uncertainty. It lacks the apparent (and illusory) precision of many legal systems – the so-called transparency models of supervision. In many respects, the Bank of England's philosophy is much closer to the economist's ideal – it leans more towards a market-orientated approach (Model F of Chapter 2). It is flexible and recognizes the role of the market.

In this general context, the modern historical evidence – such as it is –

does not come out in complete support of any definitive supervisory philosophy. Both highly regulated, transparent systems (like those in the US and West Germany) and more freely regulated systems (like the UK system up to the 1973–5 events) have experienced problems, crises and some failures. Despite the potential dilemmas raised by these observations, this historical evidence does at least support the need for some supervision. The supervisory system that develops in any country is a complex phenomenon. It is the product of several major forces – like the political, social, cultural and institutional environment – and it is often a reaction to specific events, particularly crises.

The new prudential returns following the supervisory reorganization of 1974 were usually required on a quarterly basis. An important supervisory function was to monitor a bank's risk positon. Capital adequacy and liquidity measures are regarded as central tools in this supervisory process, and in 1975 the Bank discussed its evolving views on these areas. In capital adequacy analysis, the Bank began to look more closely at risk assets measures, besides the traditional capital : deposits (the gearing ratio) measure. The concept of free capital – broadly defined as total capital, less fixed assets – was given more emphasis in the risk assets measure. The free capital approach obviated the artificial boosting of capital ratios by such accounting means as revaluing fixed assets.

The Bank regarded liquidity as probably more important than capital adequacy. Its traditional liquidity yardstick was to relate a bank's quick assets to deposits. This approach, however, was recognized to be increasingly defective with the rise of liability management. Wholesale banking operations required a more sophisticated analysis – for example, matching principles needed to be developed. The importance of cash flow forecasts was emphasized. It seems that the Bank devoted considerable resources to the prudential monitoring of liquidity in the new and more complex banking environment.

The Bank of England has not employed supervisory techniques like inspection. No team of Bank of England inspectors periodically samples the credit files of supervised banks. In this area the Bank relies on its own supervisory process, supplemented by various channels of market intelligence. Particular events in the market may alert it to possible adverse developments in individual banks. The Bank's adoption of the so-called CAMEL approach summarizes its main emphasis in practical supervision. CAMEL reflects the main areas covered in supervision – **C**apital adequacy, **A**sset quality, **M**anagement quality, **E**arnings, and **L**iquidity. The present arrangements flow from the 1979 Banking Act.

The present arrangements

Pressures for new and more formal supervisory measures in the UK made themselves felt during the 1970s. An important impetus was given by the

December 1977 adoption in Brussels of the First Directive of the EEC on the co-ordination of laws, regulations and administrative provisions concerning the taking up and pursuit of the business of credit institutions (document 77/780/EEC). The 1979 Banking Act formalized the powers of UK banking supervisors and clarified several points. It removed uncertainties about the Bank of England's powers and the scope of supervision. At the same time, it strengthened the Bank's powers in areas previously shown to be weak.

The 1979 Banking Act was a landmark in that it was the first time that the Bank of England's regulatory powers were enshrined explicitly in specific legislation. The new Act, however, was more evolutionary than revolutionary. The Bank of England's supervisory philosophy and style of the 1970s were not seriously undermined. In many respects, the legislation was similar to corresponding bank laws in Continental countries. It required banks to be authorized, criteria were laid down for authorization, and a Depositors' Protection Scheme (deposit insurance) was established. But unlike the bank laws in many Continental countries, it did not specify minimum balance-sheet ratios for liquidity and capital adequacy. The Act was not designed to control and regulate every aspect of banking business. Clear scope was preserved for the continuance of the Bank of England's particular supervisory style.

An important aim of the Act was to prevent any bank or other financial institution – existing or newly formed – from accepting deposits without the prior authorization of the Bank of England. The Act defines the institutions subject to the legislation and specifies the criteria which must be satisfied to obtain Bank of England authorization. The Act requires banks to be either recognized as banks or licensed as deposit-taking institutions. It lays down the procedure for revocation or recognition of a licence. The Act provides statutory authority for the Bank of England to supervise all authorized institutions, and it controls the use of banking names and descriptions. A number of institutions that accept deposits were exempt from the Act, and these included the National Savings Bank, the National Girobank and the building societies. The exemption from the Act of the trustee savings banks (TSBs) is due to expire in 1986.

Banks seeking a licence or recognition must meet the relevant criteria specified in the Act. As a minimum, an applicant must satisfy the Bank of England as to its solvency and the competence of its management. Applicants for recognized status must also show that they can provide a wide range of banking services, and satisfy the Bank on their standing and reputation in the financial community. Many of these general criteria were not new to supervised banks in the UK. The five kinds of banking service required of a recognized bank are specified in the Act, and the Bank was given powers to excuse a bank from some of these in certain cases.

Although the Act was silent on supervisory controls like minimum balance sheet ratios, the Bank was given statutory power to supervise that banks continued to satisfy the conditions for authorization. The Bank's supervisory style of dialogue and flexibility, and its special relationship with supervised banks, were not altered by the Act. Supervisory controls on liquidity, capital adequacy and foreign exchange were the subject of a separate series of discussion papers issued by the Bank of England following the 1979 Act. These papers invited comment and debate, and the current Bank of England approach is the product of the ensuing dialogue. This process was particularly evident in the liquidity paper first published in March 1980. The debate which followed its publication helped shape the modified proposals contained in the 1982 paper. As in previous years, the Bank of England continues to regard ratios as no more than initial screening systems.

The Deposit Protection Scheme which came into being in February 1982 was a particularly novel feature of the Act. It invoked considerable hostility at first. The large banks baulked at their implied subsidizing of the frailer institutions, especially in the light of their experiences with the Lifeboat following the fringe banking crisis. Many also argued that no depositors had lost money in the fringe banking crisis. It was pointed out that the Act itself – without deposit insurance – should strengthen and consolidate a supervisory process designed to ensure that an event like the fringe crisis never got under way again. Others felt that simple guarantees from all banks were all that was needed. These arguments were not ignored, but they did not prevent the Scheme becoming operational. Initial contributions to the fund were made in July 1982.

The Scheme insures 75 per cent of the deposits of any single depositor, up to a maximum of £10,000. It is limited to sterling deposits. Secured deposits and those with an original maturity of more than five years are excluded. These provisions were designed to satisfy the philosophy of consumer protection; larger deposits were not protected in the same way. Initial bank contributions to the fund were computed as a fixed percentage of each bank's 'deposit base', subject to a minimum contribution of £2,500 and a maximum of £300,000. The first call on the fund was a sum of £1.2 million to depositors with Merbro Finance (NI), a licensed deposit-taker which went into liquidation in May 1982.

International aspects

Although the traditional focus of supervision seemed to be on business denominated in domestic currency and retail banking, international developments could not be ignored. As we have seen, many important banking risks and problems originated in the international banking system. This stimulated concern with international banking supervision and a growing Bank of England interest in foreign exchange risk-exposure and international banking risks generally. In practice, supervisors cannot segment neatly domestic and international banking. The banking structural developments of the 1960s and 1970s were partly a continuing trend towards a more global banking and money market. Similar globalization trends have been evident in capital markets.

Following the 1974 measures, the Bank of England had clarified with banks in London associated with overseas banks where supervisory responsibilities lay. These overseas banks included the banks' shareholder banks and other central banks. The Bank of England also set out to secure a much closer liaison internationally with its opposite numbers. At the same time it emphasized generally to all banks in London the need for much tighter internal control systems on foreign exchange.

A major development has been the growing internationalization of banking. Banks have spread their activities into other banking systems through vehicles like foreign subsidiaries and branches. At the same time, home-banking systems have been subjected to the growing presence of foreign banks. These structural developments have posed major supervisory problems. The supervisors of the parents of foreign banks will be concerned that the foreign offices are properly supervised. Host countries will also be greatly concerned that these foreign banking operations can be subjected to effective supervision.

It is clear that these structural developments can cause major problems. These became evident following the 1973/4 events in the international banking system. The result was the establishment by the governors of the central banks of the Group of Ten major industrialized countries and Switzerland and Luxembourg of a standing committee of banking supervisory authorities. The Concordat followed in 1975, and it specified the responsibilities of the host supervisory authorities and the supervisors of the parent bank. The primary objective of the Concordat was to ensure that no bank operating internationally escaped supervision.

The Banco Ambrosiano collapse in June 1982 brought the Concordat into sharp focus again. It re-emphasized the need for international supervision to keep pace with a fast-changing banking market-place. Cooper (1984, p. 277) suggests that had the Bank of Italy been able to supervise Banco Ambrosiano's affairs on a consolidated basis – the practice which evolved in Britain during the 1970s from the Concordat – the problems would have been detected much sooner. The Bank of Italy, however, did not possess the legislative power to supervise that was given to the Bank of England under the 1979 Banking Act. Nor did the Bank of Italy enjoy the kind of mutual trust with Italian banks under its control which is a core feature of the British supervisory system. Nevertheless, no supervisory system is watertight, as recent events in Britain have shown. The troubles of Johnson Matthey Bankers in the autumn of 1984 sent shivers through the British banking community.

The 1975 Concordat was revised in May 1983. The revision included a refinement of the principle of consolidated supervision first enunciated in the 1975 Concordat. It also contained several other modifications. For example, it sought to fill in supervisory gaps arising from inadequate supervisory standards in some countries. The committee has not addressed the question of responsibilities for lender of last resort. This is a central bank function and supervision in many countries party to the Concordat is not carried out by the central bank.

A useful survey of this and other related areas of international supervision (like the EEC's role) is provided by Cooper (1984, Ch. 5). Dudley Peake explores several aspects of this general field in the following Chapter 11. International supervision is undoubtedly a major policy area and it would take several volumes to discuss all the issues. The focus of this book, however, is more on domestic banking supervision. Having provided a general perspective of the field, we can now turn our attention to the specialist contributions. The first collection of four papers examines the evolution and practice of all UK bank supervision.

References

Bank of England (1971), 'Competition and credit control', *Bank of England Quarterly Bulletin*, vol. 1, no. 1 (June), pp. 189–93.

Bank of England (1974), Speech of the Governor to the Institute of Bankers at Bristol on 5 February 1974, *Bank of England Quarterly Bulletin*, vol. 14, no. 1 (March), pp. 54–5.

Bank of England (1975), 'The capital and liquidity adequacy of banks', *Bank of England Quarterly Bulletin*, vol. 15, no. 3 (Sept.), pp. 240–43.

Bank of England (1978), 'The secondary banking crisis and the Bank of England's support operations', *Bank of England Quarterly Bulletin*, vol. 18, no. 2 (June), pp. 230–39.

Bank of England (1980), 'Banking supervision and the Banking Act', *Bank of England Quarterly Bulletin*, vol. 20, no. 2 (June), pp. 205–8.

Bank of England (1980), 'The measurement of capital', *Bank of England Quarterly Bulletin*, vol. 20, no. 3 (Sept.), pp. 324–30.

Bank of England (1981), 'Foreign currency exposure', *Bank of England Quarterly Bulletin*, vol. 21, no. 2 (June), pp. 235–37.

Bank of England (1982), 'Prudential arrangements for the discount market', *Bank of England Quarterly Bulletin*, vol. 22, no. 2 (June), pp. 209–11.

Bank of England (1982), 'The measurement of liquidity', *Bank of England Quarterly Bulletin*, vol. 22, no. 3 (Sept.), pp. 399–402.

HMSO (1979), Banking Act, 1979.

Blunden, George (1975), 'The supervision of the UK banking system', *Bank of England Quarterly Bulletin*, vol. 15, no. 2 (June), pp. 188–94.

Committee of London Clearing Bankers (1978), *The London Clearing Banks*, Evidence by the Committee of London Clearing Bankers to the Committee to Review the Functioning of Financial Institutions (Longman).

Commission of the European Economic Community (1977), *First Banking Co-ordination Directive* (published as document 77/780/EEC 1977).

Cooke, W. P. (1982), 'The role of the banking supervisor', *Bank of England Quarterly Bulletin*, vol. 22, no. 4 (Dec.), pp. 547–52.
Cooke, W. P. (1983), 'The international banking scene: a supervisory perspective', *Bank of England Quarterly Bulletin*, vol. 23, no. 1 (March), pp. 61–5.
Cooper, John (1984), *The Management and Regulation of Banks* (London: Macmillan).
Edwards, F. R. (ed.) (1979), *Issues in Financial Regulation* (New York: McGraw-Hill).
Gardener, E. P. M. (1983), 'The Bank of England's approach to banking supervision', *Issues in Bank Regulation*, vol. 6, no. 3 (Winter), pp. 14–17.
Morison, Ian, Tillet, Paul and Welch, June (1979), *The Banking Act, 1979* (London: Butterworth).
Revell, Jack (1975), *Solvency and Regulation of Banks*, Bangor Occasional Papers in Economics, No. 5 (Cardiff: University of Wales Press).

PART B

Evolution and Practice

Part B is devoted to a further examination of how UK supervision developed, and its operational philosophy. The opening paper by Peter Cooke, Head of Banking Supervision at the Bank of England, discusses the evolution of UK supervision, and he reconciles the traditional and self-regulation approach practised in the UK with the new Banking Act. A central thesis of this paper is that the supervisor's role is to arrive at the appropriate balance between methods of self-discipline and legal rules. Margaret Reid goes on in Chapter 6 to discuss the influence of the secondary, or fringe, banking crisis on UK supervision. This crisis was one of the major driving forces behind the rapid development of UK supervision to its existing form. The following paper by Jane Sargent reminds us of the role of politics and pressure groups in the formation of banking regulations. Jane Sargent examines the role of the British bankers' associations since 1972 in helping to shape important supervisory legislation. The last paper in Part B by Les Metcalfe studies the transition of UK supervision from self-regulation to what he calls 'a more open-ended preventive medicine approach'. He explores from an organizational perspective how UK supervisors are developing a more rigorous appreciation of the banking system as a collection of interdependent units.

5 Self-Regulation and Statute – the Evolution of Banking Supervision

PETER W. COOKE

Associate Director and Head of Banking Supervision, Bank of England

This is the text of the Ernest Sykes Memorial Lecture given at the Institute of Bankers on Tuesday, 26 April 1983. It is reproduced with kind permission of the Institute of Bankers.

Ernest Sykes died 25 years ago. This annual series of lectures which is dedicated to honouring his memory is also an occasion to pay tribute to the work of the Institute of Bankers itself which he served so long and so well. Sykes was Secretary of this Institute for some thirty years at the start of this century and more than any other he was instrumental in transforming it from what had been a modest professional association to an institute of national stature in which the greatly-expanded constituency which it serves can take justifiable pride. As a student of banking at the turn of the century, Sykes won the Institute's essay competition with a paper entitled 'A History of the Growth of London as the Financial Centre of the World and the Best Means of Maintaining that Position'. I fear I cannot compete with the breadth of his vision tonight but there is one essential requirement for a flourishing financial centre that he would have recognised and that is that the institutions which operate in such a centre should enjoy an undoubted reputation for fair dealing and the financial soundness which derives from observance of prudent business principles. It is to the process involved in overseeing these aspects that I propose to address my remarks today.

I have taken as my theme 'Self-regulation and statute – the evolution of Banking Supervision' not because I see the pursuit of supervisory endeavour as being a choice between methods of self-discipline and law, but because, I would suggest, it is the characteristic of all regulatory arrangements that they are most effective when they combine both these influences. It is the essence of the supervisor's role to arrive at that delicate balance of both these factors which best suits particular national marketplaces. These marketplaces of course vary and it is because banking systems and the supervisory system within which they operate have grown up within different national frameworks that the process of arriving at an appropriate homogeneous framework for an international system of banking supervision has proved so elusive and difficult.

Although the City of London is the last place to ignore the international dimension, it is to the domestic system that I want to concentrate most of my remarks. It will be a recurring refrain, however, that the domestic situation in the United Kingdom cannot be addressed in isolation. Nonetheless it does seem timely, almost ten years on from the onset of that shock to the domestic banking system in this country which became known as the secondary banking crisis, to stand back and review the developments in the supervisory framework and in supervisory practices which have occurred since those troubled days late in 1973.

Half-way through this span of almost ten years came the drafting of the Banking Act, which eventually received the Royal Assent in April 1979, and I would like to spend a little time recalling the circumstances and the thinking which led to its enactment and the system onto which it was grafted. I shall then move on to consider how the statute has settled down and how the current arrangements operate and finally conclude with a few thoughts about the issues likely to concern us as we look into the future.

It is right to give considerable weight to this statute in discussing supervisory developments over the past decade but at the same time, as I will endeavour to demonstrate, it is only up to a point correct to describe it as a watershed; in many respects the legislation was designed to interfere as little as possible with what was regarded as good in what had come before and only to add to the earlier arrangements new features where the previous system had been found wanting. In this process the Bank fully recognised that it was necessary to move with the times – acknowledging, with the old Arab proverb, that men are more like their times than their fathers.

There are few, I think, who would seek to contest the view that the supervisory arrangements which had been in place before the secondary banking crisis had not sufficiently kept up with the times. This has been frequently remarked in the international context in relation to the rapid growth in international markets through the 1960s, but it was equally true of domestic business. The Discount Office combined the handling of the daily operations with the Discount market with the Bank's banking supervisory responsibilities serviced by only a handful of staff. The Bank concerned itself primarily with a limited number of substantial and long-established banking businesses. It relied heavily on the fact that the City was a compact community exercising its own disciplines where prudential and ethical shortcomings would usually produce market-induced reflexes which only required the Bank's intervention in extreme cases.

But the marketplace and the players were changing. More and more foreign banks were coming to London. Domestically, the period of relatively rapid economic growth (at least as it seems today) in the 1950s and early 1960s had led to significant expansion of the consumer credit industry. Many new institutions had grown up to service these and related businesses and through the 1960s these had received an added stimulus first through being outside the credit control regime applied to the banking system and then from the expansion in credit, particularly in the property field, following the removal of those controls after the publication of the Bank's paper 'Competition and Credit Control' in 1971.

A number of these institutions grew up outside the traditional purview of the Bank and without the internally applied restraints which obtained among established City institutions. At the same time, the existing statutes were of limited effectiveness. The act of taking deposits from the public required no statutory permission and the Section 123 'banking' certificate which these newer institutions sought to obtain from the Department of Trade, thereby exempting them from the provisions of the Moneylenders Acts, was essentially designed to protect the institutions themselves against repudiation of debts by borrowers rather than to protect depositors. The Protection of Depositors Act, enacted in 1963, only applied to institutions wishing to advertise for deposits; but the rules on the content of advertisements and the balance sheet information which such institutions had to supply did not adequately alert depositors to the degrees of risk present in the different companies. Most importantly, once authorisation for a particular purpose under one or other of these statutes had been given, there was inadequate provision for monitoring the subsequent performance of the institution.

Many of the new institutions developed out of businesses with no banking traditions and with little, if any, banking expertise. The dangers posed by these essentially unregulated businesses were exacerbated by the growth of the wholesale money markets which enabled them to expand their balance sheets rapidly without a sound base of established customer relationships. At that time also there was little statistical data available to provide some early warning of any general flouting of traditional prudential standards by these companies and the data available in audited accounts was not sufficient to enable the wider public, or indeed often sophisticated financial observers, to make informed judgements about the soundness of their business.

When the events of the winter of 1973/4 revealed the extent of these lacunae in the system, the Bank acted swiftly to fill the void which had been identified, but very much on an *ad hoc* basis. In the course of 1974, most of the larger companies registered in the United Kingdom holding sizeable deposits from the public were identified by the Bank and brought within a system under which they voluntarily submitted themselves to its supervision. Before the end of 1974 all banks and other deposit-taking companies of any significance, other than those groups of institutions already covered by alternative supervisory regimes, e.g. building societies, had agreed to participate in an enlarged and intensified system of prudential supervision. Under these arrangements they were required to submit quarterly statistical returns revealing the main components of their business and to attend interviews at the Bank to discuss the position revealed in those returns. The Discount Office was reorganised, its staff significantly increased and a new supervisory office formed. At that time only the clearing banks and the British overseas banks were not covered by these new arrangements. At a time when priorities had to be established quickly, they were not felt to be a cause of particular prudential concern and were thought unlikely to suffer any significant or sustained loss of confidence on the part of their depositors.

By this action, the Bank moved to plug the main weakness of the system and put in place arrangements for monitoring the performance of this wider group of financial institutions. At the same time the particular and acute danger for the system – the threat of a generalised loss of confidence – was met through the establishment of the Support Group, popularly known as the Lifeboat. Formed by the Bank of England and the London and Scottish Clearing Banks, it set out to provide support for those institutions which found themselves in liquidity difficulties which could not be handled within the normal market mechanisms.

It is difficult, looking back even from some years away, to highlight any particular landmarks to mark the steps as the banking system slowly climbed away from crisis. It was a gradual evolving process but as the immediate pressures eased, increasing attention began to be given to the way in which more permanent arrangements should be structured. At the heart of this scrutiny was the question whether what had been done as an immediate response needed to be supplemented, reinforced or comprehensively redefined in legislation.

It had become fairly clear within the Bank in the course of 1974 and 1975 that some new legislation was both inevitable and desirable. Over long years, the exercise of the customary authority of the Bank, coupled with the absence of any major or generalised crisis in the primary banking sector, had meant that there had been no pressures for the passage of comprehensive legislation governing the regulation of banking activity as existed in all other developed, and indeed most developing, countries. But the very fact of an absence of legislation in this area in the United Kingdom was of itself provoking some hard questioning. The existing statutes addressed particular aspects of banking business, not the business as a whole, and they left, as mentioned earlier, significant gaps in supervision. They were less than clear when it came to pointing up the status of different deposit-taking institutions and there were inadequate controls over the use of banking names and descriptions. There was no definition in statute of a bank and the majority judgment in the Court of Appeal in the case of UDT v. Kirkwood had demonstrated the difficulties and uncertainties of applying the common law to fill this statutory vacuum.

Furthermore, an important new dimension had been introduced as a consequence of the United Kingdom's entry into the European Economic Community in January 1973. It is not the place here to pursue in detail the full legal and legislative implications of that event, but initiatives already under way in the field of harmonisation of banking regulation at the time of UK accession had to be examined and a national position established. In the course of this process, the United Kingdom took a strong lead in redirecting the energies of the European Commission toward an approach to harmonisation in the banking field more consistent with the realities of the marketplace. An approach, we in the Bank believed, more likely in practice to lead to agreement because it was addressing major points of principle rather than detailed statutory provisions. The outcome of this work culminated in the adoption of the first EEC Banking Directive in 1977, the most significant feature of which, in relation to domestic legislation, was the requirement that each member country needed to have in place a prior authorisation procedure for credit institutions.

Thus early on in the course of negotiating the content of this directive, the UK authorities had accepted in principle that there would be some parallel domestic legislation – and for domestic reasons. At that time, although there were certain statutory restrictions on the particular kinds of business which a deposit-taking institution could undertake, there was no statutory requirement as such which had to be met before an institution could set out to solicit deposits from the general public. So although one of the reasons for the introduction of the Banking Bill in 1978 was the need to carry into domestic legislation some of the terms of the EEC Directive, in fact the decision had been taken much earlier, and independently of EEC requirements, to enact licensing requirements for deposit-taking institutions in the United Kingdom – as indeed was made clear when the White Paper leading up to the drafting of the bill was published in August 1976.

The proposals for legislation and the discussion in the White Paper acknowledged the importance of preserving the Bank's existing informal approach to the supervision of the primary banking sector which was seen to have a number of advantages, notably in its ability to be adapted to the changing circumstances of different banks and the marketplace. While describing the intended framework of law, the White Paper acknowledged that 'the customs and conventions of a self-regulatory system are likely to command more willing and effective support than formal rules imposed by law'. These indications were welcomed in the financial community and, although the proposal to set up a Deposit Protection Scheme was greeted with a good deal less than rapture by established banks, the approach signalled in the White Paper was generally well received in the City.

Alongside these developments, however, a wider-ranging discussion was taking place domestically about the whole nature of regulation as it affected all aspects of the City of London's activities. This arose out of the deliberations of the Committee to Review the Functioning of Financial Institutions set up in January 1977 under the Chairmanship of Sir Harold Wilson.

In the course of developing its evidence to the Wilson Committee, the Bank analysed in considerable depth the nature of the supervisory arrangements in the City of London, not only for the Bank itself in the area of its particular responsibility to the banking community, but also in other areas of City activity, notably the securities markets and the commodity markets. The Bank drew a distinction between two different forms of non-statutory regulation which had long applied to financial institutions in the City. One of these, defined as self-regulation, implied readiness by an institution or group of institutions to adhere to a set of commonly accepted business standards. So in the banking field prudential principles had come to be reinforced over time by the establishment of associations which grouped together similar institutions, conferring status on the members in return for acceptance of a code of conduct. The other form of regulation not based on law – non-statutory regulation – consisted of the exercise of authority by one institution over others, the effectiveness of which depended on it being accepted by those over whom it was exercised. Such was the traditional exercise by the Bank of its customary authority over the banking system deriving from its operational central banking role, out of which, as students of banking know well, grew its responsibility for the good conduct of financial markets and the soundness of the institutions which participated in them.

This work was helpful to the Bank and the Treasury in clarifying its thinking on a number of aspects of the proposals for legislation which were eventually put forward to Ministers in the draft bill. In particular, in settling the framework within which banking business should be conducted, the relative roles of self-regulation, non-statutory regulation and statute were considered in some detail. The central issue to be resolved was whether, in the circumstances then prevailing or in prospect, the Bank's customary authority could be relied upon. Despite the extent to which the enhanced supervisory arrangements instituted by the Bank in response to the secondary banking crisis had been accepted voluntarily by deposit-taking institutions, it was concluded that it would be unwise to rely on the Bank's traditional authority being accepted comprehensively by all the institutions prospectively involved – particularly outside the City itself.

Critical decisions of principle were settled – to legislate to provide both a prior authorisation procedure and an outline framework of supervision (although one which would still rely heavily on the Bank's traditional approach and existing practices and procedures). Consequences of these decisions were that first, the legislation was formulated as part of an evolutionary process, not as a completely fresh start; and secondly, the authority designated to exercise the statutory responsibilities for authorisation and supervision of deposit-taking institutions was the Bank, not a government department or governmental agency specially created for the purpose.

The other important feature of the Act to note was that it addressed itself particularly to the act of deposit-taking. The preamble to the Act begins with the words 'An Act to regulate the acceptance of deposits in the course of a business'. Much of the rationale for the legislation, as indeed for the earlier supervisory arrangements, derives from the special fiduciary responsibilities which attach to deposit-taking and the need to ensure that the public interest is adequately protected by some form of external supervisory oversight of such businesses.

I do not need, nor do I intend, to outline the particular provisions of the Banking Act to this audience. It will be familiar to you all. But there are certain features of the legislation which merit comment in a description of the evolution of supervision over the past decade.

The first of these – just touched on – is the extent to which the general approach to the structuring of the Act set out to preserve the enhanced non-statutorily-based arrangements which had been put in place in 1974. That system of supervision, with its roots going back much earlier, was characterised by my predecessor as personal, participative, progressive and flexible. Personal and participative because it gave a major role in the supervisory procedures to the development of close and frequent contacts between senior management in banks and other deposit-making institutions and the Bank's supervisory officials. The objective was to come alongside management and to share in their perspective of the business, although never to get into the position of taking managements' decisions for them. This continues to be at the heart of our supervisory processes since the Banking Act.

The system was progressive because over many years there had grown up a variety of requirements related to banking functions and activities, either based on statute, for example, exemption under the Protection of Depositors Act or authorisation under the Exchange Control Act; or non-statutory, for example, eligibility of bills for discount at the Bank or membership of a particular club or association of banks. Each particular recognition had its place as a step on a ladder of progression from a lowly to the highest status and standing. The new Act and the introduction of the two types of authorisation – to which I shall come back in a moment – did away with some of the rungs in the ladder but it was not designed to remove, nor has it done away with, the concept of progression, both within the two categories and from one to the other.

Then there was flexibility. It was, and it remains, a fundamental precept of the Bank's approach to supervision that the system should be able, subject to satisfaction of basic prudential guidelines, to accommodate rather than constrict the very many different kinds of banking business built up over the years. This approach was sustained in an Act deliberately structured to avoid overturning the Bank's pre-existing flexible approach. It set out statutorily-based authorisation procedures for the carrying on of a deposit-taking business and made the Bank responsible for exercising that function. But whilst it set out certain basic requirements of adequate capital and prudent conduct of the business which had to be satisfied before an initial authorisation would be forthcoming, it did not prescribe in any detail the ongoing procedures for the conduct of day-to-day supervision or any precise balance sheet requirements or prudential ratios (with the one exception of a minimum capital figure) which had to be satisfied. Thus the Bank, subject to an over-riding obligation to be satisfied that the rather generally framed legal requirements continued to be met, was left free under the Act to conduct ongoing supervision under established procedures, although with the power inherent in the statute behind it.

A second particular feature of the legislation – already touched on – merits further comment. That is the two categories of authorisation. Much has been said about this aspect of the Act and there is no doubt that it has posed some administrative problems as the Bank has set out to apply evenhandedly the provisions of the Act and the associated complexities of rules on the use of banking names and descriptions. Much concern was expressed about the classification process and the potential for discrimination and commercial disadvantage. It was, of course, inevitable that classification for authorisation purposes into two broad groups would, at the margin, establish a boundary line which did not exist before between similar but not identical institutions. It presented some problems for the Bank and required careful explanation of how we saw the system operating. The Governor speaking to the foreign banking community in May 1980, in often quoted words, said about the two-tier system:

> It is not intended, and was never intended, to be a great divide. We are concerned, as we have always been, to permit and encourage progression for those institutions which may wish to move from the licensed deposit-taker category to that of recognized bank. Classification as a licensed deposit-taker is not to be seen of itself as impugning the status of an institution – and certainly not the integrity and competence of its management or the good name of the institutions generally.

I think these comments are worth recalling, if only to remind ourselves of the way in which these matters were being viewed during the initial running-in process of the new legislation. I do not believe it is necessary to keep repeating those words today because I believe that the market understands and accepts them. At the same time there are concerns, not totally allayed with the passing of time, that even if institutions in the market are generally treated on their intrinsic merits, the tendency to resort to categorisation based on Banking Act classifications can be an easy option. It would also be closing one's eyes to the real world if we were to suggest, for example, that if an institution was reclassified other than of its own volition, as a licensed deposit-taker after having enjoyed recognised status, this would not be regarded as a demotion. The merit of the two-tier approach, however, is that it has allowed the Banking Act to span the whole range of deposit-taking institutions without destroying the essential homogeneity of the traditional international marketplace in London, while at the same time bringing a necessary legal basis to the conduct of many smaller businesses round the country not formerly within the ambit of the Bank's customary authority.

The third aspect of the Act to which I would like to refer briefly is the Deposit Protection Scheme. Naturally, the major banks felt it was unnecessary for them and indeed contrary to their commercial interests. The Bank shared the view that some element of *caveat emptor* was a necessary part of the operation of any market, so when it was concluded that this scheme – essentially a consumer protection arrangement – should form a part of the Act it was introduced with limited coverage, a ceiling of £10,000 and only 75% protection. We felt, and continue to feel, that the scheme strikes a reasonable balance between the wish to give some protection to the small depositor and the need to apply some market discipline to greedy or imprudent lenders. What it was never intended to do was to serve as an arrangement for the comprehensive underpinning of the institutions covered by the legislation.

Now let us turn and look at the system as it is today. The Banking Act has now been in place and running for three years and more and the institutions and the markets have settled down with it. I hope I am right in the assumption that the worst fears of some bankers have not been realised. Perhaps you will allow me to quote again from remarks of the Governor in 1980 referring to the concerns about the Bank's role under the statute:

> The images that some have presented of the Bank in this debate call to mind the ghosts that appeared before Scrooge in Dickens's *Christmas Carol*. There is the ghost of Christmas Pxst – a romantic image of a benevolent and benign Bank of England presiding over an exclusive 'club' of bankers where everyone knew how to behave and thus where no one ever needed to be reminded what to do. It all, as the song has it, came naturally. Then we have the ghost of Christmas Present – a baleful Bank blinking in the bright light of a new Banking Act and deciding that it must carry newly-discovered convictions about how banks should run their businesses into the furthest corners of the banking system. The last spectre is the ghost of Christmas Future – a malevolent Bank wielding its authority arbitrarily as the willing tool of a doctrinaire regime,

setting out to manipulate a helpless financial sector into becoming a mere extension of government.

I hope and believe that such concerns still exist only in the realm of caricature and that the system of supervision now operating is not greatly changed in philosophy or style from earlier years. It would be unrealistic, of course, to maintain that the system has not undergone some change, or that it will not continue to change. It is also probably true to say that it is difficult to move back off the statutory road once embarked along it. But as the Wilson Committee concluded, the central issue is not 'whether statutory or non-statutory methods of supervision are preferable in some absolute sense, but whether the existing balance between the two, and equally if not more importantly, the type of each presently used for the different groups of institutions, are appropriate for their particular circumstances'.

The Act and the manner in which the Act is administered I hope represents a reasonable balance but it would not be right to regard the system as now set in tram lines. Change may well be necessary. There are many influences at work on markets to which flexible supervisory responses will be needed. The national and international macroeconomic environment, the realities of international banking involvements, the measured progress toward European integration, the pressures brought about by competition, institutional and technological changes and the lessons of unsuspected failures will all need to be a part of the supervisor's wider perspective. And, of course, in due time the legislation itself may need to be reviewed in the light of experience of its operation.

But before indulging in a little crystal-ball-gazing to assess the impact of some of these various factors for change in the period ahead, I would like to pause to look – as a snapshot – at the broad elements of the system as it is today – three years after the implementation of the provisions of the Banking Act.

We have a supervisory system with authorisation deriving from statute but the running of the system still depending to a large degree on moral suasion. Powers exist to reinforce the system, but not so draconian as to leave no room for debate, reasoned discussion and persuasion – of bankers by supervisors and vice versa. Broad criteria are applied to all authorized institutions on an individual basis to take account of particular circumstances but always with an eye to peer group analysis and the avoidance of competitive inequality as a consequence of supervisory arbitrariness. The cornerstone of the system is close and regular contact with management based on the submission of quarterly statistical returns which are closely analysed and monitored. Discussion documents on capital adequacy, liquidity and foreign exchange exposure have been circulated and debated with the industry and in their final form – final, that is, for the time being – represent agreed understandings on the systems of measurement and monitoring on which the Bank bases its supervision of these important aspects of banks' business.

With each institution, understandings of the parameters within which the Bank would expect business normally to be conducted are established and regularly reviewed with management. Close attention is paid to the analysis of risk, and its distribution and concentration. The examination and classification of individual loans is not a part of these procedures. We prefer to allow the banker to take the decision on risk and assess his overall performance by careful monitoring of provisions and write-offs and the evolving pattern of overall profitability. In eschewing inspection, however, it must be said we are able to do so at least in part because of the reliance we have over the years felt able to place on the professionalism and integrity of the external auditors. In reserve, however, powers exist under the Act for the carrying out of special investigations of the books if this is thought necessary, although there continues to be an assumption that traditional relations with fully-fledged banks will not require the invoking of statutory authority. Should it seem desirable in particular circumstances to look at a bank's loan book in detail, we would expect to do so with the full co-operation of the institution concerned.

The constituency is almost six hundred strong and still growing. There are currently 291 recognised banks and an almost equal number of licensed deposit-taking institutions, serviced by a division within the Bank currently some eighty strong. Over two-thirds of the institutions supervised are foreign-owned or foreign-controlled, so as mentioned earlier, looking at the market merely through domestically-focused spectacles is only a part of the picture. It is outside the scope of these remarks to discuss international developments in detail but of course the past ten years have also seen major developments in international supervisory co-operation and co-ordination. Understandings on supervisory principles and contacts between supervisory authorities are now an integral part of the supervisory process in major industrialised countries, and these contacts have, I believe, contributed significantly to the improvement of supervisory arrangements around the world, this country included. On the basis of the understandings reached at the Bank for International Settlements in Basle, we, as the host authority for the branches here of the major banks of the world, have some supervisory reponsibilities, for example, over the general conduct of their business in London, the quality of their management and the monitoring of control systems and reporting lines to head office, but we expect the primary role to rest with the parent bank's supervisor. Similarly, we have greatly extended the coverage of our supervisory arrangements to cover the global activities of indigenous UK banks.

Implicit in our approach to supervision is that there is an essential identity of interest between supervisor and banker in ensuring that individual businesses are conducted with integrity, soundness and profit. But of course there may always come a point where the supervisor's view will differ from that of the banker and if the banker cannot be persuaded, the supervisor's view must prevail. At the same time, the variety of institutions necessitates differences of approach in particular cases. There is inevitably a great difference between the way we relate to a clearing bank with huge resources of experience and expertise and detailed and well-proven control systems, and to a small deposit-taking institution, with the same handful of people all performing the different roles of controllers, directors and managers and where not infrequently our concern is to avoid becoming too involved in the running of the business. There are other cases where, in dealing with a few of our newer charges, there must remain a question whether gentlemanly discussion and exhortation to observe prudent practices will on their own always produce the desired result.

We are well provided in the Act to deal with the recalcitrant and it is right and necessary that these powers are available; and indeed they have already been used. At the same time, I am sure such powers should be used sparingly and I find it difficult to contemplate a supervisory regime in which compulsion becomes the order of the day. But for the system to remain on the present basis, it requires the continuing full-hearted commitment of the participants – particularly the major players – if what the Bank believes to be the advantages of the present system are to be maintained. Pressing the supervisor to the limits of tolerance may appear individually to produce the best commercial advantage but I am reminded of the analogy, by Keynes, I think, when describing the damaging effect of inflation, of the brick at the end of a length of elastic. As you pull, the elastic will stretch so far, but there comes a point when eventually the brick flies up and hits you in the face.

Let me now, in concluding, try to peer a little into that crystal ball. As all who attempt this know, the future invariably comes out looking rather cloudy and my comments will be long on diagnosis and short on prescription. But let me try and pick out particular areas where the supervisors' art will be tested in the years ahead.

As I have said, it is certainly my hope that the traditional ethos and philosophy which, as I have tried to demonstrate, has been sustained through fire and statute, can be continued. But, as also stressed, it will not be sustained without support; and it will need to be nimble in its assessment and identification of the risks in banking business if it is to remain abreast, and as far as possible ahead, of the developments taking place in the market.

There will be many dilemmas. For example, the Bank has to find the right balance between, at the one extreme, the rigorous pursuit of professionalism in its supervision with the attendant danger of excessive refinement of the system and, at the other, a fetish of flexibility which can only lead to flabby and complacent supervision and an unsound base for the system. The present very broad-brush nature of the risk assets ratio when calculating capital adequacy is a prime example of this dilemma. It cannot be denied that the weightings are imprecise, but would adding te= more categories of asset with minor variations in the weighting increase the effectiveness of the overall measure as a supervisory aid? I doubt it, but that is not to say that no modifications can be contemplated. I confess, however, I have always tended, with Keynes again, to side with those who believe that it is better to be approximately right than precisely wrong.

In the European context, banking supervision, like other areas of activity, will continue to be affected by the pursuit of the dream of the founding fathers of the Community. The debate will before long be engaged on the controversial subject of disclosure and I will not be rash enough to make predictions about the outcome; although underlying the discussion I think it is correct to discern a secular trend toward greater disclosure in many areas of economic activity. On the wider international stage, the problems of sustaining the soundness of individual banks and of the system as a whole in current circumstances have been extensively debated. While there is unlikely to be any alternative to make do and mend at present, I believe the events of the past few months will lead over time to some significant reappraisal of the proper role for commercial banking intermediation in international banking flows, to sounder judgements on levels of exposure and to more effective procedures by international banks for monitoring their global business. In considering these processes I believe it will be timely for bankers to pay a good deal more attention than has been evidenced recently to the liabilities side of the balance sheet which has all too often been starved of proper attention by excessive management concentration on marketing and asset-led growth. May it never be forgotten that at the heart of banking business is the banker's fiduciary responsibility to his depositor, whoever that depositor may be.

Domestically, as both new technology and the pressures toward a greater integration of the various constituent elements of the financial services industry gather pace, the supervisor is going to be faced with formidable challenges and difficult judgements in determining how far the authorities should lead and how far they should follow market forces. As with most dilemmas of this kind, the answer will probably be a mixture of the two. Can managements keep proper control over very complex multi-faceted financial services supermarkets? Can supervisors devise adequate supervisory arrangements? How far will the pressures of increased competition which come with increased sophistication of management and customers put too much strain, through top-heavy infrastructures or inadequate margins, on the capacity to sustain profitability – the dynamic of the business? In another important area, both domestically and internationally, I believe there is likely to be an increasing dialogue between external auditors and supervisors which still preserves the proper sphere of each but recognises their complementary roles.

In facing up to all these developments, the objectives of the Bank, at least as I see the exercise of its supervisory function, will be to sustain a high level of professional competence and intellectual commitment in its task; to encourage a probing and restless spirit of enquiry and a regular testing of received wisdom whether of its own making or deriving from the experience of bankers; at the same time, to continue to profit from the experience and the disciplines which the market can contribute. We shall strive to strike the right balance between the soft voice and the big stick, between persuasion and the rigours of the law, between flexibility and soundly-based supervisory rules, so that bankers can continue to run their own business with prudence, expertise and innovative skills for the benefit of their customers and the community at large.

6 Lessons for Bank Supervision from the Secondary-Banking Crises

MARGARET REID

Finance Editor of the Investor's Chronicle *and author of* The Secondary Bank Crisis 1973–75 (*Macmillan, 1982*)

The strengthened system of UK bank supervision developed in the few years before the Banking Act, 1979 and, legally underpinned by it, had its origins to an important degree in the banking crises of the mid 1970s. There is no doubt that the Act was the result of dual influences[1], the British secondary banking upheaval of 1973–5[2] and the European Economic Community directive on credit institutions, adopted in December 1977. However, the EEC's requirement that there should be formal arrangements for the licensing of deposit-taking institutions was itself not wholly unconnected with the extensive previous banking disturbances as manifested in various countries, notably by the collapse of the West German bank ID Herstatt in June 1974. The present extensive and legally-based supervision arrangements are thus doubly traceable to the storms which blew through the banking world (not excluding the US) during the 1970s. And those upheavals, for their part, can be seen as the outcome of the blows caused by the first oil shock to the economies of the West after a long era of prosperity which had latterly encouraged much haphazard and little controlled growth in new banking businesses.

In Britain, the banking crisis sparked off by the darkening financial climate in late 1973 was specially severe because of the scale on which newer, so-called secondary or fringe banks had previously grown up alongside the established primary banks. In many cases these proved to be without the strength, substance and general disposition of business which would have safeguarded them from trouble when conditions became harsh.

Frequently a drastic mismatching of borrowings and lendings meant that, when short-term deposits drained away in the crisis atmosphere, there were not corresponding liquid assets to provide the means of repayment, nor were other resources or stand-by borrowing rights available to bridge the gap. Still more serious than this 'liquidity' aspect of the crisis was the subsequent revelation of a 'solvency' problem in various cases. In other words, the assets in which resources had been placed – often property, loans to property companies and investment stakes in other companies – turned out, in the troubled climate, to be worth nothing like their book value. Frequently, particularly as the property and stock markets plunged in 1974, the assets of the secondary banks were shown to be worth less even than their borrowings, implying that capital had been more than wiped out; such a situation carried the threat of insolvency in the absence of rescue action.

While such difficulties were generally most acute in the secondary and fringe ventures engaged in general lending and 'investment banking', some independent finance houses were also susceptible to the problems. A strong habit of reliance on short-term deposits increased their vulnerability on the liquidity front when, from late 1973, market lenders began switching funds away to the safe haven of the big banks. In so far as these concerns had stuck to their last and kept their business to the financing of a wide range of consumer and industrial customers, asset losses were not too serious. But in a number of instances where companies had branched out into property-lending and other fashionable diversifications in the early 1970s money boom, assets proved far more at risk, losses were often substantial and solvency problems were not unknown.

To grapple with the crisis once it had broken out in December 1973, the big banks and the Bank of England responded swiftly with the Lifeboat rescue operation. This took the form of the Lifeboat group's lending funds to the cash-starved, crisis-ridden fringe banks – on the condition that remedial retrenchment action was taken as far and as soon as possible to improve their positions. What was in essence a cash recycling exercise was thus the first response of the major banks (to which much of the nervous funk money had retreated) to deal with a problem which first presented itself as a liquidity crisis in the fringe sector. Later, as the problem deepened with the onset of the 1974 property and stock market slumps, the Lifeboat group – led by the Bank of England and chaired by its then Deputy Governor, Sir Jasper Hollom – took a closer grip on the problem, monitoring and supervising in some detail the fortunes, or misfortunes, of the afflicted concerns for which solvency problems were frequently in the offing. In due course, some recovered in certain cases after capital reconstructions and/or the injection of new resources by large shareholders. Others faced the prospect of too much uncertainty to be capable of a viable independent long-term future and were taken over by stronger groups, the Bank of England often acting as 'marriage broker'. In a number of instances, help was eventually withdrawn and the business collapsed: in one or two cases, failure occurred from the outset, Lifeboat support having been refused.

In all, twenty-six banks and financial concerns were assisted through the Lifeboat and at least the same number received forms of support[3] from their own banks or major shareholders. In the well-known cases of Slater Walker and Edward Bates, extensive and costly support was provided by the Bank of

England itself, which also assumed responsibilities in some other cases. The approximate sum set aside by the Bank of England for its rescue role was some £100 million. The total lent through the joint Lifeboat operation exceeded £1,300 million at the peak. Most of this was repaid in due course, often by strong groups which took over hard-pressed rescued concerns. In addition, the big high street clearing banks, which financed the main Lifeboat operation – and shared its losses – on a 9:1 basis with the Bank of England (the Bank also carrying many heavy special costs itself), were involved separately in directly helping various struggling property and financial borrowers not in the Lifeboat. The total burden on these banks of the whole rescue strategy, though never publicly quantified, was certainly very substantial.

The lessons from this major upheaval – the biggest UK banking crisis this century, though it was kept short of catastrophe by the rapid remedial action – have not been neglected. Indeed, they appear to have been well learned in general and in particular.

The obvious broad inference was that it had been a mistake to have let such a significant sector of Britain's banking activity grow up without a system for its adequate monitoring and supervision. The fact that the Bank of England's supervisory system under the Banking Act, 1979 (first introduced on an informal basis from mid 1974) now spans the whole range of deposit-taking institutions shows that this message has been absorbed. The more detailed basis on which supervision is now administered – with regard to known standards on such matters as capital, liquidity and limitation of foreign currency positions – also illustrates that the experience of the secondary banking affair has not been neglected.

Faults of Original Supervisory Arrangements

Before the 1979 Act, there was no legal definition of a bank as such in Britain, in contrast with the position in most other developed countries. Nor was there any specific legal requirement governing the setting up of a deposit-taking business. However, certain Acts were relevant. Under Schedule 8 of the Companies Act 1948 (which consolidated and continued earlier legislation), the Board of Trade (or its successor) can exempt banking companies from the obligation to publish accounts in full. Those exempted are able to maintain hidden reserves and, in their annual profit and loss accounts, may disclose net figures after unspecified transfers to or from inner reserves. For many years, exemption under this provision (later provided under Section 127 of the Companies Act, 1967), was a sign that a company was fully recognized as a bank. A further indication of good standing – acceptance as an 'authorized' bank under the Exchange Control Act, 1947 – was available to a wider range of banks, including many British offshoots of foreign-based groups.

Those in these two (partly overlapping) categories were considered fully accepted as banks and the Bank of England maintained regular contact with them. However, other concerns taking deposits from the public were not similarly regulated and were able readily to go their own way. If smaller, they were also not caught by the official requests on loan restraint and other matters which were frequently issued by the Bank of England in the two decades up to the early 1970s. Consequently, they often showed above-average, unrestricted, growth in this period. These companies were, though, subject to the requirements of the Protection of Depositors Act, 1963, which restricted their freedom to advertise for deposits unless certain information, such as on the maturity of their deposit book, was included in their accounts. This Act had been passed after certain well-publicized collapses of deposit-taking concerns in the early 1960s.

A significant development in 1967 was the passing of a further Companies Act which, via its Section 123, introduced a new category of banking business. Section 123 was included following a celebrated case, UDT v. Kirkwood, which concerned the question of which companies were exempt from the Moneylenders Act, 1900 on the ground that they were 'bona fide carrying on the business of banking'. In line with a suggestion of the Appeal Court, the Act gave the Board of Trade responsibility for recognizing which institutions were, for the purpose in question, conducting a bona fide banking business. The upshot was the creation of a numerous new class of 'Section 123 companies', many initially quite small. By the autumn of 1973, on the eve of the secondary banking crisis, no fewer than 133 concerns held this status. While a good many were, or were offshoots of, substantial banks, others were of much less strength and of the latter many proved vulnerable to the upheaval when it occurred. Certain banks and finance houses enjoying a higher degree of pre-crisis status were also hard hit when the storms blew.

As the Bank of England has pointed out in evidence to the Wilson Committee,[4] one drawback of this situation was that it did not give the government departments concerned with the issue of certificates any powers of prudential supervision over the institutions concerned. In other words, once a company had received a Section 123 certificate, there was no adequate system for keeping track of its activities or requiring the regular submission of information necessary for a satisfactory supervisory watch over it. The Bank kept touch with the fully recognized and authorized banks but, as it subsequently stated, 'the Bank did not maintain any formal or regular contact with companies which did not fall within the banking sector proper, seeking to develop such relationships only when a company became a serious contender for full recognition as a bank'.[5]

The problems of monitoring events in the banking and 'sub-bank' sectors were the greater in view of the very rapid expansion in the size of the banking community in Britain during the fifteen years up to 1973.

Compared with a relatively small number of primary banks in the 1950s (mostly high street clearers, senior merchant banks, British overseas banks and London operations of foreign groups), there were, by late 1973, 323 full banks (many foreign) in business in Britain, along with a further 133 Section 123 banking companies. This was a massive family which had, by the eve of the crisis, far outgrown the traditional official monitoring system (through the Bank of England's Discount Office) which had been geared to a far sparser banking population. The huge growth in the little-overseen part of this numerous banking fraternity was the more dangerous since so many were, in the money boom of the early 1970s, heavily tapping the wholesale markets for short-term deposits which, in a harsher climate like the one which lay just ahead, they were to have difficulty in repaying.

Remedial Moves From Mid 1974

In the years between the full emergence of the crisis in 1974 and the passage of the Banking Act five years later, the basis of the present reformed and strengthened supervision system was laid. In the troubled atmosphere of the mid 1970s, the Bank of England met with no real resistance in its moves towards a tougher and all-embracing surveillance: conditions at the time were such that financial businesses readily saw the merits of an official watchdog and were not inclined to oppose it. The improved system operated from mid 1974 – in essence a forerunner of present arrangements – lost none of its effectiveness through lacking a legal foundation.

Just how great the change was after June 1974 can be gauged from the increase in the staffs involved. Compared with the previous fifteen-strong Discount Office, which had run the earlier informal surveillance, the successor Banking and Money Market Supervision section (BAMMS) had, by 1978, a staff of about seventy. It was presided over by a more senior official than had headed the Discount Office: the first holder of this new post was Mr George Blunden, who later became an executive director of the Bank.

The new system of supervision was immediately extended to cover more than sixty non-bank deposit-taking companies, including finance houses, and one hundred banks outside the clearers and other top groups. These were normally required to submit quarterly returns revealing the main components of their business and to attend interviews at the Bank to discuss and elaborate on the position reported. The process, useful as an early warning indicator of new trouble, was designed, for instance, to pinpoint situations of excessive mismatch, undue concentration of business with one client and undesirable illiquidity.

A good sketch of the procedure for all those outside the ranks of the clearing banks, British overseas banks and large foreign banks – for which separate arrangements were made – was set out by the Bank of England in evidence to Wilson in 1978. Here is an extract[6] which gives a clear impression of the new approach, which still broadly prevails.

> The intensification of the Bank's supervisory procedures has taken place in a number of areas. For the 160 or so institutions now involved, returns are submitted and reviews undertaken at least once a quarter. These returns break down the balance sheet into its components, display the maturity structure of liabilities and assets both in sterling and in other currencies, provide details of large deposits and loans (together with those made by or to others with whom the company or its directors have a connection) and of bad loan provisions, and provide a breakdown of the purposes and country destination of loans. In addition, information on profitability is received on a regular basis. All these returns are analysed . . . and certain key ratios are derived, covering capital adequacy, liquidity and the matching of maturities of liabilities and assets in sterling and eurocurrency . . . The interview . . . can and does range far wider . . . (aiming) to build up within the Bank an intimate picture of the institution, its business and its objectives, and to assess the capabilities of its management to control the business and fulfil its objectives.

In a clear allusion to the preceding crisis, the passage adds:

> This emphasis on qualitative assessment has been born of experience, as management problems and inadequacies have typically provided the first sign of difficulty.

Present System Reflects Crisis Lessons

If one looks at the present supervisory system, as formalized under the Banking Act, 1979, one can see that in its key elements it reflects the lessons of the secondary banking crisis. In the first place, the Bank of England's legal authorization is now required – in the form of recognition as a bank or through a licence – by any concern, large or small, whose business involves taking deposits from the public. This is the first basis of the control system operated for the protection of the public and of the financial community generally. Next, authorization is not a once-for-all official stamp of acceptance on the banking business in question. Supervision is a continuing process and, in the last resort, if all is not going well, authority to operate can be withdrawn. Finally, the principles on which the Bank administers its supervision, particularly the standards it applies on capital adequacy, liquidity and limits to currency exposure, are – like the system itself – the product of experience.

The fact that the system is now legally based and has teeth – the sanction of refusal or withdrawal of authorization – is an admission that the previous informal method of supervision lacked the firmness sometimes required. The extension of authorization across all deposit-taking shows a lesson learned from the previous unsupervised growth of many secondary and fringe businesses not caught even by the old voluntary contacts with the primary banks. Continuing supervision is a sequel to the frustrating inability of earlier watchdogs to keep track of companies once banking certificates had been issued; it also reflects the greater international conviction that more effective banking supervision is needed in the modern world.

Another sign of learning from experience is the stress placed on quality of management in current supervision. The depth of many fringe banks' problems in the crisis suggests that the foresight, judgement and prudence of their managements had often not been of the highest quality. Under the Banking Act, recognized banks must be managed with integrity, prudence and professional skill, while licensed institutions must be run by 'fit and proper' persons and with prudence. Obviously managers with criminal records are hardly likely to be acceptable. Under the Act the Bank can require the disclosure of previous criminal convictions (notwithstanding the normal law on spent convictions). And the handbook of guidance to applicants makes it clear that 'It is not expected that the Bank will be able to regard as "fit and proper" persons who are undischarged bankrupts or persons with criminal records, especially in connection with fraud.' (In the secondary banking crisis, prosecutions were not frequent but there were some cases of convictions on criminal charges.)

The division of authorized concerns into 'recognized banks' and 'licensed deposit-taking institutions' under the 1979 Act is perhaps an echo of the old 'status ladder' of acceptance for particular purposes which did prevail under the previous more informal system. However, it is probably implicit in the nature of bank supervision that the authorized community should take the shape of a double-tier system. Thus, inferences from the banking crisis are not so clearly perceptible in this aspect of the structure.

Lessons from the mid 1970s upheaval, can, however, be discerned in the three papers issued by the Bank to indicate the principles it applies in its supervision. The paper on 'The measurement of capital', issued in September 1980, for instance, deals with the need for a proper basis of capital to support a banking business and the importance of some of its being in the form of a readily available cushion to absorb losses, if need be. The acceptable constituents of capital (for example, subordinated loan capital, as well as share capital and reserves) are indicated, and weights allotted to different assets according to their possible fluctuation in value. Precise objectives for ratios of capital to total assets are not spelt out, though, as the Bank prefers to maintain some flexibility in its judgements. The importance of proper standards here is the better appreciated when it is remembered that in the secondary banking crisis various groups incurred losses which nearly or totally absorbed all or more than all their capital. In the most serious cases, this threatened insolvency, in the absence of rescues.

Similarly the Bank's paper on 'The measurement of liquidity' (July 1982) outlines principles designed to avoid banks running into the situation of cash famine which faced many fringe concerns from December 1973. The third paper – 'Foreign currency exposure' (April 1981) – seeks to control the general banking risk that excessive currency positions can lead to loss if exchange values swing adversely.

Limited protection fund

One novel aspect of the present supervisory system which is a sequel to, and partial consequence of, the secondary bank crisis, is the £5–6 million[7] Deposit Protection Fund set up under the Banking Act in February 1982. Providing cover for 75 per cent of deposits up to £10,000 with a failed banking company, it is there to safeguard personal and other smaller depositors rather than the larger lenders which place bigger deposits with banks through the wholesale markets. The banking system would have been unwilling to put up the vastly greater sums that would have been needed for a full-scale permanent Lifeboat fund. In any case, it would have disapproved of such a permanent measure, regarding it as an undue encouragement to rash management by over-bold concerns at the expense of more prudent concerns. If the collapse of an ill-managed bank could not hurt any of its depositors because fellow members of the banking community would compensate them, restraint on the wilder spirits would inevitably be weakened.

With toughened supervision, the scope for failures has doubtless lessened anyway. Even so, were any major disaster none the less to happen in the future, the need for special rescue measures might still arise afresh.

International aspects

One important sequel to the events of the 1970s – a decade which saw major national banks greatly expanding their overseas networks and, from 1974, lending vastly more world wide – is the new international dimension of supervision.[8] Following the shock of the Herstatt bank collapse, the leading central banks increasingly co-ordinated their anti-crisis defences, and established a system of co-operative monitoring, formalized through the Standing Committee of Banking Supervisory Authorities, chaired by Mr Blunden, and later Mr Peter Cooke, both of the Bank of England. One important point of agreement is that, where supervision of a bank operating in various countries is concerned, responsibility is split between the supervisors in the headquarters and host countries but that the chief say lies with the former. This is known as the parental principle, while the arrangement is called the Concordat. The differing nature of supervision and of accounting standards in various countries makes the Concordat still a less-than-perfect means of regulation, but efforts towards its improvement continue. The international banking supervisors' co-operation developed over the past nine years proved valuable when the problems of Mexico and other troubled Third World debtors to the banks broke out in 1982.

Conclusion

The first years of the new UK supervisory system have been encouraging, in that new failures have been few and of relatively little significance. Fortunately, any fear which may have existed that the authorities would be insufficiently tough in administering the law have proved unfounded – and supervisors' hands have been strengthened by the new international banking tremors. At least one or two applications for authorization have been refused and in some other cases licences have have been provided in response to requests for the higher recognized status, the latter having, on occasion, been conceded later. In two instances action has been taken by the Bank to withdraw licences and wind-up deposit-takers.

One problem posed for central banks by the present international financial turmoil is the need to reconcile the quest for careful management of banks with the encouragement of new lending, perhaps beyond managers' wishes, to stave off disaster among hard-pressed borrower nations. In fact, central bankers have lately been performing a difficult balancing act, enjoining reasonable prudence on the banks in their flocks, while at the same time urging new bail-out loans to troubled Third World states. This is how the Bank of England's chief regulator, Mr Cooke, recently struck this delicate balance:[9]

> There has been some comment recently that the current pressures on the banks will inevitably mean an erosion of prudential standards. I do not accept this view. While taking due account of the need for time for adjustment (by hard-pressed debtor countries), I cannot see that any significant erosion of prudential standards will necessarily have to, or will in fact, occur over the next few years. The world's banking system is going to be with us for a lot longer than the particular concerns of the moment, whether in Eastern Europe, Latin America, or closer at home in the domestic portfolios of major banks in a number of industrialized countries . . . It must retain the confidence of those who use it and it must retain confidence in itself. This, however, is not to say that absolute adherence to some fixed supervisory standards at all times is an essential prerequisite for dealing with the present situation. How can soundness be reconciled with keeping the system going? Here is a supervisor talking about the need for prudence, including careful

> attention to new lending propositions and prudent provisioning policies, while elsewhere among the authorities calls are being made to commercial bankers to stay in international business and, indeed, in some cases increase their commitments in areas where they have doubts about the soundness – at least in the short term – of doing so. I have to say I do not find this apparent contradiction very troublesome intellectually, and certainly not practically . . . [It] does not appear to me to fly in the face of reason to suggest that new lending, often with a tinge of doubt attaching to it, may on occasions be the best way of protecting the quality of the existing lending and ensuring its ultimate soundness . . . [The] time factor will be important as . . . IMF programmes [of adjustment for improvement of the debtor economies] may take some time to bring results . . . Burdens are best sustained when they are shared. But even the strongest can eventually become over-burdened and it will be important in shaping the system for the future that commercial banks are not asked to do too much and that governments and international agencies should take their proper share of the load.

Notes

1 In introducing the second reading of the Banking Bill, Mr Denzil Davies, MP, Minister of State, Treasury, said:

> Unlike most other advanced countries, we have never had a comprehensive system of authorisation for banks . . . The Bank [of England] has traditionally supervised the primary banking system on an informal non-statutory basis . . . But, especially in the late 1960s, many institutions grew up outside the primary banking system. The secondary banking crisis of 1973/4 led to a general recognition that it was necessary to take a comprehensive look at the regulations of institutions which took deposits from the public. At the same time, the EEC was devising plans for the first stages of harmonization of European banking systems. (House of Commons *Hansard*, 21 Nov. 1978, col. 1,500.)

2 Considered fully in the present writer's *The Secondary Banking Crisis, 1973–75* (Macmillan, 1982).

3 *Ibid*, pp. 89–90, quoting a speech by Mr George Blunden, Director, Bank of England.

4 'Regulation in the City and the Bank of England's role', June 1978. Part of written evidence by the Bank of England to the Committee to Review the Functioning of Financial Institutions. (See also *Bank of England Quarterly Bulletin*, June 1978, pp. 230–9.)

5 *Ibid*, section on 'Supervision of Banks and Other Deposit-Taking Institutions', paragraph 5.

6 As in note 4, paragraphs 8 and 9. A useful description of the new approach was also given in a survey by Mr George Blunden, reproduced in the *Bank of England Quarterly Bulletin*, Sept. 1975, pp. 190–93.

7 Fed by certain cash contributions and larger back-up guarantees from recognized banks and licensed deposit-taking institutions.

8 See *The Secondary Banking Crisis, 1973–75* (as in note 2 above), pp. 116–19; also *Bank of England Quarterly Bulletin*, Sept. 1977, pp. 325–9.

9 Speech on 9 December 1982 to a *Financial Times* conference.

7 Pressure Group Development in the EC: the Role of the British Bankers' Association*

* Reprinted with permission from the *Journal of Common Market Studies*, March 1982, pp. 269–85

JANE A. SARGENT

London School of Economics and Political Science

This present article is part of a Ph.D. research project supported by the Social Science Research Council, for the London School of Economics. It is a revised edition of a paper presented at the Annual Conference of the Political Studies Association, 6–8 April 1981. The author would like to thank Ian Morison and Jane Welch formerly of the Inter-Bank Research Organisation, Paul Taylor and Dr Gordon Smith of the London School of Economics and two BBA officials who prefer to remain anonymous, for their helpful comments on earlier drafts.

On accession to the European Community (EC) the British banking community was faced with a draft proposal[1] which threatened to destroy the flexible system of banking which operated in the UK. At the time, associations representing bankers in the original Six were actively engaged in presenting to the Commission not only their individual views, but also their collective views, through the European Banking Federation (BFEC) in so far as this was possible.

As a central bank the Bank of England, the traditional spokesman for the UK banking community, could not join the BFEC. UK views on Community matters could, of course, have been submitted by individual banks or groups of banks to UK authorities involved in the work of the Council of Ministers but this would have secured access for the banking community only at a very late stage in the Community legislative process. A united approach could not, thereby, have been made directly to the Commission (the most important Community body at the initiation and formulation stages), as neither Commissioners nor Commission officials have national mandates and thus cannot be contacted directly through national level channels. As the BFEC is comprised of only one national association per Member State it became clear that a single organisation was needed to put forward the views of bankers in the UK on Community matters. Yet, the banking community had no peak association.[2] An organisation was needed, however, and the British Bankers' Association (BBA) was chosen.

This paper examines how the BBA had developed since 1972, particularly during the passage of the draft proposal and the ensuing legislation: the 1977 'EC Banking Directive'[3] and the UK Banking Act, 1979. Some implications of these developments for the role of national pressure groups in the European Community are then discussed in a concluding section.

To begin the present task we must agree upon what we mean by the term 'pressure group'. Unfortunately, there is no clear and consistent usage of the term, although a review of various definitions adopted in studies of British 'pressure group' behaviour[4] indicates that four characteristics are integral to any understanding of the term. These are as follows:

1 A membership open to those who share a particular interest.
2 A structured organisation designed to promote and defend this common interest.
3 Access to decision-making bodies.
4 Exertion of continuous effort to try to impress upon decision-making bodies the merits of this common interest.

Although this is a list of only the minimum defining characteristics of a pressure group it applies equally to different types of pressure groups, be they classified in terms of the type of access sought and/or obtained, types of interest represented or the internal characteristics of pressure groups. Although these criteria allow for a pressure group to exist without being effective they do not entail the notion of an inactive pressure group. They allow, therefore, for a distinction to be made between a pressure group and a 'latent' or 'potential' pressure group. Further, because the first three characteristics are mutually exclusive, as are the fourth and the first two, a 'latent' or 'potential' pressure group cannot be expected to mature automatically or inevitably. Therefore, if the BBA proves to be a 'latent' or 'potential' pressure group a clearer definition of its present form will be required.

The BBA was chosen to represent the UK banking community on Community matters largely because it had maintained regular, albeit informal, contact with the BFEC since 1961, and in 1964 a contact committee had been established to create a formal link between the two organisations.

The BBA was established in 1920 following the merger of the Central Association of Bankers and the Association of English Country Banks. By 1972, however, the BBA still shared its staff and offices with the Committee of London Clearing Bankers and only represented approximately one-third of some 300 banks then operating in the UK. The Association's role was also limited, it worked on an *ad hoc* basis and was discouraged from representing any but the collective views of its members. As consensus amongst bankers was rarely sought, or possible, the Association was of little value as a representative association between 1920 and 1972, indeed, a former president of the Association has referred to the BBA as 'a moribund institution' for many years.[5]

To qualify for membership of the European Banking Federation the BBA was required to widen its membership. In 1972 the interests of bankers were channelled through various associations of groups of banks and a high level of divergence between the interests of the different associations had always acted as a deterrent against creating a single representative association. Absence of a legally accepted definition of a bank had created further difficulties, especially concerning the criteria for establishing eligibility for membership of such an association. In 1971, however, the Bank of England introduced Competition and Credit Control which involved a requirement for banks to maintain a certain reserve assets ratio, which in turn necessitated publication of a list of commercial banks, recognized as such, by the Bank of England. During the following year, therefore, eligibility for membership of the BBA was established on the basis of this list. Publication of the draft proposal in question, meanwhile, convinced bankers in the UK that they should act collectively to oppose the proposal, hence, towards the end of 1972 the BBA's membership increased threefold to about 300 banks.

The 1977 'EC Banking Directive'

By May 1973 such consultations as had taken place on the draft proposal established that the four principal issues of contention for Britain were: 1. the notion of a system of prior authorisation (a licensing system), 2. the elaboration of ratio provisions, 3. supervision and the various credit-reporting requirements, and 4. the regulation on branching and participations. The intractable issue for bankers in Britain was licensing as no licensing system operated in the UK at the time, a 'ladder of recognitions'[6] operated instead. The categories of recognition overlapped, however, and had been criticised by the Crowther Committee,[7] hence, bankers in the UK generally accepted that the ladder needed some reform. Although some legislation, whether from the Commission or from the UK Government would, therefore, have been welcome, the banking community had not at that time accepted the need to introduce a licensing system into Britain, and was therefore opposed to the provisions which threatened to render the banking activities of people or companies not on the proposed approved lists of banks, an offence. Consequently, members of the UK banking community tried to rally support on the Continent for a drastic simplification of the proposal. They argued that the basic objective – the equalisation of conditions of competition amongst banks by official regulation – could be achieved by a much simpler directive which should be based on a philosophy of flexibility rather than control.

Britain's bankers claimed that the draft proposal threatened the status of London as the world's leading financial centre, a status which they were convinced had been acquired because of the very flexibility of the UK banking system:

> The supremacy of London as an international banking centre is founded on a freedom from vexatious banking legislation equalled in few countries in the world . . . It would be a tragedy if this position were radically altered simply to satisfy bureaucratic tidiness.[8]

The draft was ultimately withdrawn by the Commission because of dissatisfaction expressed not only by Britain but also by other Member States.

Members of the British banking community, however, had begun to realize that Community legislation could provide a means to overcome the limitations of the 'ladder of recognition', limitations which were becoming increasingly apparent as the secondary banking crisis, which had begun in November 1973, continued to escalate.[9] Thus, the BBA suggested to members of the European Banking Federation that a new directive should be drafted which embodied the principles on which the British banking system was based. The BBA's proposal, therefore, was that 'harmonisation should be limited to as few issues as possible and be based on the principles of maximum flexibility and self-regulation.[10] This proposal was accepted *in toto* by the other members of the BFEC who thereby decided to substitute approximation of the banking laws of the Member States for the Commission's objective of unification.

Having persuaded the Commission to withdraw its initial proposal, the European Banking Federation was keen for the Commission to adopt the new one. In this the BFEC was successful, not least because a British official, Robin Hutton, with experience as a London Merchant banker, was appointed director of the then recently established Directorate-Generale (XV) for Banking, Insurance and Financial Institutions.[11] Hutton, not surprisingly, was sympathetic to the BBA's proposal and it came as no shock, to the British banking community at least, that within weeks of taking office Hutton announced that the Commission's whole approach would probably be changed. Speaking at the first of the Ernest Sykes Memorial Lectures in 1973, organized by the Institute of Bankers, Hutton declared himself in favour of harmonization on a number of crucial points only and called for a more urgent approach to the problem by British institutions in view of the rigid approach of a number of people in Brussels.[12]

The Commission later argued that a fresh approach, amounting to a U-turn, had been required by the new situation created specifically by

Britain's accession to the EC which no longer made it possible to attempt to unify all the banking laws of the different Member States in one all-embracing set of proposals such as the 1972 proposal. In other words, the Commission agreed to replace its idealistic approach with the pragmatic, British one.

The new proposal was for an 'umbrella' directive to come first which would seek common acceptance of certain basic principles concerning issues on which the Commission had initially intended to legislate. The issues included conditions under which banking licences could be issued; minimum levels of liquidity risk and solvency; rules of competition; definitions of banking operations and arrangements with third countries; preparation of accounts and methods of 'winding up' a banking enterprise. The Commission also suggested that this directive should be followed by other, more specific measures which would deal with these issues separately, as developments and circumstances dictated.

The main features of the draft directive, published in December 1974,[13] were that it should be applied to all institutions that take deposits and make advances but that it should be limited initially to a hard core of institutions which would be formed on the basis of lists drawn up by the national authorities in each member state. Attached to the draft directive were provisions for the creation of a contract committee which was designed to oversee implementation of the directive. The Commission submitted amendments to the proposal in July 1975 following receipt of comments from the European Parliament and the Economic and Social Committee. These amendments were accompanied by a request for a quick decision on the provisions for establishing a contact committee because the Commission hoped that such a committee might help to contain the risk of further banking crises in the Community.

Britain's attitude towards the draft directive had changed by this time. In August 1974 *The Banker* recorded that the reaction of Britain's bankers to the draft which was modelled on their proposal was about: 'whether there is any point in subscribing to an ineffective statement of intent – other than just to satisfy some Commissioner's desire to show he has got something "on the books" – if there is no political likelihood of agreeing to something substantial.'[14] This dissatisfaction arose partly from two developments in Community law during 1974 which rendered redundant many of the provisions of the 1973 Directive on the abolition of restrictions on freedom of establishment and freedom to provide services in respect of self-employed activities of banks and other financial services.[15] Dissatisfaction was also due, however, to a growing concern that the draft directive would not be capable of protecting the interests of legitimate banks against the activities of 'cowboy' banks, and would thus not be capable of preventing a repetition of the 1973/74 secondary banking crisis. Nevertheless, throughout the 1975/76 Parliamentary session members of the BBA, together with other representatives of the banking community, pressed UK government officials directly and through the EC scrutiny committees of the two Houses of Parliament to make haste in reaching a decision on the draft directive in the Council of Ministers. At the same time, representations were made to MEPs to raise questions on the progress of the draft in the European Parliament and contact was made with Commission officials, directly by BBA representatives and through BFEC, in order to express the banking community's sense of urgency on this issue.

The Directive was finally adopted on 12 December 1977. It embodied a marked shift from the gradualist approach initially proposed by the Commission. The principal credit for turning the Commission's head must certainly go to the British although quite how much influence the BBA had on events is difficult to establish beyond stating that together with Robin Hutton, the Bank of England, the Treasury and the Minister for Trade and Industry, the clearing bankers and the Inter-Bank Research Organisation it played a leading role. R.K.C. Giddings, then Secretary General of the Association, is more specific. He has stated that:

> Long and detailed study by a few dedicated representatives from member banks of the newly-reconstituted British Bankers' Association and subsequent discussion in the EEC Banking Federation led to a change of heart over the basic concept of this document, first by many bankers in the original six member states and then more importantly, in the Commission itself.[16]

Clearly the Association's role should not be underestimated, particularly as by 1974 the BBA led the UK banking lobby in the EC and was becoming an important component in the Community banking lobby.

Although the Association's attitude towards the Commission's two proposals corresponded to that of the UK Government, pressure from the latter alone would probably not have been sufficient to persuade the Commission to withdraw its initial proposal, even though the Director of D-G XV was also opposed to it, and would certainly not have justified adoption of a totally different set of proposals in 1974. The BBA had a special role to play on both occasions. With respect to withdrawal of the 1972 proposal the BBA's opinion had a special significance for the Commission both because it expressed the views of bankers in the UK and because the Association reiterated the views of the UK Government and the Bank of England (the supervisory authority), and thereby consolidated British opposition to the proposal.[17] Concerning the 1974 proposal the BBA was the body which provided a new set of proposals and secured their acceptance by representatives of bankers in the other Member States before they were submitted to the Commission by the leading European banking organisation: the BFEC. Several factors explain why the Association was able to play a leading rather than a supporting role on behalf of bankers in the UK and in the EC generally, throughout the passage of the 1977 Directive.

First, the Bank of England did not speak on behalf of banks in the UK on this occasion partly because it was not able to join BFEC and partly because it was concerned to defend its role as a supervisory authority against certain provisions of the Commission's proposals. Secondly, banks in the UK united their efforts against the common enemy: the Commission's 1972 proposal, and, to the satisfaction of the UK Government and the Bank of England, agreed to invest in the BBA authority to speak on their behalf. Thirdly, by mid 1974 bankers in other Member States had begun to accept the need for some legislation to contain the risk of further banking crises in the Community and they felt that the BBA's proposals filled this need. At the same time these bankers had come to share the British doubts about the Commission's philosophy towards Community banking law and wished to prevent legislation which might allow for a Lloyds Bank, for instance, to be set up in every high street in the Community. Other supplementary factors were the status of London as an international finance centre and absence of any other positive alternatives to the 1972 proposal. Of major significance, however, was the fact that the BBA's proposals, whether by chance or design, provided an initiative when one was needed but lacking. Further, the Association's representatives exercised great political skill in securing acceptance of their proposals first by members of BFEC and then allowing the BFEC to submit this proposal to the Commission.

Whatever the degree of influence exerted by the BBA on the details of the final document the process of lobbying Community institutions certainly affected the Association, in particular, its membership, its organisation and its functions. We have seen that the Association's membership was widened to about 300 banks in order for it to join the BFEC and thereby to influence the attitudes of the Commission and bankers in other Member States towards Community banking law. Reconstitution of the BBA in 1973 also provided it with a committee-based decision-making machinery which proved capable of promoting consensus amongst the BBA's membership on Community matters. In addition, an amendment to the BBA's constitution in 1973 which made provisions for a president to be appointed by the General Council and a decision taken in 1974 to separate the BBA's Secretariat and administrative services from those of the Committee of London Clearing Bankers rendered the Association a more identifiable spokesman for the banking community than it had previously been. With respect to the Association's access to decision-making bodies throughout the passage of the Directive the BBA concentrated on building up contacts with members and officials of Community institutions and committees; consequently, by 1977 the Association had established an extensive network of contacts at the Community level and in the UK.

The BBA's attention was mainly directed towards the Commission during the passage of the Directive, largely because the Association was anxious to dissuade the Commission from publishing the 1972 proposal and because, later, the BBA wanted the Commission to initiate a particular set of alternative proposals. The European Banking Federation was evidently the most important channel of contact with the Commission for the BBA at these stages as the Commission was more likely to act on the collective views of bankers in the Community than on the proposals of a single national association. Concerning withdrawal of the 1972 proposal, however, the BBA utilised its direct links with the Director of D-G XV and with UK Commissioner Tugendhat who had special responsibility for financial institutions. Regular, direct contact was also established and maintained with officials at all levels in Ds-G XV and III (Internal and Market Affairs). During 1975 close liaison was maintained with British members of the European Parliament by members of the BBA's working party on harmonisation of banking law. Several bankers, including the President of the BBA, even sat in the gallery as the Parliament debated the draft directive 'and were available to the British members . . . to answer their questions and brief them as to what it might be appropriate for them to say'.[18] The Association also contacted British representatives of the Economic and Social Committee, and close contacts were maintained with UK members of the Council of Ministers and UK members of the relevant Council working party after the Commission published its proposed amendments to the 1974 draft directive. Contact with members of the Council and its working party were maintained through UK channels, in particular via the Bank of England, the Treasury and the Department for Trade and Industry; consequently, the BBA was able to strengthen and extend its network of UK contacts during the passage of the Directive. Contacts with other associations of groups of banks were also cultivated during this period, for instance, representatives of the British Overseas and Commonwealth Banks' Association and the American Banks Association of London attended a meeting of the BBA's working party to discuss the draft proposal in 1974.[19] And through the BFEC, BBA representatives liaised with UK members of other Community-level banking organisations, for instance the Association of Co-operative Saving and Credit Institutions of the EEC and the Savings Banks Group of the EEC.[20]

The future of the Association's role as spokesman for the UK banking community on Community matters seemed, then, to be assured partly because its members, the UK Government and the Bank of England all accepted that the Association should continue to perform this function, and partly because the 1977 Directive was intended to be but the first in a long series of directives designed to harmonise the banking systems of the Member States. By looking at the Association's experience during the passage of the subsequent UK legislation, the Banking Act, 1979, we shall see whether or not the development of its role has been restricted to the Community level and Community matters, or whether its domestic activities have also been developed even though a conscious decision was never taken concerning the Association's domestic role when the BBA was rejuvenated.[21]

The UK Banking Act, 1979

Existence of a draft directive on aspects of banking activities was only one reason behind the publication of a White Paper on 'The Licensing and Supervision of Deposit-Taking Institutions' in August 1976.[22] Article 3(1) is the key requirement of the Directive which made UK legislation essential: 'Member states shall require credit institutions subject to this Directive to obtain authorisation before commencing their activities . . .'[23] The White Paper, however, was not intended to pre-empt the pending Community-level agreement, largely because the draft directive had been modelled on the BBA's proposals. In fact, members of the UK banking community had begun to doubt the ability of the proposed directive to regulate the activities of banks in accordance with the requirements that had become evident during the secondary banking crisis. Hence, the White Paper proposals went much further than the Directive's provisions.

The BBA was not involved in consultations with the Government prior to publication of the White Paper as it was confident that its members would convey to the Government, through the Bank of England and their respective associations their views about the type of legislation that was needed in view of the pending Community policy and experience of the secondary banking crisis. Yet, although the BBA agreed with many of the provisions of the White Paper it disagreed with the proposal to exempt building societies, trustee savings banks and the National Girobank, and denied the need for the proposed deposit protection scheme. Consequently, the Association became involved at every stage during the passage of the subsequent Act.

Following publication of the White Paper a consultation paper on details of the proposed deposit protection scheme was circulated amongst the banking community. The BBA endeavoured to reach a consensus of opinion among its members concerning the details of the scheme but each of the different types of banks had their own views on the proposals. As contention between the members increased, in particular over an alternative to the Government's proposed method of allocating contributions to the deposit protection fund embodied in the scheme, the BBA had a hard task to aggregate these diverse interests. As no consensus emerged it was left to the Government to decide, on the basis of further consultation with bankers, how to implement the White Paper proposals. Thus, there ensued a period of intense discussions on the proposals between the banking community and Bank of England and Treasury officials before the Government published the 'Banking Bill' in July 1978.[24] Commenting on this consultation stage, a leading banker observed that: '. . . comments were prepared in writing and several meetings took place, in which the bankers were represented separately by the Committee of London Clearing Bankers (CLCB) and the British Bankers' Association (BBA)'.[25] As the BBA was never expected to speak for the banking community when a collective view on a particular issue could not be reached[26] many associations, other than the CLCB, put their views individually to the authorities, on the deposit protection scheme in particular. There thus arose a situation in which the banks agreed with the proposals put forward in Part One (Control of deposit-taking) and Part Three (Advertisements and banking names) of the Bill but were in conflict with the authorities and divided amongst themselves concerning Part Two (the deposit protection scheme). On this occasion, therefore, the Association's members did not invest in the BBA the authority to act as their main spokesman and the BBA, consequently, 'contented itself with putting forward various alternative formulae for allocation (of which that chosen was effectively one) and noting the interests of the various types of banks in relation to each'.[27]

The BBA claims to have been closely involved in discussions with the authorities throughout the passage of the Act prior to its adoption on 4 April 1979. This involvement enabled the Association 'to achieve a number of useful modifications to the proposed legislation'[28] with the end result being reasonably satisfactory to the Association's members, claimed the BBA's President in 1979. He went on to make the following comment:

> H.M. Treasury and the Bank of England offered full consultation at all stages and the Act itself, as finally adopted, took account of many of the Association's representations. Although the banks' attempts to have the deposit protection scheme dropped and to bring the National Girobank within the terms of the Act were unsuccessful, the Treasury did concede that all contributions paid into the scheme would be regarded as deductible for tax purposes. In the closing stages of the debate, a major step forward was achieved by the inclusion of amendments to certain parts of the Consumer Credit Act, 1974 relating in particular to the Director-General's power to issue directions regarding overdrafts.[29]

It should be noted, however, that those issues concerning which the BBA claims to have had some success were not the most contentious issues associated with the Act and, more important, this success was not achieved alone. The CLCB played an equally, if not more important part, especially in achieving inclusion of amendments to the Consumer Credit Act. These amendments[30] were tabled through the House of Lords and were accepted purely because of the political situation at the time, viz. the Government was about to fall and therefore most of the proposed amendments were accepted without debate as this was the only way of ensuring that the whole

Bill was not lost. Yet, the supporting role of the BBA should not be underestimated. Had the Clearing Banks not been able to claim that they had the rest of the banking community behind them, represented by the BBA, their influence on the details of the final Act may well have been much less than it actually was.

Although the Association was rejuvenated in order to represent the interests of the UK banking Community on Community matters to members and officials of Community institutions, members of the BBA are not inhibited from making their own representations concerning EC legislative proposals or subsequent UK legislation. However, in order not to render representation of British banking interest fragmented, uncoordinated and thus weak, the associations of groups of banks expressed their views on the Commission's proposals through the BBA.[31] Conversely, various associations of groups of banks presented their views on the proposed UK legislation through UK channels individually. This different reliance on the BBA was due to a number of factors. First, the contentious provisions of the proposed Banking Act did not relate to provisions in the pending Community directive; they thus comprised, in effect, non-Community derived legislative provisions, and as such did not fall automatically within the scope of the BBA's activities. In addition, as members of the UK banking community were unable to agree on their response to details of the proposed deposit protection scheme, recourse to the BBA as their principle spokesman was not considered save by the small banks, which agreed to defend their views on contributions to the proposed deposit protection fund against those of the big banks, through the BBA.[32] Finally, whereas the BBA represents members of numerous associations of groups of banks at Community level, these banks can be represented in the UK by their respective associations and through them by the Bank of England, the traditional UK spokesman for the banking community. In other words spokesmen, other than the BBA, exist in the UK through which members of the banking community can represent their views, but there are no other spokesmen for the UK banking community as a whole, or the majority of UK associations of groups of recognised banks at Community level, as these associations cannot be represented by any Community-level banking organisation other than the BFEC, which restricts its membership to one association per member state.

Although the BBA has always been concerned with domestic legislation, it was rejuvenated in 1973 specifically to act as the banks' spokesman on Community matters. It would seem, however, that not only has the Association extended its role in the UK to cover Community legislation and Community-derived legislation, it has also extended its role to include non-Community-derived legislative proposals. Progress in this direction is slow, however, commented the BBA's Secretary-General in 1976:

> Whilst the advantages of presenting a collective view of EEC matters

> has been readily accepted, the realisation of similar advantages when dealing with domestic issues, on which all banks operating within the UK are likely to take a similar view, is proceeding rather more slowly.[33]

Progress has, nevertheless, been made. The Bank of England has adopted an increasingly favourable attitude towards the BBA and over the past five or six years has encouraged various associations of groups of banks to present their views on particular issues collectively through the BBA rather than individually.[34] In fact, the Association has gained competence to speak on behalf of its members in the UK, in the EC and even in third countries, for instance the United States, on particular subjects such as banking law, foreign exchange and money markets, company law and capital markets, accounting matters, fiscal matters and consumer protection. This development is reflected in the Association's decision in 1978 to cease distinguishing in its annual reports between 'activities in the domestic field' and 'EEC matters'.

It would seem, then, that Britain's accession to the EC has had a direct effect on the organisation and representation of UK banking interests. Accession first prompted development of a single representative association which had a membership open to all recognised commercial banks in the UK, and which had an independent secretariat and independent administrative and financial resources. This association quickly gained access to Community decision-making bodies, partly by building on its existing UK contacts and partly by establishing new contacts at Community level. Publication of numerous proposals for further Community legislation in the banking field[35] has since enabled this association to continue to present the views of the UK banking community to Community bodies and, thereby, to maintain and strengthen its network of contacts. Clearly, then, accession prompted development of an association which with respect to Community matters has acquired the four minimum characteristics of a pressure group outlined at the beginning of this paper. As a by-product of this development the same association has acquired the potential to become a pressure group with respect to non-Community-derived legislative proposals, and has begun to extend its scope of activities in this direction, particularly with respect to issues concerning which bankers think that there are advantages to be gained from coordinating their views through this association.[36]

Consequently, the BBA can no longer be classified as a moribund institution. The Association is, however, an obscure organisation and a flexible one which has some of the features of both a pressure group and a research organisation reflected in its primary objects: '. . . to provide facilities for the discussion of matters of interest to the British Banks and to make representations on their behalf.[37] If a single term were needed to describe the BBA in its present state perhaps the best choice might be a contact committee, by virtue of its intermediary role and its style of organisation (responsibility for the day-to-day business of the Association is invested in the Executive Committee, which is composed of practising bankers, rather than in the Secretariat). Although the BBA does not have the status of a peak association, since Britain joined the EC the Association has become an organisation in which the banking community could, if it wished, consolidate its representation on a more permanent and wide-ranging basis than hitherto.

Some implications for the role of national pressure groups in the EC

The BBA established its present network of contacts with members and officials of Community institutions through three channels: through membership of the European Banking Federation, through direct Community-level contacts and through UK contacts. Although each channel has particular significance for the BBA in particular contexts – depending upon the stage a proposal has reached in the Community legislative process, the nature of a proposal, and the attitudes of bankers and governments in other Member States towards a proposal – in general the Association places greater emphasis on the first two channels than on the third. This is because these two can provide access to the Commission which is an important contact for the Association because it is responsible for initiating and formulating Community policy, i.e. for setting the parameters for discussions, and for amending policy proposals.

During the passage of the 1977 'EC Banking Directive' the BBA's contacts with the Commission were conducted mainly through the BFEC. Yet, the BBA also had discussions with members and officials of the Commission, not only about the technical details of the proposals but also about what the Association was likely to accept in the way of community banking law and how much it was willing to compromise. In other words, the Commission discussed the political position of a national association towards the proposals with the Association itself, even though the Commission is said to prefer to discuss these issues with the European-level associations to which national pressure groups belong.[38] In the past, this preference has enabled the Commission to rely on European-level associations to aggregate the interests of their national components. Our findings may apply to an isolated case when the representations of a European-level association were supplemented by the direct representations of one of its members. Yet, the fact that the BBA has built up a network of direct contacts with various Community bodies, which enable it to express its views at every stage in the Community legislative process, suggests that this was not an isolated case. A review of the Association's annual reports shows that on several occasions each year since 1975 the BBA has made direct contact with Commission officials, members of the European Parliament and the Economic and Social Committee concerning Commission proposals about which, in general, it has also made representations through the BFEC. This may well indicate a failure on the part of the BFEC to aggregate its members' views, yet the following comment has been made by the Economic and Social Committee:

> The BFEC . . . demonstrates organisation cohesion. Although there were cases where the BFEC was unable to reach a common stand and had to submit both a majority view and a minority view, it appears . . . that 'normally' solutions can be found on which all nine member affiliates of the BFEC agree . . .[39]

If the views presented by the BFEC and the BBA coincide, why should the latter, or any other national component, duplicate the efforts of its European-level association? Various explanations suggest themselves: a national group does not have confidence in its European-level association's ability to represent its members' views; a national group finds the compromise solutions put forward by its European-level association too weak; a national component's views do not coincide with those of its European-level association; and/or there is a greater openness on the part of some Community institutions towards national pressure groups than hitherto.

Only detailed study of the attitudes of national pressure groups towards their European-level associations will establish the significance of the first two explanations. With respect to the BBA's attitude towards the BFEC, prior to 1979 the former felt that the Federation had insufficient staff and proposed the appointment of an adviser 'to consolidate and expand links between the Federation and the various Community organisations in Brussels'.[40] Yet there is no evidence from interviews with leading members of the BBA or from its annual reports of dissatisfaction with the 'strength' of the BFEC's opinions. The third explanation would seem to have some significance as many European-level associations, including the BFEC, submit both majority views and minority views when their members cannot reach agreement on Commission proposals, although the possibility of the BFEC's opinions differing from those of the BBA was possibly reduced in 1979 as the BFEC's newly appointed Adviser was a British banker put forward by the BBA. Finally, explanation four would seem to have some significance, for the BBA at least, as both the European Parliament and the Commission have been more accessible to its representatives in recent years. On the part of the EP this is probably due to the fact that MEPs have become concerned, since they were directly elected in 1979, to be seen to represent actively the interests of their (national) constituents. Hence, the BBA has been able to increase the number of UK MEPs with which it has contact and to extend its contacts to include the secretariat and research organisation of the European Democratic Group, and the technical and personal assistants of particular UK MEPs.[41] The Commission has become more open to the BBA both before proposals are published and afterwards, which indicates that the Association has information which the Commission requires but which the

BFEC is unable to provide, and that the Commission wishes to guarantee for itself that the Association will support certain of its proposals, rather than rely on the BFEC to secure this support. Extension by a national group of its direct links with Community institutions need not, therefore, indicate dissatisfaction with the ability of its European-level association to represent its views. It is more likely to be a result of the natural instinct of any representative group to make contact with any accessible bodies that are involved in the decision-making process.

To conclude, there seems to be evidence from this case study that the effects of membership of the EC on interest organisations at the national level can be quite considerable, especially in sectors which have no peak association prior to membership and which are represented at Community level by associations which restrict their memberships to one organisation per Member State. This case study also suggests that the role of national pressure groups in the Community legislative process is far greater than that envisaged by the drafters of the treaties. This penetration of Community bodies by national pressure groups is likely to continue because by dealing directly with these organisations Community bodies could undermine the authority of the European-level associations to which they belong. As a consequence of such a development a situation could arise in which ever more direct contact between national pressure groups and Community bodies becomes both a cause and an effect of the erosion of the role of European-level associations.

Notes

1 Draft Directive for the co-ordination of the legal and administrative provisions for the taking up and exercise of the self-employed activities of credit institutions XIV/508/72–E Orig.; D. July 1972. The proposal was for all the banking rules of the Member States to be harmonised in a single piece of legislation.

2 For an excellent discussion of the reasons that the banking community has not produced a peak association see Michael Moran, 'Finance Capital and Pressure Group Politics', paper presented to the Conference on Capital, Ideology and Politics held at the University of Sheffield, 8–9 Jan., 1981.

3 First Council Directive on the co-ordination of laws, regulations and administrative provisions relating to the taking up and pursuit of the business of credit institutions 77/789/EEC. Printed in the Official Journal of the European Communities (OJ) No. L322 of 17 December 1977, pp. 30–37.

4 See, for example, Robert, J. Leiber (1972), 'Interest Groups and Political Integration: British Entry into Europe', *American Political Science Review*, vol. 66 (March); Harry Eckstein (1960), *Pressure Group Politics: The Case of the British Medical Association* (London: George Allen & Unwin); S. E. Finer (1966), *Anonymous Empire: A Study of the Lobby in Great Britain* (London: Pall Mall Press); Allen Potter (1961), *Organized Groups in British National Politics* (London: Faber & Faber); Timothy C. May (1975), *Trade Unions and Pressure Group Politics* (Farnborough: Saxon House); Brian Frost (ed.) (1975), *The Tactics of Pressure: A Critical Review of Six British Pressure Groups* (London: Galliard); Peter Hain (ed.) (1976), *Community Politics* (London: John Calder); Patrick Rivers (1974), *Politics*

by Pressure (London: Harrap); Bridget Pym (1974) *Pressure Groups and the Permissive Society* (Newton Abbot: David and Charles); Graham Wooton (1963), *The Politics of Influence: British Ex-Servicemen, Cabinet Decisions and Cultural Change (1917–1957)* (London: Routledge & Kegan Paul); and Graham Wooton (1978), *Pressure Politics in Contemporary Britain* (Massachusetts: Lexington Books); J. D. Stewart (1957), *British Pressure Groups: Their Role in Relation to The House of Commons* (Oxford: Clarendon Press); Peter Shipley (ed.) (1979), *Directory of Pressure Groups and Representative Associations* (London: Witton House Publications); and D. Marsh & W. Grant (1977), *The Confederation of British Industry* (London: Hodder & Stoughton).

5 Minutes of Evidence taken before the House of Lords Select Committee on the European Communities (Sub-Committee A) Wednesday 10 May 1976 (unpublished).

6 For details of the 'ladder of recognitions' see *The Banker*, May 1972, pp. 639–42, and I. Morison, P. Tillet and J. Welch (1979), *Banking Act 1979* (London: Butterworths), pp. 12–17.

7 Reference in *The Banker* (May 1972), pp. 639–42.

8 Address to the Scottish Institute of Bankers by Sir (later Lord) Leslie O'Brien, Governor of the Bank of England, quoted in *The Banker* (Feb. 1973), p. 125.

9 For details see the *Bank of England Quarterly Bulletin*, vol. 18, no. 2 (June 1978), pp. 230–39.

10 *The Banker* (Dec. 1973), p. 1,421.

11 This appointment was secured chiefly by the efforts of the Governor of the Bank of England. Minutes of Evidence taken before the House of Lords Select Committee on the European Communities, op. cit.

12 Quoted in *The Banker* (Dec. 1973), p. 1,421.

13 O. J. No. C 12, 17 January 1975, pp. 7–13.

14 *The Banker* (December 1973), p. 1,421.

15 O. J. No. L 194, 16 July 1973, pp. 1–10. These were the van Binsbergen case (case 33/74 (1974)) ECR 1299 and the Reyners v. Belgian State case (case 2/74 (1974)) ECR 631.

16 *Journal of the Institute of Bankers*, vol. 97, Part 1 (February 1976), p. 14.

17 In the French case the Government's view differed from that of the banks, consequently the bankers' influence was less than it might have been. For full details of the views of other Member States towards the proposal see Alan Butt-Philip (1981), 'A Tale of Nine Cities: Pressure Groups and Policy in the European Communities', paper presented to the Political Studies Association Annual Conference 1981 workshop on 'Pressure Groups and Economic Policy' (Hull: University of Hull).

18 Minutes of Evidence taken before the House of Lords Select Committee on the European Communities, op. cit.

19 Report of the British Bankers' Association for the year ended 31 March 1974, p. 3.

20 Interview with the Adviser to BFEC's board, 3 July 1980.

21 Interview with the Deputy Secretary and an Assistant Secretary of the BBA, 25 August 1981.

22 HMSO, Cmnd 6584.

23 I. Morison, P. Tillet and J. Welch (1978), *The Banking Act, 1979* (London: Butterworth), pp. 21–4.

24 HMSO, Cmnd 7303.

25 *The Banker* (Oct. 1978), p. 19.

26 Interview with the Deputy Secretary and an Assistant Secretary of the BBA, 25 August 1981.

27 *The Banker* (Oct. 1978), p. 20.

28 Foreword to the British Bankers' Association Report of the Association for the year ended 31 March 1978, p. 1.

29 *Ibid.*, p. 2.

30 For details of these amendments see I. Morison, P. Tillet and J. Welch, op. cit.

31 Only one member bank, The Co-Operative Bank Ltd., is eligible to join a European-level association: the Association of Co-Operative Savings and Credit Institutions of the EEC. As a member of this European Association the Association of Co-Operative Banks

Ltd., expressed its views on the draft directive and the original proposal; however, these did not differ from the views of the BBA. Interview with a Research Officer, International and Plannning Dept., Co-Operative Savings Bank Head Office, 18 July 1980.

32 The principle enshrined in the Government's proposal was that the 'strong' institutions should 'bail out' the weaker ones in the event of a crisis. This principle was contested by the larger banks.

33 *Journal of the Institute of Bankers*, vol. 97, Part 1 (February 1976), p. 13.

34 Interview with a manager, Banking Supervision Division, Bank of England, 11 December 1981.

35 Commission proposals which affect the activities of banks are now so numerous that the BBA publishes a check-list of these proposals annually.

36 This is not to say that the BBA would never have been rejuvenated and developed in this way had Britain not joined the Community in 1973. These changes would almost certainly have come about in the wake of the secondary banking crisis; membership of the Community, however, accelerated these developments.

37 Rules of the British Bankers' Association.

38 For further details of this and the following point see James A. Caporaso (1974), *The Structure and Function of European Integration* (California Goodyear Publishing Company), pp. 30–31.

39 Economic and Social Committee of the European Communities, General Secretariat, *European Interest Groups and their Relationships with the Economic and Social Committee* (Saxon House: Farnborough, 1980), p. 27.

40 British Bankers' Association, Report of the Association for the year ended 31 March 1979, p. 7.

41 Interview with the Deputy Secretary and an Assistant Secretary of the BBA, 25 August 1981.

8 Self-regulation, Crisis Management and Preventive Medicine: the Evolution of UK Bank Supervision*

* Reprinted with permission of Basil Blackwell from the *Journal of Management Studies*, vol. 19, no. 1, 1982, pp. 75–90.

J. L. METCALFE

Civil Service College

Abstract

This article examines the transition in bank supervision from an ideology of self-regulation to a more open-ended, preventive-medicine approach. It explores the processes by which the supervisors are developing a realistic and relevant appreciation of the banking system as a network of organizations.[1]

Introduction

The 1979 Banking Act marked an important departure in the development of UK banking. In place of traditional, non-statutory self-regulation, it established a comprehensive, statutory framework for the authorisation and supervision of deposit-taking institutions. The Act established the Bank of England as the supervisory authority for all banks and deposit-taking institutions except those, such as savings banks and building societies, which are subject to other legislation.

This break with tradition was partly prompted by an EEC call for statutory bases for bank supervision in all member countries by the end of 1979. But the reform was not intended simply to tidy up an untidy situation and to meet EEC requirements. Another, more important reason, was a major crisis in banking in 1973/4. The secondary-banking crisis, as it is usually termed, was the most serious to hit the industry in this century. It involved the collapse of some banks and heavy losses by others, and for a time, it threatened the integrity of the whole banking system. The National

Westminster Bank was forced to deny rumours that it was in difficulties, and not all observers have accepted that denial (Opie, 1977). Although the worst consequences of the crisis were averted, the costs of doing so were very large. A major operation was needed to guard against chain reactions that might have undermined otherwise viable banks.

One estimate is that 'not less than two billion pounds was deployed during the crisis, which began in late 1973, to guarantee the liquidity of secondary banks and the property companies which the banking system had so heavily financed' (Reid, 1978, p. 22). Exact figures are not available, but about 600 million pounds of support loans were outstanding in 1978; the Bank of England provided for losses of over 50 million pounds; the large clearing banks (Barclays, Midland, Lloyd's and National Westminster) also made substantial provisions for losses, in the region of 200 million pounds.

Though banking is usually associated with values such as caution, prudence and risk avoidance, crises are recurrent phenomena in banking systems. The generic characteristics of banking crises have been succinctly described by Kindleberger (1978). Crises originate with events which significantly increase expectations of profit in one sector of the economy, stimulating demand for finance. Extension of bank credit increases the money supply and a self-exciting euphoria develops. As individuals begin to believe that the sky is the limit, realistically grounded expansion turns into a speculative mania.

> When the number of firms and households indulging in these practices grows large, bringing in segments of the population that are normally aloof from such ventures, speculation for profit leads away from normal, rational behaviour to what has been described as 'manias' or 'bubbles'. The word 'mania' emphasises the irrationality; 'bubble' foreshadows the bursting (Kindleberger, 1978, p. 17).

Even the suspicion that this tissue of expectations is weakening can precipitate a crisis. Only a small incident is needed to transform manic behaviour into panic behaviour – a destructive, devil-take-the-hindmost process which inflicts widespread damage.

More broadly, banking exemplifies a general problem of all organised social systems: the management of a system of expectations under conditions of risk and uncertainty (Deutsch, 1966; Parsons, 1963). Like all social systems, the effective functioning of the banking system depends on a fabric of co-ordinated expectations. Mutual expectations guide the behaviours of the participants and, in turn, are modified in the process of interaction. In forming expectations and defining their own interests, individuals draw on assumptions and beliefs about roles and values. Although value consensus cannot be assumed, values do coalesce into more or less coherent doctrines, myths or ideologies which provide the intellectual rationales and moral bases for legitimate actions.

This facet of social organisation is especially obvious in banking, where the extension of credit creates explicit webs of rights and obligations distributed over time. Fulfilment of expectations depends on confidence in the continuing viability of the whole system, and vice versa. But, as Hicks (1967) pointed out, the stability of a banking system should never be taken for granted. The system is potentially unstable in two directions. In one direction, performance will fall short of potential if there is lack of confidence. In the other direction, overconfidence, as in the build-up to a crisis, will produce unrealistically high expectations.

Since expectations are never precisely fulfilled in any moderately complex social system, there is a continuing management problem of avoiding the extremes of mistrust and over-confidence. Maintaining a balance requires an institutional framework which encourages confidence but also restrains the constituent organisations. The problem is partly one of supervising the behaviours of individual organisations and partly one of regulating the environments created by their interactions (Metcalfe, 1974, 1979).

In banking, there are doctrinal differences about how responsibility for regulation should be discharged. A central issue is the extent to which supervisory activities should be reduced to the application of predetermined rules, and the extent to which supervisory discretion is required to recognise new situations and to solve unexpected problems.

The case for rules is overwhelming if we accept the assumption of ideal rules and incompetent and arbitrary administrators. It is conclusive for discretion if we accept the assumption of all wise adminstrators and all foolish rules. At any point between the extremes the conclusion must be qualified and indefinite. Yet it is only this intermediate zone that is relevant to the world that is and can be expected to be (Whittlesey, 1968, p. 256).

Statutory control versus self regulation

In the UK, the choice between rules and discretion in the design of a new supervisory system has generally been formulated as a debate between ideologies of statutory control and of self-regulation.

The change from non-statutory self-regulation to regulation within a statutory framework was an important shift in bank supervision, particularly because there was strong opposition from the banking community and the Bank of England. Statutory control was regarded as too rigid, too detailed, and self-defeating, since it would encourage banks to seek loopholes in the law. Self-regulation, by contrast, has long been regarded as flexible, responsive, more acceptable and hence more effective.

This paper, based on interviews conducted within the Supervision Division of the Bank of England, seeks to show that this ideological dispute reflects some dimensions of the changes that are being made, but obscures other dimensions which have important bearings on the ways the emerging system of supervision is likely to function. A brief description of the crisis and the process of crisis management will be followed by an analysis of the changing roles of values and ideologies in supervisory policy-making.

The Origins of the Crisis

The 1973/4 banking crisis had complex roots. A number of processes interacted, gradually creating unstable conditions and then suddenly precipitating a collapse. A detailed description can be found elsewhere (Channon, 1977). Through the 1960s and into the early 1970s, important changes took place in the structure, functions and composition of the UK banking system. The organisational population of the banking system expanded in two directions. First, with the development of Eurodollar markets, London experienced an influx of foreign banks. Secondly, new sterling money markets grew up parallel to the established primary banking system, and with them a new network of secondary banks.

Notwithstanding the strongly held belief that self-regulation was adaptable and responsive, these important extensions of the banking network were not matched by changes in the scope of supervision. The Bank of England did not extend its supervisory responsibilities to the new institutions and markets. Some of the banks attracted by the Eurodollar markets were already well established elsewhere and ostensibly subject to supervision by their domestic authorities. But others, such as consortium banks, were organisational innovations prompted by market opportunities, such as the large financial requirements of multinational corporations, that existing banks did not satisfy. They presented novel supervisory problems to which no real response was made. Still others, operating in the domestic money markets, were what became known as secondary banks.

As the term implies, secondary banks had lower status than established, primary banks, and operated on the fringe of the banking system. They included hire-purchase companies and small institutions that could exist because the large clearing banks operated a cartel. Their right to describe themselves as banks stemmed from their meeting legal requirements administered by the Department of Trade, which lacked powers to supervise them. Nor were they supervised by the Bank of England, because they had not gone through the elaborate process of securing recognition by the Bank of England and the banking community. Recognition had many of the overtones of diplomatic recognition as a means of establishing legitimacy. Lack of recognition deprived a financial institution of full status, but it did not prevent the institution from calling itself a bank or from developing relationships with supervised banks.

By the late 1960s, the expansion of the banking system led to dissatisfaction with the interest-rate cartel of the clearing banks and with the restrictions upon the primary banking system as compared with the freedom of the secondary-banking system. This led, in 1971, to a new policy of competition and credit control, designed to place all banks on the same footing. The change was justified on the grounds that old demarcations among financial institutions were obsolete and should be removed. But, little attention was paid to the diversity of institutions that had been created by expansion, even though this diversity added substantially to the interdependence, heterogeneity and, hence, the potential instability of the whole banking system. Hardly had this new policy been instituted when, in 1972, the government sought to increase industrial investment by pursuing an expansionary monetary policy. Unfortunately, instead of channelling funds into manufacturing industry, funds flowed in large quantities from the primary to the secondary banks, and into property-development companies. Euphoria developed as property values rose sharply, and a speculative mania ensued. The established system of self-regulation failed to provide advanced warning and also failed to diagnose accurately the problems which followed.

Crisis Management: the Lifeboat Operation

In December 1973, a secondary bank, London and Counties Securities, failed. Its failure signalled the beginning of the secondary-banking crisis. Moves to mount a rescue operation were overtaken, as a crisis of confidence led to a panic (Channon, 1977, p. 97). It was unclear how serious the situation might become. Before 1973 ended, the Bank of England established the Lifeboat operation. This was an exercise in crisis management, designed to rescue foundering financial institutions. The Lifeboat Committee was chaired by the Deputy Governor of the Bank of England, and not by the head of the Discount Office, who had been responsible for bank supervision. The Committee was composed of representatives of the main clearing banks; representatives of leading insurance companies and pension funds were co-opted later.

The lifeboat operation sought to restore confidence in two ways. Symbolically, it acknowledged that the Bank of England had wider responsibilities for supervision than it had previously exercised. Co-opting leading financial institutions demonstrated that there was a shared responsibility for restoring confidence (Metcalfe, 1976; Selznick, 1949). The financial institutions sought to do this by replacing the funds that had been withdrawn from fringe institutions and deposited in the more secure and established banks. Thus, at this stage, the problem was perceived as a liquidity crisis to be met by solidarity and by channelling deposits to the threatened, secondary institutions.

Very soon, the initial definition of the problem was shown to be inadequate. Interest rates rose sharply, international economic and monetary uncertainty linked to the oil crisis increased, as did political and industrial conflict on the home front. Further financial collapses occurred, including, embarrassingly, First National Finance Corporation, which was represented on the Lifeboat Committee. Capital losses of substantial, but indeterminate, proportions loomed in prospect.

The lifeboat metaphor does not describe how the crisis was managed. The process was more of a salvage operation; less concerned with rescuing the sometimes motley crews of sinking institutions than with salvaging some of the institutional vessels themselves. Some secondary banks were allowed to collapse. Others were taken over and reconstructed. One eye was kept on the wider damage that might be done by not salvaging particular institutions.

The clearing banks limited their financial commitments to the lifeboat, so the Bank of England was left with residual responsibility as guardian of the whole system, secondary as well as primary. The Bank's activities also extended to the property industry. The lifeboat operation averted the worst consequences of the crisis. Nevertheless, the severe shock raised basic questions about the adequacy of bank supervision and prompted reform.

The following sections consider why the crisis was not foreseen and what is now being done to ensure that such problems do not recur. These questions are significant, not just because British banking is so important, but also because the banking system illustrates the problems facing regulatory bodies that supervise populations of organisations. Regulatory bodies have to decide how to define and enact their roles. On the one hand, they may limit their functions to reacting to crises. On the other hand, they may seek to identify future problems, particularly those which are not apparent to individual organisations or which are beyond their control. The latter approach raises broad theoretical questions about the ways organisations secure and evaluate information about problems emerging in their environments and transform that information into operational policies.

Values, Ideologies and Policy-making

All policy-making depends on theories of organisations' roles and their relations with their environments (Boulding, 1956). Such theories are embedded in organisational constitutions (Schon, 1971; Starbuck, 1965), and organisational constitutions govern policy-making in two interrelated ways. First, they provide designs for attention management. To economise on limited information-processing capacities, a constitution distributes responsibility for monitoring different facets of the environments. Secondly, to compensate for the divergent perspectives encouraged by specialisation, decision-making procedures assign different weights to the views of sub-units. The power structure embodied in the weighting system defines the values that are considered in organisational policy-making and the priorities among them (Metcalfe, 1981; Stinchcombe, 1960; Zald, 1970).

If policy-making is to be realistic, information which challenges the validity of existing policies and structures should be reported, as well as information that reinforces them. When this is not the case, organisations become rigid, current policies are invested with absolute value, and closed ideologies which put some assumptions beyond discussion become institutionalised. Whether power structures overdetermine what phenomena individuals are allowed to perceive and believe, or whether individuals anticipate unfavourable responses from power-holders and tailor reports to fit their preconceptions, the results are similar. Policy-making is immune from corrective feedback, and decisions are dictated by unrealistic ideologies.

The Bank of England's paradoxical adherence to a supervisory policy of self-regulation, despite the value it attaches to flexibility, evolution, and adaptation, illustrates some of the damaging consequences of unrealistic ideologies. The policy of self-regulation was underpinned by a belief that the banking community shared a normative consensus which assured responsible, prudent behaviour. The theory was that gradual incorporation of new banks into the system, together with their desire for recognition, provided conditions for socialisation and opportunities for existing institutions to observe and penalize deviant conduct. Acceptance of the spirit of self-regulation and awareness of the penalties of misconduct supposedly made the banking system self-equilibrating. The Bank of England's supervisory role could, therefore, be minimal. The light touch of moral persuasion, rather than the heavy hand of the law, was all that was needed.

This theory continued to be the basis for supervisory activities even though the events preceding the secondary-banking crisis changed the banking system in ways inconsistent with the assumption of self-regulation.

It is useful to consider two latent functions performed by maintaining closed ideologies in the face of contradictory evidence. First, associated with any belief system there is a disbelief system, and disbelief systems are more sharply distinguished when belief systems are closed than when they are open (Rokeach, 1960). The disbelief system associated with self-regulation was statutory control, and the contrast helped to maintain loyalty to self-regulation. Polarisation of alternatives helped to cope with contradictory evidence. Whatever deficiencies might be seen in self-regulation, the deficiencies of statutory control appeared worse.

Secondly, ideological analysis looks for discrepancies between the professed and the real intentions governing the exercise of power. Often, an ideology is perceived as a cloak which disguises the deliberate misuse of power. But in the case of bank supervision, the ideology of self-regulation disguised the Bank of England's lack of clearly established supervisory authority. The Bank relied on self-regulation because of ambiguity about its own supervisory status, as well as out of a genuine belief in the superiority of this approach.

Ideologies and frames of reference

One of the universals of organisational behaviour is that people seek to make sense of events by placing them within established frames of reference. But incongruities which do not fix existing frames of reference may foreshadow important changes. Making sense of incongruities depends on reconstructing frames of reference; but some ideologies impose rigidities of perception and interpretation which obstruct this process of adaptation. A critical issue for organisational adaptation is, therefore, the extent to which frames of reference can be modified to accommodate events which contradict preconceived beliefs. McCall (1977) suggested several ways in which incongruities might prompt changes in frames of reference. Jönsson and Lundin (1977) approaching the problem from an organisational rather than an individual standpoint, proposed another way of removing ideological blinkers. They suggested that organisations' statements of purpose 'develop in wave patterns around consecutive myths'. Myths are the values and beliefs that people live by and for (MacIver, 1965), and they are parts of the socially constructed reality. There is no contrast between myth and reality. Organisational myths guide policies by creating shared frames of reference within which solutions to problems can be negotiated. However, they are temporary bases for integrated action; leads and lags in the emergence of new problems and in the formulation of new myths may cause periods of disorientation.

To avoid these difficulties, organisations should behave as learning systems, and should develop effective processes for problem setting as well as problem solving. Instead of grafting on new myths when existing myths fail, adaptive organisations would slough off obsolete solutions as they evolve new ones (Jantsch, 1975). The main challenge is 'to allow for solutions to an endlessly and rapidly evolving set of problems, taking into account changes in one's own comprehension of the problems as well as changes in the problems themselves' (Starbuck, 1975).

Meta-level analyses require frames of references for analysing and comparing frames of reference. Yet, research on policy and decision making has tended to sidestep the problems this raises, particularly the problems associated with analyses of value systems. March (1978) observed that rational choices involve two guesses – or sets of expectations – guesses about the future consequences of current actions, and guesses about future preferences for those consequences. Research has attended to the former. The problems associated with the second guess – ambiguity and conflict over future preferences – have received much less attention. Values and preferences have generally been assumed to be stable, known and exogenously given. But ambiguity and conflict about preferences and values contribute as much, if not more, to the complexity of policy making as do uncertainties about consequences. Moreover, judgements about values, as much as judgements of fact, are liable to change during policy making, and any satisfactory scheme for analysing frames of reference must allow for this change.

Vickers' (1965, 1970) concept of appreciative behaviour provides a useful tool for analysing frames of reference. Appreciative behaviour has three facets: the observation and prediction of actual performance, the generation of norms, and the comparison of performance with norms. Comparison is central to policy-making and to the evaluation of organisational behaviour. Readiness to reconsider and reorganize appreciative systems is one hallmark of an adaptive organization.

Ignoring terminological discrepancies, there is a one-to-one correspondence between Vickers' three-fold distinction and basic distinctions between normative reference groups, comparative reference groups, and conditional reference groups (Kelley, 1952; Merton, 1968; Runciman, 1966; Turner, 1956). Using these reference-group concepts, the next sections of this paper examine the appreciative systems that now guide bank supervision.

Bank Supervision as Preventive Medicine

The approach to bank supervision whiph has evolved since 1974 is neither a simple continuation of what preceded it nor a violent reaction against it. Legal constraints have been introduced, but a large measure of discretion persists. For the first time, the Bank of England has a legal basis for supervising the whole of the banking system.

'Preventive medicine' is the phrase used to characterise the new approach. Preventive medicine has suitably reassuring connotations – no one wants to repeat the secondary-banking crisis. The new guiding myth prescribes a professional-client relationship between supervisors and supervisees. This calls for diagnostic expertise and the capacity to head off potential problems. Implementing this conception of supervision requires a supervisory organisation geared to learn and contribute to the adaptation of the banking system. Otherwise, preventive medicine could degenerate into a superficial surrogate, and the organisational capabilities for gathering, interpreting and evaluating information about the banking system could fail to develop.

The Supervision Division of the Bank of England was established after the secondary-banking crisis began. Since 1974, its staff has grown to over seventy, and it has undergone three reorganisations. Investigation of this new unit provides an opportunity to delineate appreciative systems at a formative stage. Interviews were held with individuals responsible for general supervision policy, and with the heads of sections concerned with clearing banks, accepting houses and merchant banks, consortium and other foreign banks, and other deposit-taking institutions, including finance houses. The interviews were tape recorded, the full transcriptions were made to ascertain the interviewers' frames of reference, the sources of information available to them, and the organisation of supervisory activities. The following sections consider normative reference groups first, then conditional reference groups and, lastly, comparative reference groups.

Protecting depositors and the health of the system

Organizational objectives rarely afford clear-cut guides to action, and bank supervision is no exception. However, a consistent, if incomplete, picture of the values guiding supervision emerged from the interviews.

Two main reference groups act as sources of values for supervisors: depositors and the banking industry as a whole. The risks inherent in banking create problems for depositors and for banks, which deposit funds with each other. These risks give rise to two basic supervisory values: protecting depositors, and safeguarding the health of the system. These values provide broad criteria for supervisory policies, and their generality does not make them so vague as to be all-embracing. Protecting depositors does not extend as far as guaranteeing depositors against all possibilities of loss. A bank that is guilty of persistent imprudent conduct could forfeit help from the Bank of England in time of crisis.

However, protecting depositors and the health of the system do not provide detailed formulae for evaluating the conduct of banks and banking. Operational criteria developed more quickly in relation to the protection of depositors than in relation to the health of the system. Liquidity and capital adequacy provide guiding principles for evaluating the conduct of banks. Each of these is operationally specified by financial ratios for groups of banks, and even individual banks. A great deal of technical expertise and effort is needed to arrive at satisfactory measures of liquidity and capital adequacy. Measures are revised as new information is acquired and, thus, the meanings of liquidity and capital adequacy evolve, without destroying the relevance of the concepts themselves.

Respondents found it much more difficult to specify the operational policies aimed at safeguarding the health of the system. Threats to the health of the banking system as a whole are difficult to specify, and this creates problems in policy-making. But the respondents also view the banking system as more than the sum of its component parts, as the following discussion of conditional reference groups shows.

The banking system as a network of organisations

The interviews indicated that bank supervisors see the banking system as a complex and highly interdependent network of organizations. However, they build their perceptions of the system on knowledge of individual banks, and they emphasize differences among banks and play down similarities. The supervisors attach considerable importance to detailed knowledge of how individual banks function: their motivations, objectives, corporate strategies, structures and managerial competences. Such detailed knowledge is insufficient for building a model of the system as a whole, as is required for regulatory purposes (Conant and Ashby, 1970). Despite the acknowledged precariousness of interbank relations, the supervisors lack a framework for analysing them. This is an important gap.

The supervisors do perceive similarities among banks which enable them to formulate partial models of the banking system. The divisions of supervisory responsibilities imply classes of banks, although the bases of classification are unclear in some cases. Consortium banks, clearing banks and accepting houses form organizational sets with interfirm organization of different degrees of cohesiveness (Caplow, 1964; Phillips, 1960). Elsewhere, categorical distinctions with little or no sociological justification are used to group institutions together merely for adminstrative convenience, as in the case of miscellaneous deposit-takers A–K and the miscellaneous deposit takers L–Z.

Interdependence among banks and among banking sectors creates two supervisory problems. First, prudent conduct by individual banks involves diversification of lending and borrowing. Unacceptable risks arise from too heavy dependence on a few sources of funds, or too heavy commitment to a particular industry such as shipping, or to a country such as Iran. However, sound policy for individual banks may increase risks for the system as a whole if diversification creates patterns of interdependence among banks which are unaware of, or indifferent to, the aggregate effects of their policies. The second supervisory problem is how to deal with lending among institutions that are connected by ties of ownership. This problem recurs in a different form in large, diversified organizations such as the clearing banks. It is not obvious whether such banks should be regarded as integrated units or as loosely coupled systems of separate businesses.

Comparisons and norms

The acid test of the discretionary, supervisory system is its ability to evolve appropriate norms for evaluating banking conduct. All respondents stressed that the same criteria should not be applied uniformly to all banks. Institutional diversity demands that general concepts be tailored to particular circumstances. For example, liquidity problems are less complex for finance houses providing domestic consumer credit than for international banks making long-term, large-scale commitments which have to be matched in several currencies. At the same time, there is an acknowledged need to go beyond the question-begging cliché that every case should be treated on its individual merits.

Norms are being generated inductively. Supervisors build up notions of best practice by comparing the experiences of similar institutions and by comparing over time the track records of individual organisations. As yet, this structure of comparative reference groups is fragmentary and localized. At the system level, there is a more firmly defined comparative reference group – other centres of international banking. The standing and performance of the

UK banking system are explicitly compared with those of other centres of international banking, and considerable importance is attached to maintaining what is perceived as London's pre-eminence. This aspiration limits the depth and scope of supervision. There is a conflict between maintaining adequate prudential standards and maintaining London's position in international finance, since banks can easily shift their operations from, say, London to Luxembourg if supervisory requirements become too onerous. A partial resolution of the conflict may result from closer international co-operation in bank supervision (Blunden and Farrant, 1977).

Supervisory organizations as a learning system

Because the basic values are underspecified and subject to re-interpretation in response to changes in the banking system, effective supervision requires a learning system. One requirement for this is feedback of information from the environment. Information is secured from the environments in two ways: statistical data are collected and analysed every three months, and prudential interviews are also conducted quarterly with the top management of each supervised institution. These provide a regular flow of information which is more up-to-date and more extensive than any published data. Supervision Division compares financial ratios over time and across comparable institutions, where possible. Analysts, who work with interviewers, are expected to offer their interpretations of figures and to propose questions for interviews.

A second requirement of effective supervision is that the appreciative systems of supervisors should be open to modification in response to feedback. In other words, supervision should be information-based with respect to values, norms, and perceptions of reality. Since much information is collected with an individual organization as the unit of analysis, the Supervision Division needs internal mechanisms for treating different cases consistently, and for diagnosing inter-organisational problems. Without such internal mechanisms, inconsistencies would develop, problems in the relations between banks would be overlooked, and the supervisory system would become less and less reliable. Without efficient internal communication and systematic compilation of data, divergent or even contradictory supervisory criteria might be applied to different parts of the banking system.

Policy implementation and policy-making

One question this raises is whether the internal organisation of the Supervision Division facilitates early detection and correction of discrepancies and thus promotes reliable implementation of current policies. In general, organizational reliability can be increased by designing overlap and duplication into organisational mechanisms (Landau, 1969). Interviewers and senior staff have regular daily meetings at which they report on the previous day's meetings, discuss the current day's workloads and highlight policy issues. Responsibility for interviews with particular sets of banks is assigned to specific individuals, but there is some overlap in assignments; someone who is primarily responsible for miscellaneous deposit takers may participate in interviewing consortium banks. Continuity is important in building up good external relations; overlap is important for ensuring internal consistency.

The leaders of the analysis groups also meet weekly to keep track of general problems. As well as moving people around to give them wider experiences, the analytical work is redistributed as variations in workload occur. Analysis groups are not strictly compartmentalized, and leaders of analysis groups attend interviews.

One significant exception is the clearing banks: a supervisory approach to them has developed slowly, partly because of their size and complexity and partly because of their sensitivity about being supervised.

A second important question is whether internal organization facilitates policy making as distinct from the consistent application of existing policies. The interviews revealed awareness of the tentativeness of existing policies and of the wider implications of particular decisions. Emergent problems and proposed decisions are reported internally before public commitments are made; and when they raise general issues with unclear policy implications, working groups research them. Studies may seek to develop more appropriate measures of capital adequacy for the clearing banks, or investigate connected lending among associated companies. At this early stage, many strategic questions have yet to be analysed in depth.

Conclusions

By comparison with the minimal supervision that preceded and contributed to the secondary-banking crisis, the new system is a substantial improvement. It provides regular feedback to the Bank of England about the conduct of commercial banks without imposing bureaucratic straitjackets on them. The new system also incorporates mechanisms which should prevent its degenerating into a superficial substitute for effective supervision. In this respect, the preventive-medicine doctrine motivates supervisors to build up their knowledge of the behaviour of banks and to improve their understanding of what constitutes best practice. Potentially, supervisory performance can improve by learning from experience.

The establishment of a legal framework for bank supervision has not created a corporatist system of state control over the banking system. Statutes have strengthened the Bank of England's position *vis-à-vis* the commercial banks, but the Bank has not used its authority unilaterally. Appropriate criteria have been defined through negotiations between the Bank and the commercial banks, and appropriate criteria of liquidity and capital adequacy have been the subjects of protracted and detailed negotiations.

There is some doubt about the robustness of the present system. One basic problem, enshrined in the statutory framework itself, is the lack of a general purpose legal definition of a bank. The supervisory system covers banks and other deposit-taking institutions, but the distinction between these has never been explicated. Banks have been identified by enumeration rather than conceptually. Appeals against the Bank of England's decisions to refuse full banking status to particular financial institutions could result in an unsatisfactory legal definition, out of touch with organizational realities, or they could erode the distinction between banks and other deposit-taking institutions.

A second potential source of problems is that supervisors judge the quality of management in banks and base decisions on those judgements. Quality of management, rather than adherence to prescribed financial ratios, is the yardstick supervisors prefer. However, quality of management remains a nebulous concept that is far from being defined operationally. The supervisors' emphasis on quality of management is partly due to their desire to avoid second-guessing the decisions of commercial banks. But even though they avoid claiming to make better commercial judgements than commercial bankers, they are claiming a more sophisticated and abstract competence, the ability to judge the managerial skills of commercial bankers. In doing this, they ignore conceptual problems that intimidate academic students of management.

Perhaps the most serious gaps in the preventive-medicine approach occur in treatment of interbank relations. The supervisors lack the analytical tools to model the banking system as a network of organisations even though public discussions of supervision generally give a good deal of attention to the dangers of domino effects in interbank relations. Moreover, there is emphasis on keeping British banking open to the international banking community in order to retain the pre-eminent position of the City of London in international finance. The price of this emphasis is increased vulnerability to world events. In effect, reliance is placed on international arrangements to buffer disruptive changes. Should these arrangements, together with the new domestic system of supervision, prove inadequate, the banking system could collapse like a house of credit cards.

Note

1 The research on which this paper is based was conducted at the London Graduate School of Business Studies with a grant from the Social Science Research Council. The Bank of England co-operated in granting access for a series of interviews. The views expressed are solely the responsibility of the author.

References

Blunden, George & Farrant, R. H. (1977), 'International co-operation in banking supervision'. *Bank of England Quarterly Bulletin* (Sept.), pp. 325–9.

Boulding, Kenneth F. (1956), *The Image: Knowledge in Life and Society* (Ann Arbor: University of Michigan Press).

Caplow, Theodore (1964), *Principles of Organisations* (New York: Harcourt, Brace & World).

Channon, Derek F. (1977), *British Banking Strategy and the International Challenge* (London: Macmillan).

Conant, Roger C. & Ashby, W. Ross (1970). 'Every good regulator of a system must be a model of that system'. *International Journal of Systems Science*, vol. x, pp. 89–97.

Deutsch, Karl W. (1966), *The Nerves of Government* (London: Collier-Macmillan).

Hicks, John (1967), *Critical Essays in Monetary Theory* (Oxford: Clarendon Press).

Jantsch, Erich (1975), *Design for Evolution* (New York: Braziller).

Jönsson, Sten A. & Lundin, Rolf A. (1977). 'Myths and wishful thinking as management tools'. In Nystrom, Paul C. & Starbuch, William H. (eds), *Prescriptive Models of Organisations* (Amsterdam: North Holland), pp. 157–70.

Kelley, Harold H. (1952). 'Two functions of reference groups'. In Swanson, G. E. (ed.), *Readings in Social Psychology* (New York: Holt).

Kindleberger, Charles P. (1978), *Manias, Panics, and Crashes* (London & Basingstoke: Basic Books, Macmillan).

Landau, Martin (1969), 'Redundancy, rationality and the problem of duplication and overlap'. *Public Administration Review*, vol. 29, pp. 346–58.

March, James G. (1978), 'Bounded rationality, ambiguity, and the engineering of choice', *The Bell Journal of Economics*, vol. 9, no. 2, pp. 587–608.

MacIver, R. M. (1965), *The Web of Government* (New York: Free Press).

McCall, Morgan W., Jnr (1977), 'Making sense with nonsense: helping frames of reference clash'. In Nystrom, Paul C. & Starbuck, William H. (eds), *Prescriptive Models of Organizations* (Amsterdam: North-Holland), pp. 111–23.

Merton, Robert K. (1968). *Social Theory and Social Structure* (London: Collier-Macmillan).

Metcalfe, J. L. (1974), 'Systems models, economic models and the causal texture of organizational environments: an approach to macro-organization theory', *Human Relations*, vol. 27, pp. 639–63.

Metcalfe, J. L. (1976), Organizational strategies and inter-organizational networks', *Human Relations*, vol. 29, pp. 327–43.

Metcalfe, J. L. (1979), 'A strategy for economic development', Working Paper, London Graduate School of Business Studies (March).

Metcalfe, J. L. (1981), 'Designing precarious partnerships'. In Nystrom, Paul C. & Starbuck, William H. (eds), *Handbook of Organizational Design*, Vol. 1 (New York: Oxford University Press), pp. 503–30.

Opie, Roger (1977), 'Time for a radical re-appraisal'. *The Banker* (Feb.), pp. 101–103.

Parsons, Talcott (1963), 'On the concept of influence'. *Public Opinion Quarterly*, vol. 27, pp. 37–62.

Phillips, Almarin (1960), 'A theory of interfirm organization', *Quarterly Journal of Economics*, vol. 74, pp. 602–13.

Reid, Margaret (1978), 'The secondary banking crisis – five years on'. *The Banker* (Dec.), pp. 21–30.
Rokeach, Milton (1960), *The Open and Closed Mind* (New York: Basic Books).
Runciman, W. G. (1966), *Relative Deprivation and Social Justice* (London: Routledge & Kegan Paul).
Schon, Donald A. (1971), *Beyond the Stable State* (London: Temple Smith).
Selznick, Philip (1949), *The T.V.A. and the Grass Roots* (Berkeley, California: University of California Press).
Starbuck, William H. (1965), 'Organizational Growth and Development'. In March, James G. (ed.), *Handbook of Organizations* (Chicago: Rand McNally), pp. 451–533.
Starbuck, William H. (1975), 'Information systems for organizations of the future'. In Grochla, E. & Szyperski, N. (eds), *Information Systems and Organizational Structure* (Berlin: deGruyter), pp. 217–29.
Stinchcombe, Arthur L. (1960), 'The sociology of organizations and the theory of the firm'. *Pacific Sociological Review* (Fall), pp. 75–82.
Turner, Ralph H. (1956), 'Role-taking, role standpoint, and reference group behaviour'. *American Journal of Sociology*, vol. 61, pp. 316–28.
Vickers, Geoffrey C. (1965), *The Art of Judgement* (London: Chapman & Hall).
Vickers, Geoffrey C. (1970), *Value Systems and Social Process* (Harmondsworth: Penguin).
Whittlesey, Charles R. (1968), 'Rules, discretion, and central bankers'. In Whittlesey, C. R. & Wilson, J. S. G. (eds), *Essays in Money and Banking in Honour of R. S. Sayers* (Oxford: Clarendon Press), pp. 252–65.
Zald, Mayer N. (1970), 'Political economy: a framework for comparative analysis'. In Zald, Mayer N. (ed.), *Power in Organizations* (Nashville: Vanderbilt University Press), pp. 221–61.

PART C
Related Issues

The opening four chapters in Part A discussed some of the important problems associated with the supervisory process. Some of these were taken up and developed in Part B. The following collection of papers concentrates on three specific problem areas. Marco Onado's opening paper examines the objectives of banking regulation. He explores the problems of balancing efficiency and stability in the regulatory process. Banking regulation is explored from the institutional point of view. In Chapter 10, Jack Revell tackles the important problem of reconciling competition and regulation. His thesis is that regulation and supervision are required to foster a competitive financial system. Chapter 11 concludes this section with a general perspective of international bank regulation and support issues. Dudley Peake covers this ground.

9 Objectives of Banking Regulation: the Trade-off Between Efficiency and Stability*

* This paper was received in December 1982

MARCO ONADO

Professor of Banking, Facolta di Economia e Commercio Universita degli Studi di Modena, Italy

Scope of the Paper

Banking regulation is a typical field of research where theory must rest on the solid ground of institutional facts and the actual behaviour of financial intermediaries. As such a statement might seem biased coming from a teacher of banking, I will have recourse to the authority of a distinguished economist and Nobel prize-winner, James Tobin (1967), who as a discussant to a famous Meltzer paper (1967) said:

> I have no conclusions or recommendations to offer, only perplexity. I hope that those who continue to work on this fascinating and important subject will not hesitate to take from time to time a fundamental and radical look at the institutions they are appraising.

Strangely enough, that recommendation has been largely disregarded by most scholars. They have seemed more interested in monetary theory rather than the micro-economic side of financial activity. In doing so, they even changed the traditional approach to banking. As Revell (1980) pointed out:

> Starting with Adam Smith and Ricardo through Walter Bagehot and George Rae, and up to Richard Sayers, the English literature was greatly concerned with the institutional facts of banking. After that the emphasis shifted markedly towards macro-economic and monetary policy in practically all countries. What little was written with a micro-economic approach was usually concerned with the effects of monetary policy.

In this paper banking regulation will be explored from the institutional point of view. The next section will deal with basic definitions concerning objectives and and instruments. The third section will review the theoretical debate. Assuming the necessity for most banking systems of a rather broad regulatory framework, the fourth section will examine the problem in a world where bank innovations and institutional evolution continuously challenge the effectiveness of controls. The fifth section, taking the Italian situation as a typical case, will try to point out the conditions under which the authorities can use regulation as a means to foster efficiency.

Bank Regulation: Some Definitions

Regulation is normally defined broadly by most scholars as all interventions by banking authorities which do not lead to changes in the supply of monetary base. According to Greenbaum (1967):

> The term regulation encompasses all manner of direct intervention in the prerogative of commercial banks, including control of entry, merger and branching; portfolio regulation – asset, liability, and capital account structuring; regulation of interest rates on time and demand deposits; and usury laws. Unlike reserve requirements, open market operations by the Federal Reserve System need not be viewed as a form of direct intervention. Operation of the discount window occupies a middle ground. To the extent that the System merely posts an interest rate at which it stands ready to lend to qualified borrowers, there is no interference with the operations of the banks. However, the practice of 'wrist-slapping' can be viewed as a form of portfolio control.

This definition is generally accepted. There is, therefore, widespread agreement on a dichotomy between instruments and objectives concerned with control of the monetary base (and hence of the money supply) on the one side, and instruments and objectives applied to regulation on the other. While there is a well-known debate about the rationale of monetary control and its theoretical underpinnings, the discussion about regulation is much more limited.

It is normally admitted that the objectives of regulation are twofold. First, to foster the efficiency of a banking system in respect of: 1. the level and structure of interest rates; 2. the allocation of resources; and 3. the transmission of monetary policy. Second, to preserve the soundness of individual banks and the stability of the banking system as a whole. Generally, three arguments are used to assign this final objective to regulation. We can call them the monopolistic issue, the financial instability issue and the efficiency issue.

A. Monopolistic issue. According to this, the banking industry can create conditions of monopoly, i.e. restrict output and raise prices as a way to maximize profits. In a different version it is alleged that if conditions of monopoly cannot exist on the credit market as a whole, they can arise in single local markets. This view is therefore consistent with the hypothesis of segmentation of banking output and banking markets.

Whether the real market behaves according to one hypothesis or the other depends on the slope of the average cost curve. If the cost function is shaped in the way described in textbooks (i.e. if there are economies of scale), the big bank could eliminate competition by fixing loan rates at a level lower than the average cost of the smaller bank, and thereby force it out of the market. Afterwards, the large bank could raise prices and exploit its monopoly position. In a slightly different version, the more powerful bank could enter the market, assume the price leadership and permit the smaller bank to survive only if it 'follows the leader'.

On the other hand, if economies of scale do not exist, there is the possibility for the local bank, sheltered by market segmentation, to operate in less competitive markets and then to charge higher prices. In some areas, for a given total quantity of deposits and credit, banks would hold more securities and less loans than banks operating in competitive markets. The individual local bank would therefore have the possibility – which the banking system as a whole has not – to restrict output and raise prices.

B. Financial instability issue. One of the key problems of banking has always been to preserve stability. Under any theoretical approach, a bank crisis is a danger which the authorities have to prevent in any possible way, and whenever it happens they have to intervene promptly to absorb the shock. Needless to say, the public authorities' concern ought to be concentrated not on the individual failing bank, but on the general effects of the crisis. There is no general interest to protect if a small bank with a low level of employment is closed after its net worth is destroyed. The failure of the only bank in a town is normally less worrying than the failure of the only factory in the same town.

C. Efficiency issue. Competition and stability are elements of efficiency. They facilitate the lowering of the total costs of intermediation and allow the reduction of risks for surplus and deficit units. Efficiency must be reached also from the point of view of the capacity of the banking system to transmit impulses coming from monetary policy at a reasonable speed and precision, without side effects. Moreover, efficiency must be seen also from the allocative side, i.e. viewed in the capacity of allocating resources in the most appropriate way.

These are the final objectives. Using the usual terms for monetary policy, we can also identify the intermediate objectives – these are the elements which form the structure of the banking system and which determine the actual behaviour of banks. According to Monti–Padoa Schioppa (1978), structure refers both to the characteristics of individual banks (ownership, objectives, specialization, branching, asset and liabilities composition, etc.) and the relationships between banks (markets and their elements, concentration, size distribution, etc.).

As for monetary policy, the transmission process from intermediate to final objectives – from structure to efficiency and stability – is the crucial and controversial point for theory and empirical research. The problem relates particularly to the forms of competition and their capacity to prompt efficiency. The debate on how much competition is necessary to reach the final objectives focuses on two different hypotheses. One assumes that efficiency is a positive function of the level of competition and is somehow independent of stability. The other affirms that competition does not necessarily lead to a higher level of efficiency – there is an inverse relationship between efficiency and stability. It follows that efficiency and stability cannot be optimized at the same time, and a trade-off between them is required. These hypotheses will be dealt with in the following two sections.

The instruments used to achieve intermediate and then final objectives can be classified into three main areas, each composed of different powers.

1 *Structural regulation* aims to modify the structural conditions of the banking system, as previously defined, in order to influence its performance. Having in mind the situation within most European countries, we can include in this area controls such as barriers to entry (branching, mergers, operating areas of banks); controls on interest rates (both for lending and deposit operations); controls on assets and liabilities (reserve requirements, assets and liabilities restrictions, capital adequacy and liquidity measures, etc.); and foreign exchange controls. We can also include in this area the power of nominating the directors of the banks, normally in public-owned institutions.

2 *Prudential regulation* refers to the control of bank risks both for particular operations and for the banks. According to Gardener (1981) prudential regulation should ensure that banks do not follow imprudent policies to the extent that their operational viability or solvency is threatened. Traditionally included in this category are controls on specific risks (limits to fixed assets, to loans to a single client, to medium-term loans, etc.). Moreover, authorities are given powers to obtain data and information regarding bank activity, and also powers to supervise and inspect the banks.

3 *Fair play regulation* aims to assure the diffusion of information on bank markets so as to put every participant on an equal basis. It is typically an area of disclosure and consumer protection, and includes measures such as limits to insider trading, controls on loans to directors and members of the staff, publicity of market conditions, truth-in-lending measures, etc.

More important from a practical point of view for the actual functioning of the regulatory mechanism is the kind of power system through which the authorities activate the tools they possess. For each area and each instrument there are five alternatives, each one identifying a different relationship between the regulators and the bank.

1 Total freedom of banks (i.e. no control);
2 Rules prohibiting or imposing limits to specific bank choices: these rules are issued and enforced on an equal basis for all institutions or at least for homogeneous categories. Banking ratios are a typical example in this field.
3 Authorizations issued on the basis of banking objectives and intended spheres of operation (as with the kind of authorization embedded in the first EEC Directive).
4 Authorizations issued on the basis of a discretionary appraisal of the bank application. An example can be found in the kind of authorization to bank entry issued by the Bank of Italy, especially during the 1960s when disclosure of regulators' criteria was carefully avoided.
5 Complete discretionality of the central bank which, lacking specific powers, uses moral suasion or other instruments to pursue efficiency or stability objectives of regulation. This situation is frequent in cases of bank crises.

The regulatory structure of each country is in fact a sort of grid of the three main instrument areas and the above five power systems. One can even say that the latter are of the utmost importance in identifying the specific characteristics of each institutional framework. Each banking legislation covers all the areas, so what really matters is the kind of instrument and the powers by which the regulators activate it. It is this institutional element which determines the relationship between the regulators and the individual bank, and actually influences the behaviour of the latter.

Looking at the regulatory framework and the grid of instruments and powers, we can identify two central bank models. One where structural regulation tools are very limited and the central bank can use these tools with little discretionary power. In this case the central bank is somehow *super partes* and assures that players follow the rules of the game. We can call it the 'referee' model. Such a central bank executes monetary policy (often maximizing the use of impersonal tools such as open market operations) and tends to minimize regulatory controls. The typical example of this model can be found in Germany.

The other central bank model is characterized by wider powers of structural regulation which are activated with more discretion. This central bank executes monetary policy often using instruments of regulation as previously defined. In other words, it does not limit itself to the control of monetary base from the supply side. Moreover, it also has the ambition to mould the structure of the banking system and hence its functioning. Its ambition is to direct the performance of banks in the same way as a film director directs the performance of his actors. France, Italy and the US are good examples of this model.

Both models can be defined – in Gardener's words (1978) – as examples of 'government by law'. The difference rests particularly on the kind of legal power by which controls are activated. The UK is a notable exception as it has traditionally adopted a model of 'government by men' based on moral suasion and gentlemen's agreements. But even there, the situation has been rapidly changing since the 1973/4 crisis and more formal rules have been established. The British 'government by law' is nevertheless still characterized by a continuing reliance on the participative and discretionary approach to supervision (Revell, 1982).

By this set of definitions it follows that there is a deep difference between monetary policy and regulation (whatever model is adopted). Not only are the objectives and instruments different, but there is also a different relationship between the individual bank and the authorities. Interventions whose final effect is to change the supply of monetary base are normally carried out on a negotiating basis, rates and quantities being determined by market conditions. Moreover, in most countries the personal relationship between the bank and the central bank at the discount window (which always implies that the former is somehow subordinated to the latter) have been replaced by the impersonal relationship of open market operations, which can even have a non-bank agent as counterpart.

The instruments that are not used to control the monetary base become then the arena where banks and the authorities come into contact. No wonder it is here that frictions and disagreements arise. Having cut the direct link to the central bank in order to obtain the monetary base, commercial banks feel the burden of regulation heavier and heavier. The discretionary power of regulation is therefore fiercely opposed, especially where a 'director' model is adopted. Regulation is now the controversial issue in banking communities and there is a strong demand for deregulation or, according to the definitions given, to substitute a central bank 'director' with a central bank 'referee'.

The Debate on the Optimal Quantity of Bank Regulation

Coming to the problem of how much regulation and which kind of regulation is necessary to pursue the final objectives of efficiency and stability, the area of disagreement grows according to the assumptions about the self-regulatory capacity of the banking system. Those who believe in the capacity of individual banks to reach autonomously conditions of efficiency and stability want to minimize the regulatory framework. As a matter of fact, not a single scholar or banker rejects the desirability of a system of controls. Apparently they only ask for a rationalization and simplification. According to Edwards (1981), one of the most distinguished members of the anti-regulatory party:

> . . . the remedy is not more, but different regulation. What is needed is a regulatory system that is both more compatible with today's realities and more responsive to changes in market conditions. In most cases, this calls for less regulation, although in a few situations additional regulation may be desirable.

This is a sort of ceremonial preamble for the supporters of deregulation. Their model is Antony's funeral speech and while affirming that 'Brutus is an honourable man' they try to move their audience to the opposite idea.

What Edwards seeks in practice is a dismantling of regulation. The only controls judged necessary refer to monetary policy and prudential regulation. In the first case only reserve requirements are admitted (but it would be difficult to have different opinions for those who have a fair knowledge of the multiplier process). In the second case, only balance sheet ratios and deposit insurance are admitted. According to Meltzer (1967), the latter can even be organized on a voluntary basis.

This approach can be viewed as the extreme wing of a school of thought whose ideal of central banking is the 'referee' model. The basic idea is that banks tend naturally to conditions of competition and efficiency, and it is founded on many theoretical hypotheses which should be reviewed.

The first point is that oligopoly theory cannot be applied to the banking industry. Only public authorities and the central bank have the power to restrict the output (of money) and increase prices (rates); banks do not have this power either individually or as a banking system. If banks try to exercise monopolistic behaviour the central bank can inject any quantity of monetary base at zero marginal cost. If banks were to refuse to expand, they would also refuse the principle of the fractional reserve banking and incur heavy losses.

The existence of monopoly conditions is also rejected for local markets on two grounds. First, higher concentration rates should not directly lead to the conclusion of weaker competition. Second, as bank output is not homogeneous, comparisons between bank areas are very difficult. Banks of different size and structure offer different services at different prices. Lacking a conclusive demonstration, the argument is turned inside out: if monopolistic conditions exist in local markets they should be attributed to controls which prevent entry into the market.

As to the stability objective, theoretical positions vary from one author to the other. The common denominator is the assumption that a solvency crisis is a sort of accident, a fortuitous deviation from a normal course of stability followed by banks. Being an episode, the crisis must be immediately tackled to prevent a domino effect. At any rate, the main public interest to protect is that of depositors who are not able to judge the risk involved in their portfolio choices. The implicit point is that between efficiency and stability there is no trade-off. The two functions are fundamentally independent of each other, so that competition (and therefore efficiency) can be achieved through minimization of regulation without any side effect (or with controllable side effects) as far as stability is concerned.

Controls are therefore seen as an exogenous variable whose net effect is to impose a cost, implicit or explicit, to the banking system. Facing that cost there are no benefits for the banking system or for the economic community. Competition becomes weak and distorted, exempt institutions are unduly favoured and banks try to circumvent controls, and in so doing continuously modify the structural framework. The attempt by banks to find loopholes in the system of controls is seen as the worst effect and we will return to it in the next section. As Kane (1981) suggested:

> We can liken the evolutionary interaction of political and economic activity to a struggle between a visible and an invisible hand to determine the shape of the clay statue. Far from acting in concert, the two hands work almost completely at cross-purposes. Each hand sets out to undo what the other has just accomplished. The invisible hand is the market-place and the visible hand is that of regulatory activity.

It is important to point out that this objection can hardly be judged as a theoretical point. It is simply a conclusion about what often happens in banking systems and particularly where the banking side of the financial system is subject to the main part of regulation.

The other school of thought is based on completely different hypotheses. As will be stressed in the next section, this is the view shared in countries, like Italy, which have traditionally adopted a 'director' model of central banking. First, these scholars strongly reject the view of the banking system as a mere 'transmission box' of monetary policy having a constant and foreseeable result. They point instead to the joint capacity of banks and economic agents to frustrate central bank actions and, therefore, to contribute towards determining the total supply of money. This very reason justifies controls beyond those on the supply side of monetary base, such as credit ceilings and selective measures, at least on a temporary basis. It is interesting to note that this view is generally shared by banking economists and macro-economists who are particularly interested in institutional aspects and in actual bank behaviour. It was the scholar noted for his study of the customer relationship – Hodgman (1972) – who admitted that direct instruments might be necessary as a temporary measure to cope with lags and distortions created by firms and banks trying to resist monetary policy. It was an official report on the functioning of the banking system – the Radcliffe Report – which started the debate on monetary policy, stressing the concept of 'general liquidity of the economy'. That concept, though undefined, recognized the importance of economic behaviour of individual agents in resisting central bank policies.

Also the approach to competition of the institutional students is completely different. First of all, competition does not necessarily lead to a higher level of efficiency. If there are economies of scale, in a world without regulation one could expect an increase of concentration through mergers of smaller banks with larger ones.

Secondly, totally free competition can lead to instability. Trying to compete, banks could be willing to accept higher and higher risks, and to weaken their screening of credit demands. This situation becomes more likely when the objective function of the bank is not the maximization of growth rate. In this case banks might be willing to accept higher risk or to increase overhead costs (e.g. for branches), creating rigidities in the profit and loss account and in the expected flow of funds. A non-regulated competition could therefore lead to greater instability, not to higher efficiency (Revell, 1981). As Maisel (1981) put it:

> Without regulation an undue percentage of financial institutions are likely to take excessive risks. Because of the large amount of leverage, the difficulty of depositors' policing risk levels, the high cost of information, and the number of small, uninformed depositors, an institution can profit by raising its risk ratio. Moral hazards are also high; it is hard to protect against conflicts of interest and self-dealing.

This issue can be based on a model – mainly deriving from historical analysis – in which banks are supposed to push competition too far, to create conditions of overbanking, and eventually arrive at loss conditions as soon as the decrease in operating margins pushes average costs to a level permanently higher than average revenues. When losses have eroded the bank net worth, bankruptcy becomes inevitable.

Alternatively, the financial instability issue can be put in the framework of a Keynesian model, such as Minsky's (see, for the last version, 1982) which holds that the growing separation between owners of physical assets and holders of financial assets – which is endogeneous to the capitalist process – is the main force leading borrowers and lenders to accept a continuous increase of debt and therefore of financial risks.

The stability objective is even wider than the anti-regulatory party pretends. First of all, the interests to protect are more general than those of depositors. It is true that depositors have a lesser capacity to evaluate risks involved in asset selection and they consequently deserve a special protection. But the real problem is to assure the orderly functioning of credit mechanisms. In the past, the objective of stability was mainly a problem of maintaining confidence towards the financial system as a whole. Whenever this confidence disappeared, there were runs on banks. Nowadays the problem must be viewed from the final borrowers' side. In a world of high indebtedness, stability depends on how much of the maturing debt will be rolled over.

In the real world, the objective is not only to protect widows and orphans, but to tackle the many banking problems that arise. The function of a central bank is to validate the debt structure and to avoid a debt deflation process. For such a task, a prudential regulation based only on balance sheet ratios cannot be sufficient. As experience suggests, there are too many structural limitations of bank ratios to predict the future accurately and too-broad differences across banks. Regulatory powers must therefore extend beyond bank ratios or other simple prudential measures. They must include controls on bank entry and other controls on the degree of competition.

The final point of the school of thought which strongly favours regulation deals with the scope of the regulatory measures on the financial system. They affirm that they should not only be limited to the banking sector but also cover other intermediaries as well. Theoretically, the point is to ascertain whether banks are completely different from other intermediaries and whether their assets and liabilities have low degrees of substitutability *vis-à-vis* other ones.

As a matter of fact, the uniqueness of commercial banks has been a central element in banking theory for a long time. But these scholars emphasize that this point has been questioned, at least since the seminal work of Gurley and Shaw. The real world of banking has seen recently a dramatic increase in competition across the borders between banks and non-banks, in the field of both liabilities and assets. The only privilege remaining to banks – the payment mechanism – is likely to be lost in a few years due to technological innovations.

This is not caused by regulation favouring the unregulated firms as many have contended. In many instances we have seen the non-bank intermediaries actively competing with banks, and trying to enter sectors which were formerly typical of the latter. It is instead a natural trend of financial systems, stemming from the increase in the demand for financial services.

The conclusion is that every financial intermediary as such is liable to a kind of regulation: it goes without saying that each category of institution should be subjected to specific measures adapted to their specific activities. But the idea is to impose at least a core of regulation on the whole range of financial intermediaries. Leaving a sector unregulated could only influence competition as in Barclay's model (1978) which we will refer to in the next section.

Reactions to Bank Regulation and Financial Innovation

One of the most common criticisms of regulation is that financial intermediaries can always find a loophole in controls and create new instruments or new techniques to circumvent the authorities' intentions. Financial innovation is therefore the normal answer to regulation. In rather Hegelian terms, the thesis is the action of the authorities, the antithesis the reaction of regulated firms, and the synthesis a new situation in which the financial institutions as a whole (or at least the cleverest ones) have created an area free from regulation.

Regulation is therefore seen as the impulse modifying a situation implicitly assumed of equilibrium. The regulatory measure, no matter how good the intentions of the authorities might be, determines a reaction which automatically develops the non-regulated sector of the financial system. The net result is twofold. First, regulated intermediaries – normally banks – will try to put into effect every possible technical and formal innovation to escape from the control. The innovation process is rather easy since, unlike the industrial sector, the financial system can differentiate its product at a marginal cost which is close to zero. Second, unregulated intermediaries will be placed at a competitive advantage by the very fact of the regulatory measure: competition will be distorted and market segmentation artificially enhanced (Kane, 1981).

According to Kane, there is a difference between invention and innovation. The former is the act of finding new ways of doing profitable operations: the latter is the act of putting invention into practice. In Kane's (1981) words:

> Every invention makes one or more innovations feasible, but we can always find an *innovation lag*. Before an invention can be adopted commercially the opportunities it opens must promise enough profits . . . to counterbalance the costs . . . The burden of regulation increases the reward for doing things differently *per se* . . . For this reason regulating an industry tends to reduce its innovation lags, while ongoing acts of innovation tend to lengthen and exploit parallel *regulatory lags* that develop as regulators contemplate the unexpected problems created by specific innovations and decide what (if anything) to do about the situation.

This analysis is a good theorization of what has happened in the American financial system since the early 1960s. The main turning points in banking activity (CDs, eurodollars, NOW accounts, etc.) can be viewed as a continuous sequence of regulatory measures followed by bank innovations trying to avoid them, and again by new regulatory measures adapting to the new situation.

What does not necessarily follow from Kane's analysis is the pessimistic conclusion about the net effect on the efficiency of the financial system. Kane fails to differentiate between the innovations which improve the efficiency of the financial system and those which are mere legal subterfuges. Still taking the American experience as an example, we can say that innovations induced by regulation contributed to the diffusion of new financial instruments, to the efficiency of the money market, and in many respects reduced the segmentation of the credit market. It is difficult to look at all these years as a sort of cops-and-robbers' play where the latter always won, despite the intention of the former.

It is without doubt that many regulatory measures have created distortions. But the point here is not the technical characteristic of those measures, but the very capacity of the regulation to pursue its final objectives without creating side effects greater than the advantages reached. If we are to admit that the Federal Reserve could not be so blind or lucky (or both) to create unintentionally all those opportunities for banks, we must conclude that regulation was a basic element of the move towards efficiency.

In other words, as the existence of a lag between innovation and invention is admitted, one cannot but ask why the regulators could not shorten this lag. The lag could depend not only on pure profit expectations, but also on unwillingness to change, managerial riskiness, etc. In situations where innovation is delayed by similar inefficiences both at bank and system level, regulation could be the external stimulus pushing banks to new operations and/or pricing behaviour.

If it is true, regulation may not be an obstacle to efficiency, as many scholars contend, but the way to foster efficiency, as theory requests. The point therefore is which kind of regulation, and which grid of instruments and powers, can best reach this target.

The lesson which must be learnt from the 1960s and the 1970s is that in a world where monetary policy is often restrictive (i.e. where we are to admit at any rate a burden exercised by central banks on banks from the supply side of monetary base) and where bank conditions change very quickly (i.e. modifying the transmission mechanism between structure and performance), a rigid 'director' model of central banking is very difficult to implement. First, the burden on banks could be too heavy to leave enough elbow room for entrepreneurial activity. Second, the central bank could always risk a lagged response to bank changes and innovations.

A rather substantial change in regulation is therefore in order as far as the attitude of central banks and the grid of power are concerned. The Italian situation can provide us with a good example.

The Italian case (a conclusion)

In Italy theoretical analysis normally acknowledges the necessity for a wide network of controls on bank structure and bank activity (Dell'Amore, 1967).

Moreover, this is the idea strongly emphasized by the banking law which has been in force since 1936. The existence of a strong trade-off between efficiency and stability, together with a model of central banking which 'directs' the banking scene with wide powers of supervision, are therefore strongly embedded in the Italian theoretical and institutional climate.

Since 1973, due to a progressively harder monetary policy, direct controls have been used very strictly. Credit ceilings have been enforced for almost ten years and mandatory holdings of securities have become the main elements of central bank action. The heavier the burden of controls, the stronger the reaction of banks asking for a substantial deregulation. The net result is that in a system where wide powers of regulation were normally accepted, there is now a strong demand for the relaxation of controls.

One can therefore ask why this situation has arisen and whether the central bank was at least able to use these controls, directing the functioning of banks and the process of financial innovation, in the manner described in the previous section so as to improve the efficiency of the banking system. It is without doubt that from this point of view many advantages have been reached. The stability objective has certainly been achieved, despite two serious bank crises. As far as the efficiency aspect is concerned, it can be said that credit ceilings played a very important role in directing most categories of bank towards operations almost ignored up to then. In most banks the credit function was dramatically improved. As a consequence of the ceilings, credit demand was spread over all banks, even those which were traditionally less loan-oriented. Competitive impulses were in many instances enhanced, not lessened, by administrative measures.

Nonetheless, the situation from the point of view of efficiency leaves much to be desired while at the same time the powers of the Bank of Italy are under attack by the banks. We can point out at least three reasons for this state of affairs – one pertaining to the objective of stability and the others, respectively, to the *scope* and *kind* of regulation.

First of all it is important to remember that the authorities succeeded in maintaining a fair level of stability for the system as a whole, despite two serious bank crises in 1974 and 1982. One can therefore find in the need for stability one reason why the central bank has been reluctant to see any basic change in regulation. As to the scope of regulation, it is common knowledge that innovations in new financial sectors created an area which is almost completely free from controls of any kind. There is now too wide a difference between the strict control in banking markets and the total freedom (i.e. anarchy) on 'parallel' markets. A situation dramatically similar to that described in Barclay's analysis (1978) has therefore arisen. Besides the dangers for stability, competition is clearly distorted and as long as this situation remains, the authorities have to increase the pressure on the regulated sector of the financial system to obtain, on the average, a given objective of control. This is a sort of physical law, but the obvious consequence is that the regulated sector feels that the fairness of regulation has been lost and cannot help blaming the central bank.

Secondly, as the need for a stricter control by the central bank arises, the structural regulation tools cannot be based on high doses of discretionary power and especially on discretionary authorization. In Italy, on the other hand, this is still the normal situation. Suffice it to say that the number of authorizations that the Bank of Italy issues every year on a case-by-case analysis is dramatically high. It accounts for some 20,000, 12,000 of which concern loans (limits to credit for a single customer, etc.). Notwithstanding some efforts made by the Bank of Italy, the grid of powers leans too much towards discretion rather than on rules applied on the same basis to every institution. Opening of new branches, changes in bank by-laws, loans exceeding a certain amount (from 20 to 100 per cent of net worth), and issues of securities by special credit institutions are some of the operations which still have to be approved by the authorities.

The Bank of Italy made a remarkable effort to disclose the criteria used to control bank entry, and stressed on many occasions that control on loan limits was managed from a general point of view without getting involved in the judgement about customers' creditworthiness. Nevertheless, banks felt more and more limited in their entrepreneurial freedom. Most of them – rightly or wrongly – claimed that discretion covered an unfair treatment of individual cases. In the most delicate cases concerning loans to big private and public firms, the authorization for the loan always risked becoming a sort of political guarantee by the central bank, thereby diminishing its nature as a technical measure of prudential regulation.

The stalemate in the Italian banking system (and the situation is very similar in several countries) stems from the necessity of reconciling the need for a deeper and more effective regulation with a relaxation of the burden imposed on banks so as to leave them enough freedom for their own management decisions. This objective can be achieved not through a blind flight towards deregulation, which can prove very dangerous from the point of view of stability, but through a regulation broader in scope and less based on discretion. Authorizations based on a case-by-case analysis are a relic of the past in the toolbox of central banks: structural and prudential regulation are better achieved through controls on entry based on objective criteria (Bank of Italy's 'piano sportelli' (Banca d'Italia, 1982) is a very interesting example), through balance sheet ratios, through capital adequacy measures, etc. This does not necessarily mean shifting to a 'referee' model of central banking, relying on rules instead of discretion. The point is to put boundaries on the discretion of central banks, i.e. to build a 'participative and discretionary approach' (Revell, 1982) to rules used for the objectives of regulation.

As a matter of fact, the purpose of rules is to circumscribe discretion, not to eliminate it. In Whittlesey's words (1968): 'It is important to recognize that while rules are antithetical to discretion, the inverse does not hold true:

discretion is not antithetical to rules *per se* . . . Indeed discretion not only allows rules, but presumes them.'

At the same time, the core of regulation should apply to every firm engaging in financial activity. The essential point is to place all segments of the financial system on an even footing with a view to their competing on fairer terms. When this condition is realized, the central bank can engage in the regulatory dialectic which stems automatically from regulation without the fear of generating perverse effects on competition.

Wherever, as in Italy, history and economic theory lead to the necessity of a 'director' model of central banking, the ideal situation can be synthesised as follows: a set of regulatory powers, the core of which should apply to all financial intermediaries, based on a limited number of controls, enforced in a participative and discretionary approach by the central bank.

References

Banca d'Italia (1982), 'Il piano sportelli 1982', in *Bollettino Banca d'Italia* (January–June), pp. 225–252.

Barclay, Christopher (1978), 'Competition and financial crises, past and present' in C. Barclay, E. P. M. Gardener & J. Revell, *Competition and Regulation of Banks* (Cardiff: University of Wales Press)

Dell'Amore Giordano (1967), *La Struttura delle Aziende di Credito* (Milano, Giuffre).

Edwards, F. R. (1981), 'Financial institutions and regulation in the 21st century: after the crash?'. In Albert Verheirstraeten (ed.), *Competition and Regulation in Financial Markets* (London: Macmillan).

Gardener, Edward P. M. (1978) 'Legal rules vs. vicarious participation in bank prudential regulation'. In C. Barclay, E. P. M. Gardener & J. Revell (eds), *Competition and Regulation of Banks* (Cardiff: University of Wales Press).

Gardener, Edward P. M. (1981), *Capital Adequacy and Banking Supervision* (Cardiff: University of Wales Press).

Greenbaum, Stuart I. (1967), 'Competition and efficiency in the banking system: empirical research and its policy implications', *Journal of Political Economy*, (Aug.), pp. 461–478.

Hodgman, Donald R. (1972), 'Selective credit controls', *Journal of Money, Credit and Banking*, (May), pp. 342–359.

Kane, Edward J. (1981), 'Accelerating inflation, technological innovation and the decreasing effectiveness of banking regulation', *Journal of Finance*, (May), pp. 355–357.

Maisel, Sherman J. (1981), 'Some issues in bank regulation'. In Sherman J. Maisel (ed.), *Risk and Capital Adequacy in Commercial Banks* (Chicago: University of Chicago Press).

Meltzer, Allan H. (1967), 'Major issues in the regulation of financial institutions' *Journal of Political Economy*, (Aug.), pp. 482–501.

Minsky, Hyman P. (1982), 'The financial instability hypothesis: capitalist processes and the behavior of the economy'. In Charles P. Kindleberger and Jean P. Laffargue, *Financial Crises: Theory, History and Policy* (Cambridge: Cambridge University Press).

Monti, Mario and Padoa Schioppa Tommaso (1978), 'Per un riesame del sistema creditizio italiano'. In Guido Carli (ed.), *La Struttura del Sistema Creditizio Italiano* (Bologna: Il Mulino).
Revell, Jack (1980), 'Towards a micro-economic theory of financial institutions', Conference given at the University of Modena; Italian translation in *L'Industria*, (Oct.–Dec.).
Revell, Jack (1981), 'The complementary nature of competition and regulation in the financial sector'. In Albert Verheirstraeten (ed.), *Competition and Regulation in Financial Markets* (London: Macmillan).
Revell, Jack (1982), 'Bank regulation in the United Kingdom: the past decade', City University Conference on Financial Regulation, 22–23 September. Mimeo.
Tobin, James (1967), Comment to Allan H. Meltzer, 'Major issues in the regulation of financial institutions', in *Journal of Political Economy*, (Aug.), pp. 508–509.
Whittlesey, C. R. (1968), 'Rules, discretion and central bankers'. In C. R. Whittlesey and J. S. G. Wilson (eds), *Essays in Money and Banking in Honour of R. S. Sayers* (Oxford: Clarendon Press).

10 The Complementary Nature of Competition and Regulation in the Financial Sector*

* Slightly adapted text of a paper read by Professor J. R. S. Revell to the Colloquium on *Financial Markets: Structure, Conduct and Performance* held at the Catholic University of Leuven, Belgium, 13–14 September 1979.

Reprinted with permission from the Macmillan Press published in *Competition and Regulation in Financial Markets* edited by Albert Verheirstraeten.

JACK REVELL

The Debate on Deregulation

The main theme of this paper is that competition and regulation are not alternatives to each other in the financial sector, but that a competitive financial system requires close regulation and supervision by the authorities. I decided on this theme largely because the invitation to submit papers described the Colloquium as being on the subject of '*competition versus regulation*'. This seemed to echo the current debate in the United States on the deregulation of depository institutions, and indeed there are two papers here concerned with that debate. I think there are great dangers in transposing the debate into a European context without being aware of what it is about and what it does not call into question.

A paper by Professor Franklin Edwards and James Scott in a collection of seminar papers edited by the former (Edwards, 1979) can be taken as summarising the debate. Strangely enough, although my paper is concerned to emphasise the continuing need for regulation and the other is subtitled a *perspective for deregulation*, I find myself in complete agreement with its conclusions. It was in favour of eliminating all or most restrictions on branching, the establishment of new banks, the activities permitted to depository institutions, and pricing; in the American setting, this seems admirable. It did, however, advocate the retention of some type of federal deposit insurance, together with 'a greater reliance upon balance sheet controls, especially liquidity and equity capital requirements, which we believe are adequate to maintain bank soundness' (Edwards, 1979, p. 104). There are others taking part in the debate who advocate a greater dismantling of controls, but this quotation probably reflects the balance of opinion. If that is so, there is no necessary contradiction between that position and the theme of my paper.

The answer to this apparent paradox lies in the fact that the word *regulation* covers two rather different forms of control. The first is what I shall call *structural* regulation. It is concerned with the kinds of activity permitted to different classes of institution, the conditions for establishment of new institutions and the branches of existing ones, and various controls on interest rates and charges for services (Regulation Q and state usury laws in the American context). The second form is *prudential* regulation and is concerned with balance sheet controls to ensure liquidity and solvency. It is true that many of the structural regulations originally had a prudential aspect, but I doubt whether many of them are really necessary for the soundness of the financial system. It is the structural regulation, far more than the prudential regulation, that inhibits competition.

What makes the American debate largely irrelevant to European conditions is the fact that most of the structural regulations have either been abandoned or drastically lightened in Europe over recent years. The French abandoned their compulsory split between *banques de dépôts* and *banques d'affaires* in 1966, and even the structural restraints implied in several countries by the restriction of commercial banks to short-term deposits and short-term loans are partly lifted. The need to establish an 'economic need' for a new bank or a new branch has practically disappeared in European countries, leaving professional experience and good repute as the two main criteria for the establishment of new institutions. We have never had a parallel to Regulation Q, and the only government-administered price controls that remain are on certain types of savings deposit. In several European countries even the 'cartel' agreeements on pricing have been abandoned.

There is little doubt that the American financial system has for some time been over-burdened with structural regulations, and there is a strong case for them to be dismantled. It would be a great pity, however, if the general theme of the American debate were to be used in an attempt to call into question the need for the sort of prudential regulation exercised by central banks and banking commissions in Europe. There is room for debate about the nature and form of this regulation, and I shall return to this point later. However, the abolition of this prudential regulation is not on the agenda, either in the United States or in Europe. The participants do not see competition and prudential regulation as effective alternatives.

Competition

The discussion of competition in the financial sector is nearly always confined to retail banking services, but this is only one of many markets in which banks compete. Since the war the breakdown of specialisation among credit institutions had led to commercial banks facing competition from a range of non-bank institutions such as savings banks, agricultural credit associations and credit unions, which offer much the same range of services either individually or through central organisations, which have sometimes become major international banks. The scope of the ancillary services offered by these institutions has also been extended greatly since the war, from the traditional trust and foreign exchange business into credit cards, leasing, factoring, travel services, insurance broking and computing facilities. Each market has its own margin of profitability, its own degree of competition, and its own split between retail and wholesale elements. It is thus unrealistic to single out one of the markets as the touchstone of competition especially as the opportunities for cross-subsidisation between all the markets and within many of them are very great.

The reason for concentrating the discussion on the retail banking services is clearly because that is the only part of banking business for which information can be obtained with any facility. In retail business prices are posted and the services are standardised. In the nationwide branch banking networks that are the norm in Europe both the prices and the types of service offered by different institutions tend to be very similar if not identical, and this fact is sometimes used to point to the lack of competition. This is surely a very naïve view, because identical prices can be found in both perfectly competitive and monopolistic markets; in between these two extremes identical prices may indicate either collusion or competition between a small number of large sellers. The product offered by each bank is likely to be very similar to that of its competitors because there is no means of patenting financial innovations. Naïve though it is, this view sometimes puts pressure on banks to create differences between each other just to appear competitive.

Discussing the reality of bank competition in terms only of the retail services has never been justified, and it is even less justified today with the development of wholesale banking, both domestic and international. Competition between banks for large customers has always been particularly intense, with negotiated terms for services that are designed to suit the particular needs of the customer; identical prices for standard packages of services do not apply in this sphere.

The special significance of large customers was recognised before the war by Chandler (1938), who spoke of them as having two great advantages in bargaining over terms with banks. The first was that they tended to use the services of more than one bank, a fact that is true for very large customers in the nationwide banking systems of Europe, but presumably even more so for the geographically restricted banking system of the United States. The second advantage is that they have the further alternative of raising funds in their own names on either the money market or the capital market. Quite apart from these structural advantages, the largest of the customers are often larger than the banks themselves. They are in a specially good position to play off one bank against another and to obtain the keenest terms for the banking services that they use.

Banks react to the strength of their largest customers by arriving at conventions or explicit agreements about the greatest concessions that they are collectively prepared to grant to the most-favoured customers. Agreements on maximum rates of interest payable on current accounts (demand deposits) in some European countries probably have this significance. This, at least, is suggested by the colloquial term applied to this agreed rate when, prior to 1945, the London clearing banks paid a low rate of interest on current account balances: it was known as the 'pinching rate', the maximum rate payable on current accounts 'pinched' (competed away) from other banks. Agreements on loan rates usually specify only one rate, that charged on loans to prime customers, and price leadership secures the same result in banking systems in which cartel practices have been abandoned. In other words, the answer of the banks to their powerful customers is a suspension of interbank competition and the presenting of a united front. Somewhat paradoxically, they usually leave a loophole by diverting some powerful customers to branches outside the country that are not subject to the agreements; the branches of Scottish banks in London used to fulfil this function.

At first sight, recent developments in wholesale domestic and international banking appear to contradict this explanation of some aspects of bank agreements. These new developments consist of abandoning a prime rate convention, whatever form it may take, in favour of basing loan rates on the cost of deposits, with a margin to cover expenses and profits. They may be seen as a result of pressure from the multinationals, the largest customers of all, to pay no more to the banks than the cost of the services that they buy; the multinationals have given notice that they want to secure for themselves the economies of scale accruing to the banks from operating their large accounts and no longer to subsidise smaller organisations. The same pressure to secure the full benefits of size can be seen in other spheres, notably the abandonment of fixed brokerage commissions on the New York Stock Exchange. The important point in the banking case, however, is that the switch to the determination of loan rates by the money market has not broken the united front of the banks against their largest customers. Collectively they have had to accept narrower margins (spreads) in their business with the most powerful of their customers, but there is no scope for even the largest multinational to play off one bank against the other because the money market rates are set by competition among hundreds of banks; the only bargaining issues are the size of the margin above the money market rates and the amount of fees to be paid.

Whatever may be the position in the retail market, there can be no doubt that wholesale and international banking are highly competitive. There are virtually no agreements or conventions to inhibit interbank competition, the customers have a wide choice of banks in both domestic and international business, and they can raise money in their own names. At the present moment, the doubt is whether competition has not reduced margins to the point of zero profitability in international banking, the so-called eurocredits, although this does not necessarily affect the safety of the system because most of the participants have many other lines of business from which they can make up the shortfall in profits.

One of the most important features of competition between banks, and increasingly among non-bank institutions and between them and banks, is the extent to which they attempt to secure the continued loyalty of their customers by making it worth their while to take a whole range of services from the same institution. This is the basis of the 'customer relationship' to which Hodgman (1963) drew attention. Hodgman was talking of the position of the large customers, the prime customers of the previous discussion. The main relationship that he described was the granting of loans to large depositor customers at a preferential rate of interest, with the prime rate as an irreducible minimum. The banks were able to do this because the other services that they provided for these customers were profitable, and there are two features of the range of non-standard services provided for large customers that ensure their profitability. The first is that they often depend on the skills of specialist staff, so that one bank can successfully differentiate its services from that of another bank for a considerable period. The second feature is that it is very difficult for a bank to estimate the cost structure of a service provided by a competitor and thus to compete effectively on the price for the service.

The customer relationship is not limited to large customers, and for the present purposes the way in which it applies in the *retail market* is of even greater importance. As in the case of the large customer, the *key service* is that associated with the operation of the customer's *current account*. In most European countries some interest is paid on current accounts, but it is only at the low rate of one-half per cent or one per cent on personal accounts; in countries where no interest is paid, such as the United Kingdom and Ireland, there is no law against payment. Fees and commission are charged for current account services, but there is almost no information on the extent to which these charges cover the cost of operating the payments service. In Britain, where many persons pay no commission at all, the London clearing banks claim that charges cover only twenty per cent of the overall cost of operating the service, but this is probably exceptionally low for European countries. In these circumstances, the profitability of the payments service, taken on its own, depends entirely on the rate of interest that can be earned by purchasing assets with the current account balances, and this will vary from time to time. Generally speaking, it is probably true to say that in Europe the case of the personal current account depositor is the opposite of that considered by Hodgman: the loan margin has to be increased to make good a shortfall between costs and charges on payments services.

What makes the current account so potent a weapon for tying the customer to one bank or savings bank is that the personal account holder sees access to credit when he needs it as one of the implicit benefits of holding deposits with the institution. The same is true, but to a lesser extent, of savings deposits. Unlike the large corporate customer, whose creditworthiness is established and who can obtain credit from a variety of sources, the personal customer has to build up his creditworthiness by the prudent operation of his account, and he is loath to begin this process all over again when he switches his account from one bank to another.

The competitive process, even in the most competitive of banking systems, thus has the fatal weakness of 'bundling' services and using profits on one service to compensate for losses on another. Only rarely is the pricing of services related directly to the costs of providing those services. It is arguable that the greatest increase in competition within the financial sector and the greatest increase in allocative efficiency would come about if the institutions were forced to pay market rates for all funds they attracted and to recover the full cost of each service. Over the next decade or so the introduction of *electronic funds transfer systems* (EFTS) in all developed countries will force governments to make critical decisions that will affect the extent and nature of competition in the financial sector, and we should give further consideration to the question of competition in an EFTS context.

Electronic Funds Transfer

After many official and unofficial reports and several tentative experiments, the technical features of an EFT system are reasonably clear. There will be three kinds of terminals through which access to the system is possible. *Point-of-sale terminals* will enable shoppers to pay for their purchases without the use of either currency or a cheque; in most cases the seller will be able to verify before completing the sale that the customer has sufficient funds in his account. The other two types of terminal, *automatic teller machines in public places and push-button telephones in homes*, will both give access to a customer's accounts in a number of different institutions; the former will also dispense currency. There is nothing particularly revolutionary in the last two types of terminal: automatic machines that will dispense cash, tell the customer the balance of his account, and enable him to order a new cheque book are already in place, and the telephone facility could be provided by individual institutions without much fuss or disturbance to the financial system. It is when the use of the various machines is shared by all or some institutions and when all the terminals and all the institutions are linked together in a computer network that the fun begins.

One of the factors that will determine the shape of an EFT system is the existence of *considerable economies of scale*. These are at their greatest with point-of-sale terminals, and it is almost certain that most countries will end up with one, or at the most two, networks linking these terminals to institutions. For the purposes of the present discussion, it does not matter whether the network is publicly or privately owned. In Britain the major banks and credit card companies are already discussing with the Bank of England the feasibility of a co-operative network of point-of-sale terminals. The economies of scale are not nearly so great for *automatic teller machines*, and they do not really exist at all for home telephone terminals. Since the degree of competition within the system and customer convenience will be greatly enhanced by having the automatic teller terminals linked together rather than tied to a particular bank or other institution, it seems likely that the authorities in most countries will opt for an integrated system. What could well be the worst of all possible worlds, in my opinion, would be the system of competing groups that some writers foresee. In this each group would have one dominant institution, inevitably a major bank, and minor banks and non-bank institutions would attach themselves to one or other of the competing groups. The danger here is that the dominant institution would begin to control the others, and we should lose the benefits of innovation that smaller institutions often provide.

Since only the major banks could begin to think of establishing EFTS, the key question is the ease of access to the full facilities of the system by other depository institutions. This question has been debated in the context of the United States banking system by Flannery and Jaffee (1973) and in that of the United Kingdom by Hopton (1979). The consensus seems to be that the authorities will insist that access be free to all in the interests of greater competition. We can hope that this will be so, but not all the competitive consequences of EFTS depend on equal access to the system for all kinds of financial institutions.

The first, and in many ways the most important *consequence* arises as soon as any sort of automatic access to the computer of an individual institution is provided by a terminal in a public place or in the customer's home. The consequence is that location ceases to have any competitive advantage for routine transactions. In Europe branching on a national or regional scale has been one of the most important competitive weapons, but much of the advantage of a branch network will be lost when access through computer terminals becomes widespread. The degree of competition could obviously be greater if the terminals in public places were provided co-operatively by all institutions, but many institutions at present without branches would find it much cheaper to provide their own terminals individually than to establish and man a normal branch. In very few European countries would they have to seek permission to do this. The cost of entry into full-scale deposit business would be drastically reduced.

The *second consequence* is that of instantaneous transfer of a balance from an interest-bearing account to a current account. As recent experience in the United States shows, this so erodes the differences between a demand deposit and a savings deposit that the two become one for all practical purposes. This would largely circumvent the legal prohibition of the payment of interest on demand deposits in the United States, even if the law were not abolished, and it would remove the inhibitions of banks in most European countries against paying a market rate of interest on current accounts.

The *third consequence* is that the cost of transferring money would be so much reduced that it would be easy to move over to a position of charging the customer with the full cost even when he had become accustomed to 'free' or subsidised money transfer facilities. The marginal cost of each transaction would be little above zero, and the average cost with full recovery of overheads would be much lower than with our present paper-based system.

The *fourth consequence* that seems to be envisaged by most writers on the subject is that the customer would have access to credit lines previously authorised: in European terminology, overdrafts would once again be the norm for consumer lending. Some writers take this question even further and suggest that the consumer could automatically mobilise such assets as the surrender values of his life assurance policies. One of the main points, however, is that the personal customer will no longer be so dependent on the bank manager's knowledge of his reliability through monitoring the operation of his current account; his creditworthiness will depend far more on credit-scoring devices that give marks for such factors as his income and its assured continuance, his ownership of a house, and his possession of a telephone. The link between a current account and access to credit will be severed, and the consumer will be able to maintain his interest-bearing transactions-cum-savings account with one institution and borrow from one or more others.

No doubt, the authorities in each country could *prevent* most of these consequences of an EFT system or they could permit the dominant banking institutions to deny equal access to all deposit institutions. Even if they sought to do this, the possibility of each customer having automatic access at all hours to his account with an individual institution, which the authorities probably could not deny him, would open the door quite wide to a more competitive system. What is certain is that the authorities must shortly make up their minds what sort of deposit and credit system they want to see developing. There must undoubtedly be a long transition period, but the decisions on the ultimate shape of the system must be taken fairly soon, and they must be taken with all the technical possibilities in mind. These possibilities add up to a system in which each deposit is rewarded at a market rate of interest and each loan and service is charged at full cost and one in which the customer has the possibility of selecting a different institution for each service.

The consequences of EFTS in the retail banking market therefore provide the possibility of a fully competitive system, but they need not necessarily have the same effect in the *market for corporate financial services.* This *is already a competitive system* because prime customers have access to the services of many different banks and alternative sources of funds and because same-day transfers of funds enable them to blur the distinction between interest-bearing assets and current accounts. In the market for large customers, large banks will always have the competitive edge, and it is arguable that the safety of the financial system is best secured if large customers and large banks are paired-off in this way.

Cycles, Crises and Agreements

So far the discussion has been entirely about competition, but now the time has come to introduce the second theme of regulation. The line of argument will be that aggressive competition in the financial sector tends to lead to financial crises, and that the motivation behind the agreements into which banks and other deposit institutions enter is *as much the avoidance of risky business as the securing of abnormal profits.* The link between agreements and regulation is that the suspension of interbank competition implied by the agreements was a primitive form of self-regulation, designed to preserve the safety of the financial system and the continued existence of established institutions. In the course of the discussion we shall have to survey briefly the significance of the recent literature on the subject of financial crises associated with the names of *Minsky* and *Kindleberger.*

Over the past few years the subject of financial crises has begun to arouse interest in academic circles, following three severe crises or near-crises in 1966, 1969–70 and 1973–5. Minsky (1975, 1977) has long been arguing that the financial system of the United States shows a condition of 'systematic fragility', and the evidence that he adduces could be paralleled in most industrialised countries. The weakness of his argument, which was seized on by participants in a conference on financial crises held in 1976 (Altman & Sametz, 1977), is that he has no empirical backing for his statements. Essentially, the only evidence that he brings forward is a comparison of a few financial ratios for different sectors of the economy over the period from 1950 to 1974, showing how the position has deteriorated. This is not proof of a dangerous position at the present time because the economy of 1950 was full of wartime liquidity. We are not told at what point or over which years the economy passed from its 1950 state of 'robustness' to its present state of 'fragility'; in other words, there is no definition of either state. The acceleration in the rate of inflation must surely be an important indicator although it does not figure in Minsky's argument. I have a strong 'gut feeling' that Minsky is right, and I shall revert to this question towards the end of the paper with a suggestion on the methods that might be employed to verify his contention.

Minsky's interest is largely in the postwar period, but other writers have been driven to explore the lessons to be gained from history by going back over the important financial crises of the past, starting in the seventeenth century. Kindleberger (1978) is undoubtedly the most eminent of these, and he concludes his study with an analysis of the lessons to be drawn from history. For our immediate purposes an especially interesting study is that made by *Barclay* (1978), in which he compared nineteenth-century financial crises in Britain with our *fringe banking crisis of 1973 and 1974.* In the course of this comparison he developed a model of the way in which pockets of excess profitability attracted new entrants to an industry, reducing the level of profits down to a more normal level and often below the level that was necessary for the continuance of the enlarged number of firms in the industry. It is, if you like, a cobweb theorem model. It applies particularly to banking because it is an industry that can be entered most easily unless government regulation inhibits entry, a state of affairs that did not apply in the nineteenth century.

This model of the banking industry can be developed to show that the increase in competition led in almost all instances to the growth of bad banking practices. What makes such practices very likely is that retribution for bad banking does not follow immediately; it is delayed until the next financial crisis, which may be sparked-off by some almost fortuitous event, although it is unlikely to occur until the banking system is in a state of what Minsky would describe as fragility. The losses and failures resulting from bad banking are not spread evenly over time but are bunched. Before this crisis arrives, the profit advantage will lie with the aggressive banks that indulge in unsound and speculative practices, and the established banks will be drawn into bad banking in order to rescue their profitability. This results in a kind of Gresham's law of banking, in which bad banking drives out good banking.

At a more analytical level we can identify the *particular features of a boom period that will draw banks into unsound practices.* The general price-level is rising and the prices of equities and properties rise with it, so that capital gain looms much larger in financial calculations. Not only do banks themselves indulge in speculation on rising price-levels but they also issue loans that can be serviced only if the price of the borrower's output rises continually. During a boom period the yield curve is usually tilted, so that the financing of long-term assets with short-term deposits offers the prospect of high profits. The importance of these features is magnified when, as in the postwar period, a rising trend of inflation is superimposed on the business cycle.

The implication of the bunching of banking losses at times of financial crisis is that risk is not some immutable factor associated with a particular type of banking asset. Risk varies over time, and in general we can say that the probability of loss increases with every year that has passed since the last crisis. The behaviour of bankers completely ignores this factor. Since the provisions for loan losses and the general need for a risk cushion in the form of shareholders' funds are usually assessed by the averaging of losses over the immediate past, the amount of safety usually declines once the next cycle is well under way. This factor is reinforced by a fast rate of growth of assets that usually outstrips the rate of growth in safety resources and by a growing feeling of euphoria as speculation continues to be rewarded with profits.

This analysis, bald though it has to be for reasons of space, *provides justification for associating a high degree of competition with a high degree of risk* in banking. The next step in the argument is one that cannot be documented to any great extent. It consists of the hypothesis that one of the reactions of established banks, which had by definition survived one or two financial crises, was to resist the continuance of this cyclical process, in which increased risk and increased competition went hand in hand, by banding together to restrain interbank competition. The history of the interbank agreements that we have come to call 'cartels' has not been investigated in any country that I know of, although I hope to find some material in due course. In the meantime, I can only indicate why I think it likely that one of the main motives behind these cartels was self-regulation to make the banking industry safer. For this to be true it is not necessary to pretend that bankers are angels who never use their cartels to their own profitable advantage; all that need be done is to demonstrate that the self-advantage sought through cartels was partly the increased safety of the banking system.

I must admit that the indications are rather flimsy, but fortunately the hypothesis, interesting and useful though it is, is not essential to the general theme of this paper. The first indication is the extent to which the phrase 'excessive competition' crops up whenever restrictive measures are being considered and the way in which it is explicitly linked with risk. An obvious example is the avowed reason for the prohibition of the payment of interest on demand deposits in the United States. It was held that competition between banks over the rate to be paid on these deposits would lead them to invest in more risky assets. The fact that Cox (1966) found that the empirical evidence contradicted the 'risky assets' argument is largely irrelevant: it is what bankers 'believe to be true' that matters. The second indication is that at the time when these agreements were coming into existence large banks were acting in another way to improve the safety of the system, by acting as informal lenders of last resort to smaller banks. This was especially true of the hierarchical banking structure of the United States between 1863 and 1913. This at least demonstrates some concern with aspects of safety.

The *step from primitive self-regulation* through the suspension of interbank competition *to regulation by the authorities* was a necessary one as soon as it was demonstrated that self-regulation could break down. This point was not reached in most countries until the nineteen-thirties. The weakness of the cartel policing of the banking system was that there was no means of enforcing membership of the association maintaining the cartel, although the authorities in one or two countries stepped in to make membership a legal requirement. In general, it is significant that the various cartel agreements were continued with official blessing after the tightening of regulation in the nineteen-thirties; it was not until the widespread moves to increase competition in the financial system between 1966 and 1971 that many of them were disbanded or modified.

Recent Events

The changes in the regulatory environment that took place in Europe some ten or twelve years ago form an important link in the argument. They were designed to increase competition between banks and between different sorts of credit institution, but the significant fact is that they were followed within a very few years by the most dangerous financial crisis since the war. Competition was certainly not an adequate substitute for regulation in this instance.

These measures were nearly all structural. They did away with restrictions on branching and legally-enforced specialisation of types of institution, such as that between deposit banking and investment banking in France. In the case of the United Kingdom, the 'Competition and Credit Control' reform of 1971 changed the method of applying monetary policy regulations on banks, moving from credit ceilings to controls over a reserve assets base. In many ways the most important feature was that the new controls applied to all recognised banks instead of only to clearing banks, thus seeking to bring under official control the largely separate group of wholesale banks that had grown up during the previous decade. In some countries, including the United Kingdom, the cartels were abandoned as a result of pressure from the authorities, and the banks were set free to compete as vigorously as possible. By contrast, no changes were made in the forms and content of prudential regulation.

There is one point that makes an interesting sidelight to the discussion. *This is the suggestion that the authorities in many countries thought that competition would drive out bad banking and destroy the fringe operators.* Many of the measures were designed to remove fetters on the largest banks, and it was thought that they would be so successful that the fringe would not survive. If this is so, I do not think that I favour the use of competition to bolster the strong against the weak in this way. Big may be beautiful and big banks may be safer, but the innovations usually come from the smaller institutions, which would suffer along with the fringe. A jungle in which only the most powerful can survive is not what I understand by a competitive banking system. In any case, it did not work out that way.

What followed in late 1973 and throughout 1974 has been well documented, but there are some points that need clarifying. The first is the nature of the bad banking that led to banks in all countries failing or having to be rescued from failure by the authorities. Although much publicity has been given to losses in foreign exchange dealings, they were rarely the fundamental cause of failure. The foreign exchange market after the Smithsonian agreement was certainly a dangerous place for operators who had consistently produced good profits for their banks in the days of fixed exchange rates, when the official reserves absorbed all losses and when the only question was not whether one could make a profit but how much. As recognised profit centres the foreign exchange departments of banks were expected to produce equally good results under the regime of floating exchange rates. It is no wonder that some were led to plunge even more heavily after initial losses and that some did so for their own profit rather than for that of the bank. Even when the failure of a bank appeared to be caused by foreign exchange losses, however, closer inspection reveals that the bank was led into greater speculation on the exchanges in an attempt to recoup losses made on domestic banking. This was certainly true of both Herstatt and Franklin National.

The *pattern of bad banking* can be seen mostly clearly in the fringe banking crisis of 1973 and 1974 in Britain because many banks got into difficulties at the same time or soon after one another and because the pattern of unsound practices was consistent. On the liabilities side the banks relied on short-term deposits, drawn either from the inter-bank market or from retail operations, and they invested the funds in either longer-term loans or in speculative ventures that yielded no immediate income so that the interest due had constantly to be added to the principal – Ponzi finance. Much of the lending was to property companies, many of which were linked to the bank in common ownership. In addition to these general examples of unsound and speculative banking there were, of course, many cases of straightforward fraud and embezzlement.

The *disturbing feature* of this period of British banking was that these dubious operators were given every encouragement by the established banks; they could raise deposits on the interbank market by paying a premium of no more than one-quarter per cent over the rate paid by banks with first-class names, and the major banks helped to finance them. Such was the euphoria of the period that hardly anybody saw the dangers, and the explanation may well be that those in charge of banks had not had any personal experience of the last major financial crisis, that of the nineteen-thirties. The period of euphoria came to an abrupt end with the acceleration in the pace of inflation, the freezing of the property market, and the drop in equity prices. After the first hint of the failure of a bank (one must remember that Britain had not had a real bank failure since the late nineteenth century), the inter-bank market dried up, and only a handful of banks with first-class names were able to raise deposits at any price. The remainder of the story, particularly the Lifeboat operation of the Bank of England, is well known.

This particular episode in the history of banking had many features that were *peculiar to Britain*. Banks were free to establish themselves with a minimum of interference and to continue in their business with a bare minimum of supervision by the authorities; the Bank of England concentrated its supervisory function on those established banks to which it had given various recognitions, and it had no responsibility for the 'fringe'. These features may explain why all these fringe banks got into trouble at much the same time and also why no major bank was in trouble, but they cannot explain why much the same sort of bad banking was to be found in nearly every country at the same time.

In looking at the descriptions of the types of domestic business that was conducted by the banks that failed in European countries and the United States in 1974 and 1975 I am struck by the *similarities* to the business of the fringe banks in Britain. In nearly every case there was, for example, some connection with the property market, whether it was the involvement of American banks with real estate investment trusts or the links between small German banks and the property companies. The fact is that this phenomenon of bad banking was worldwide and it existed in countries where the prudential regulation of banks was exceedingly tight as much as it did in the permissive regulatory climate of the United Kingdom. There must be some common reasons, and the elucidation of these is essential to the argument.

The two main reasons have already been mentioned, and they are linked together. The first reason, to my mind, was *the move towards relaxation of structural controls* over banks with a view to making the banking system more competitive. I would not claim that this, by itself, could explain everything. It was rather the association of these relaxations of control with the *acceleration of inflation and the general euphoria that accompanied it*. Had the moves towards greater competition taken place at a time of general stability in the financial system, there would probably have been no ill effects, but the combination of greater competition with inflation and euphoria was lethal. Since any prudent man at the present time must reckon with the continuance of inflation, we must take heed of this lesson in deciding how much more competition the financial sector can stand in the immediate future.

To my own satisfaction at least, I have demonstrated the close connexion between competition and risk, but there remains one weak link in my argument. The regulatory changes of the period from 1966 to 1971 did not extend to a formal relaxation of the prudential aspects of control. My thesis requires me to show that increased competition in the financial system should be accompanied by increased prudential regulation, and yet during the early part of this decade even the tightest systems of prudential control in some countries were unable to prevent the unsound and unsafe banking practices that were associated with the fringe in all countries, a fringe that grew as much by the changes in the management teams of established institutions (Herstatt was established in 1720) as by the influx of new banks. Competition may not be able to ensure a sound banking system, but it is no use relying on increased prudential regulation if that too is impotent.

Part of the prevalence of bad banking even in countries with tight regulatory systems can be ascribed to the fact that the feeling of euphoria was general. All regulatory systems, even those most hedged around with compulsory ratios and formal rules, leave a lot to the discretion of the supervisors; if they are also infected with the general euphoria, they will not act to stop unsound practices that are not covered in the rules. That consideration gets me off the hook to some extent, but it leaves open the question of what sort of prudential regulation can cope with the quick structural changes and the further increases in competition envisaged in earlier sections in this paper. This is the question to which we must now turn our attention.

Forms of Prudential Regulation

A useful point at which to begin is the consideration of the *purposes* that a system of regulation of the financial sector ought to serve from the point of view of society. The supreme purpose is the safety of the financial system. The working of the system depends so completely on public confidence in the ability and willingness of institutions to carry out the contracts into which they have entered that the authorities must always seek to prevent failures and to contain the effects of those failures that are inevitable. As this formulation implies, it is impossible (and probably undesirable) to ensure complete safety, and the problem reduces itself to a series of trade-offs between safety and a number of other factors, the safety of the system remaining the paramount concern.

A number of other considerations, such as consumer interests in privacy, the prevention of conflicts of interest, and so on, enter the picture, but there are three main factors that must be balanced against safety:

1 The cost of intermediation.
2 The allocative efficiency of the financial system.
3 The ability of the system to sustain strong measures of monetary policy.

A greater degree of competition is likely to lower the cost of intermediation and to improve the allocative efficiency of the system, but it may well be at the cost of safety if institutions are not prevented from indulging in speculative and unsound banking practices. On the other hand, safety works in the same direction as the ability of institutions to sustain strong measures by the authorities in the interests of macro-economic policy: the sounder the balance sheet structures of banks and other credit institutions the greater is the power of the authorities to impose and sustain such measures until they begin to bite, and conversely, the weaker the balance sheets the sooner such measures will have to be reversed. This point has been made forcefully by Gardener (1978, p. 32).

In Europe there are as many different systems of regulation as there are countries, and none of them has much similarity to the systems used by the four or five federal agencies and fifty-odd state supervisory bodies in the United States. Not surprisingly, the United Kingdom stands out as being completely different from everybody else, although it is being forced to move in the direction of uniformity.

Until recently there was not even a legal definition of a bank in the United Kingdom, and we had to content ourselves with the circular definition that a bank did banking business and that banking business was what a bank did. In practice, a large part of the banking population was defined by various recognitions and privileges granted by the Bank of England and government departments, each for a different purpose. Only those banks that derived their recognition or privileges from the Bank of England were subject to anything approaching a rigorous system of supervision for prudential purposes. The combination of the fringe banking crisis and the pressures arising out of our membership of the EEC have changed all that, and since April 1979 we have a Banking Act. This provides for many of the things covered in the banking laws of other countries, in particular for the licensing of banks. In keeping with British tradition, however, it manages to separate them firmly into two classes, the gentlemen and the others; the gentlemen, defined as those recognised as banks by the Bank of England, are exempt from licensing, leaving only the other 'deposit-taking institutions' with the requirement to obtain a licence.

It is in the system of prudential regulation and supervision that the United Kingdom differs most from other countries because there is no specification of ratios or norms. Supervision is conducted without any published framework or description of what constitutes prudent banking. The Bank of England is gradually moving towards a system of indicating in general terms the criteria on which it bases its judgements, and it may even specify certain ratios at which it will look. The important point is that it shows no inclination to lay down acceptable levels for these ratios, stating that each bank is different and must be treated differently. This is a very flexible system, far too flexible for the taste of many others in Europe, and one that appears to run foul of the EEC passion for 'transparency'.

By contrast other European countries, whether or not they are members of the EEC, have a banking law that covers the conditions of entry into the banking market and contains a number of separate provisions on such items as participations in other credit institutions and in non-financial companies, the role of bank auditors, mergers, and a host of others, most of which come within the earlier definition of 'structural' rather than being purely prudential. The balance sheet controls almost always specify liquidity and solvency ratios. The solvency ratios are usually applied to all banks irrespective of the business that they do, but The Netherlands and Belgium work towards an overall solvency ratio for each bank by means of capital requirements against different classes of asset. The liquidity ratios tend to be somewhat more complicated. The German system is of particular interest since it formed the basis of the ill-fated EEC draft directive of 1972. It attempts to limit the degree of maturity transformation by banks through stating what proportion of each type of deposit may support long-term and short-term assets.

These European systems, based on strict legal requirements, appear to be in stark contrast to the British system, which gives almost unfettered discretion to the Bank of England. The difference between them, although great, is not in practice quite so great as it appears. All supervisory systems must give some discretion to the supervisors to deal with points not covered by the regulations and to decide how vigorously to pursue infringements of the rules. Particularly in recent years, many have turned a blind eye to capital ratios that had fallen below the stated minimum as a result of inflation. Gentlemen's agreements are not ruled out either; The Netherlands Bank managed to bring a new set of regulations into force by this means several years before Parliament could find the time to pass the enabling law. As we have seen, even the British system is moving slightly towards a more formal framework, although the Bank of England will fight hard to maintain the flexibility of the present system.

In the conditions of the early nineteen-seventies the British system failed to prevent the fringe banking crisis, but the more formal regulatory systems of the United States and Europe also failed to prevent bank insolvencies. The failure of the British system lay in the fact that most of the dubious operators escaped supervision of any kind, but the parallel failure of the other systems must have lain in the nature of the supervision. If we are to rely on regulation to permit a greater degree of competition in the financial sector, it is important to analyse the weaknesses and to suggest a more effective system.

With the sole exceptions of the British systems and some American systems, the supervisory and regulatory systems of all countries rely on a number of rules of thumb. As we have seen, these may be simple ratios, applied across the board to all institutions, or they may be based on elaborate breakdowns of the asset and liability structure of each institution. However elaborate they may be, the numbers applied to the ratios or to the capital coefficients are arbitrary, and they are usually drawn from the practice of institutions at the time when the regulations were formulated, often many years in the past. One of the main lessons to be drawn from the experience of accelerating inflation in recent years is that the rules of thumb that have served the managements of financial institutions in place of a more theoretical approach have begun to break down, in many cases completely. Regulatory systems based on such rules of thumb are also liable to break down.

Linked with this point is the fact that all present supervisory systems are much more concerned with what has happened in the immediate past *than with what is likely to happen in the months or years ahead.* The figures that are inspected are drawn from a balance sheet that is already several months out of date. The only *forward-looking elements* occur in those systems, like many in the United States, in which loans in the current portfolio that carry the seeds of trouble are identified and assessed for risk. Earlier on I made the point that risk is not an immutable attribute of a particular asset or class of assets, but varies with time; losses are bunched, so that historical experience is of limited use.

I believe that there is a *new approach* to supervision that can overcome this reliance on historical experience. This is based on *computer simulation*, and we are carrying out research in the Institute of European Finance to see how this instrument can best be applied to the problems of supervision. The approach that we are exploring goes one stage back, and focuses attention on the use of computer simulation by individual banks to assess the risks involved in projected plans; the role of the supervisor is then to conduct a *risk audit*, to satisfy himself that the bank has adequately assessed and can cover from its capital resources the risks inherent in its operations over the next year or so.

The sort of simulation that we have in mind is mechanical simulation of the effects of certain *hypothetical circumstances* (abrupt and severe changes in interest rates, exchange rates, equity prices, and the rate of inflation, for instance) and not simulation within the framework of an econometric model of the financial sector. The use of an econometric model, which is built up from the observed relationships between certain financial magnitudes over the recent past, would be merely the importation of historical experience through the back door. The first suggestion for the use of computer simulation in bank regulation was made by Vojta (1973), but his was only a halfway house towards the system that we are suggesting; the main element in the assessment of capital adequacy by simulation was historical loss experience.

Such an approach is not without its problems, quite apart from the need to gain acceptance for a major innovation. *The main problem is to determine the severity of the hypothetical tests* to which a bank is to be subject. Computer simulation offers the possibility of simulating the conditions necessary for a bank to become insolvent – testing to destruction – without causing any damage to the bank and without alerting the market to its weaknesses, but it would be pointless to do this. It can be assumed that as soon as the banking system gets into general difficulties or threatens to do so, the central bank will intervene as lender of last resort, and requiring banks to cover all eventualities would raise the cost of intermediation to an unwarranted level. The level of safety to be maintained must be a matter of judgement by the regulatory authorities. Unfortunately, this may well upset the EEC, whose doctrine of 'transparency' requires that the rules of the game must always be specified in detail and must be the same for everybody.

The *second problem* is suggested by the mention of the market in the previous paragraph. *The more sophisticated the method of supervision becomes the less can the market make its own assessment of the safety of different banks.* The supervisors will be working with information that is not available to the market; indeed, the availability of more detailed information to the supervisors is perhaps the strongest justification for superimposing a public system of regulation on top of the policing conducted by the market. Although the safety of the system may come to depend entirely on the risk audit of the supervisors, some provision must be made for the market to receive sufficient information for it to make a reasonable assessment of banking risk.

There are two other points to be made on regulation. The first is that supervision of a bank or other credit institution is almost exactly parallel to the process by which that institution assesses the creditworthiness of its customers, and the *application of computer simulation to credit analysis* is another subject which we are researching. The relevance of this point to the present paper is that the parallel can also be extended to the analysis of financial *robustness* or *fragility* in the financial system as a whole by subjecting the sector balance sheets to the same sort of extreme hypothetical conditions as in the bank simulations. This offers a way in which Minsky's hypotheses can be tested.

The second point concerns *deposit insurance,* which is being adopted in many European countries. Deposit insurance contains a double moral hazard; an insured institution may adopt less prudent methods because its operations are covered by insurance, and depositors may cease to discriminate between institutions when deciding where to place their money. The first point leads to the conclusion, brought out in the seminar papers edited by Edwards (1979), that the insuring body, whether it be public or private, will always try to control the risk by regulating the activities of banks. In any case, the established banks, which contribute the greater part of the insurance fund, always insist on the regulation of the weaker brethren. The main significance of deposit insurance, to my mind, is that it inevitably entails regulation; it is far from being a substitute for supervision. The other significance is that deposit insurance is a method of preventing runs on banks and not primarily a means of compensating the depositors of banks that fail. The moral hazard of lack of care on the part of small depositors must be accepted, and it is pointless to give less than full compensation. In the new British system depositors of liquidated banks receive only three-quarters of the first £10,000 of their sterling deposits, and this is surely a sufficient danger for a small depositor to continue to worry about the safety of his deposit and to create the conditions for a run at the slightest hint of trouble.

Conclusion

This Colloquium comes some five years after the most serious financial difficulties experienced by Western countries since the nineteen-thirties. These difficulties followed by a few years the relaxation of structural regulation in many countries and were probably caused in part by the encouragement of competition in the financial sector that promoted the relaxations. The real culprit was inflation, and we must expect the continuance of inflation for some years to come – unless we get a full-scale depression. The existing systems of bank regulation were powerless to prevent the unsound banking practices that precipitated the crisis of 1973–5.

I have argued that the development of electronic funds transfer systems gives us the opportunity to create a much more competitive financial sector. If this is not to lead to even greater financial crises after a brief period of free for all, our methods of regulation must be revised so that they are flexible enough to cope with rapid innovation and to monitor the risk exposure of financial institutions.

References

Altman, E. I. & Sametz, A. W. (eds) (1977), *Financial Crises: Institutions and Markets in a Fragile Environment* (New York: Wiley-Interscience).

Barclay, C. R. (1978), 'Competition and financial crises – past and present'. In Revell, *Competition and Regulation of Banks*, Bangor Occasional Papers in Economics No. 14 (Cardiff: University of Wales Press).

Chandler, L. V. (1938), 'Monopolistic elements in commercial banking', *Journal of Political Economy*, vol. 46, no. 1, pp. 1–22.

Cox, A. M. Jr. (1966), 'Regulation of interest on demand deposits', *Michigan Business Studies*, vol. XVII, no. 4.

Edwards, F. P. (ed.) (1979), *Issues in Financial Regulation*)New York: McGraw-Hill).
Flannery, M. J. & Jaffee, D. M. (1973), *The Economic Implications of an Electronic Monetary Transfer System* (Lexington, Mass.: Lexington Books).
Gardener, E. P. M. (1978), 'The philosophy of capital adequacy'. In J. Revell, *Competition and Regulation of Banks*, Bangor Occasional Papers in Economics No. 14 (Cardiff: University of Wales Press).
Hodgman, D. R. (1963), *Commercial Bank Loan and Investment Policy* (Champaign, Ill.: University of Illinois).
Hopton, D. (1979), *Electronic Fund Transfer Systems: the Issues and Implications*, Bangor Occasional Papers in Economics No. 17 (Cardiff: University of Wales Press).
Kindleberger, C. P. (1978), *Manias, Panics and Crashes* (New York: Basic Books; London: Macmillan).
Minsky, H. P. (1975), 'Financial resources in a fragile financial environment', *Challenge*, (July–Aug.), pp. 6–13.
Minsky, H. P. (1977), 'A theory of systematic fragility.' In Altman & Sametz (eds), *Financial Crises: Institutions and Markets in a Fragile Environment* (New York: Wiley-Interscience).
Revell J. (ed.) (1978), *Competition and Regulation of Banks*, Bangor Occasional Papers in Economics No. 14 (Cardiff: University of Wales Press).
Vojta, G. J. (1973), *Bank Capital Adequacy* (New York: First National City Bank), (privately circulated).

11 International Banking: Regulation and Support Issues

DUDLEY J. PEAKE

University College of North Wales, Bangor, Gwynedd

Background

Introduction

The debate over the need for controls over international bank lending has recently been heightened by the dramatic events in the international banking system. The possibility of the collapse of banks, following a major country default or declaration of a moratorium associated with the debt burden problem, has raised the question of whether governments should intervene in the international banking system to solve these short-term financial problems and in future provide a more comprehensive regulatory system. It is argued that banks may be unable and unwilling to provide the scale of finance needed to accommodate the repayment of the existing debt of many developing countries. Also the growing awareness of the interdependence of banks, the apparent generalization of the banking crisis, and the consequent macro-economic problems in the international economy have focused attention on the need for more comprehensive adjustment and financing solutions. Following the collapse of several banks in the early 1970s several initiatives were introduced which attempted to provide a framework for supervisory, regulation and support facilities. Some believe that this gradual and essentially market-orientated approach is sufficient and provides the only practical basis for controlling the international banking system which is complex, diverse, and subject to different legal, institutional and other aspects. Others believe that controls are unnecessary and would advocate relying on the inherent competitive and innovating nature of the market to remedy any problems that emerge.

The following discussion seeks to explore these issues by initially providing a brief outline of international bank lending and its growing importance in international finance. This is followed by a review of the response by international banks to the failure of several banks and the evolution of regulation throughout the 1970s. Finally, the effectiveness of this supervisory framework is then examined against the events of the early

1980s. Firstly, an attempt is made to examine the implications arising from the collapse of the Banco Ambrosiano for the future regulation and supervision of international bank lending. Secondly, the reaction of the international banking system to the debt refinancing problem of developing countries is evaluated. Various proposals for averting future crises are outlined.

Growth and importance of international bank lending

The gross outstanding international bank lending at the end of 1982 was $1,686 billion ($1,020 billion net) a 11.5 per cent increase compared with 1981. Over the period 1973 to end 1982 gross lending increased from $290 billion to $1,686 billion (net $155 billion to $1,020 billion) equal to a sixfold increase. Between 1976 and 1981 the average growth rate was over 20 per cent (Bank of International Settlements, 1983, p. 110). The eurocurrency market sector of international bank lending permits banks to undertake transactions in foreign currencies outside the country of origin. The crucial factor in the rapid growth of the market has been the efficiency, innovation and competitiveness inherent in the market. This has been induced to a significant extent by the asymmetry of regulatory controls over the bank deposit and loan market in the eurocurrency business compared with domestic business (Johnson, 1983). Foreign currency deposits are obtained by banks from primary non-bank sources but mainly through the inter-bank market which provides the market with its liquidity (Bank of England, 1981). Medium-term lending is undertaken on a syndicated basis with many banks participating in substantial loans which provides the market with the ability to diversify its risks and loan portfolio (Bank of England, 1980). Newly announced medium-term credits equalled $82 billion in 1981 and $90 billion in 1982 (Bank of England, 1983). Loans are made on a roll-over basis and the terms of the loan are related to LIBOR market rates. Margins above LIBOR, together with front end management fees, provide the profit for banks.

The advantage of the market to the borrowers is that they obtain large speedily arranged loans closely related to market rates. Moreover, the loans are unconditional and often directly usable for balance of payments financing rather than for beneficial domestic investment opportunities which would enable countries to service and repay loans in the future. This was particularly the case when the eurocurrency market undertook the crucial intermediation role in the recycling of oil revenues to deficit countries following the oil price shock to the system in the early 1970s (Bank of International Settlements, 1983). The problems within the world economy caused by more volatile exchange rates and interest rates together with the adjustment and financing problems following the increases in the price of oil all contributed to increase uncertainty and risk in international bank operations. Moreover, this critical financing role of the market integrated the eurocurrency market into the wider financing and adjustment aspects of the international monetary system. The eurocredit market also allowed many developing countries to borrow in order to strengthen their foreign currency reserves and finance external deficits and avoid the need for adjustment policies.

The roll-over market-related rates, which lead to adjustment of rates at the end of the usual six months period, have increased the costs of borrowing during the recent period of high interest rates and created uncertainty in the assessment of a country's ability to repay over the maturity of the loan. The consequent build up of substantial debt and repayment problems is the main cause of the rescheduling and current problems confronting the international banking and monetary system in the early 1980s. In particular the exposure of many banks to a small number of large borrowers such as Mexico, Brazil, and Argentina in Latin America highlights the dilemma facing banks.

Rationale for controls

The rapid growth of the eurocurrency market and its significance and integration into the international banking and monetary system have promoted several arguments justifying the need for imposing government and international controls over the market (Dean & Giddy, 1981). One such argument examines the fundamental issue whether the eurocurrency market has an inherent ability to create credit which could lead to an uncontrolled liquidity expansion, thus facilitating capital flows and speculation. As well as destabilizing the international monetary system it is claimed that such liquidity induces inflationary financing and frustrates attempts to control domestic monetary targets. These arguments have been the subject of extensive discussion and remain largely unresolved (Johnson, 1983, Ch. 9).

Another area of discussion attempting to justify controlling the eurocurrency market focuses on the inherent risks involved in international bank lending and the nature of the syndicated roll-over eurocredit market. Banks operating in the market are subject to a highly competitive and innovating environment which requires a flexible and responsive management. The integrated nature of the market may also inhibit portfolio and management strategies of individual banks. In particular its dependence on the wholesale inter-bank structure to sustain its liquidity and participation in loans can restrict its general strategy in times of uncertainty and tight money situations. Generalization of liquidity problems in the market may be caused by the interdependence and linkages in the system arising from the significance of the inter-bank market in provision of liquidity for eurobanks. A further concern relates to the institutional risks involved in inter-bank lending arising from the assessment of liquidity and solvency positions of other banks. This is made more complex and potentially increases risk when banks of different countries have inter-bank lines of credit with each other in the market. Such lending needs to be incorporated into country risk exposure through improved monitoring by banks. Also the narrowness of spreads and maturity structure provide potential further solvency and prudential problems.

Creditworthiness assessment by banks of sovereign lending involves wide ranging analysis requiring judgements on crucial economic indicators and political factors (Angelini, Eng & Lees, 1972). The possibility of default of sovereign loans and the substantial debt-financing involvement by banks have recently been the crucial issues underlying the concern over the ability of banks to avoid collapse. The implications of such a development for the whole banking system, together with the threat to the wider international economy, have led to renewed pressure for regulatory, supervisory and lender of last resort facilities in the market. It is argued that governments together with international institutions should initially support commercial banks to overcome the immediate global financing problems, and to prevent such international banking problems emerging again in the future they should institute wide-ranging uniform controls over the eurocurrency system (Dean & Giddy, 1981).

Evolution of regulation

The realization by banking authorities and governments that operations of eurobanks needed greater co-operation and co-ordination, based on the introduction of agreed supervisory and regulation principles, was prompted by the events following the failure of the Herstatt and Franklin banks in the early 1970s (Brown, 1980; Dean & Giddy, 1981). Thus the emergence and evolution of greater co-ordination in the international banking system were in response to the repercussions following the collapse of individual banks rather than an acceptance of the above arguments advocating controls which accompanied the growth of the eurocurrency markets from the early 1960s. This new initiative and positive response by the banking system were in essence an attempt to appraise the problems and implications arising from the bank failures and to co-ordinate information, improve understanding and formulate principles and guidelines for future prudential developments in the system.

Response to Crisis

Prior to the collapse of the Herstatt Bank in June 1974 followed by failure of the Franklin National Bank in October 1974, there were no initiatives being contemplated within the international banking system to establish prudential supervision guidelines over the market. Such matters were thought to be only necessary and practical within national banking systems. The earlier attempts by the EEC initiatives for co-ordination of supervision of banking were primarily aimed at harmonization of its banking law and thereby provided a basis for an integrated banking system as part of the wider monetary unification with the Community (Brown, 1980). However, the impact of these bank failures was far-reaching and had an immediate effect on the attitudes of banks and authorities to the need for co-ordination and controls in the future evolution of the international banking system. Precedents established following the banking failures provided a framework for examining the shortcomings of the eurocurrency system and guidelines for a future regulatory approach.

The Herstatt Bank closure by the German authorities in June 1974, following bank losses in foreign exchange dealings, without any attempt to accept responsibility for the substantial losses incurred by numerous other international banks, clearly demonstrated the system's vulnerability to widespread effects from the failure of a single national bank. The critical issue was the inability of the Herstatt Bank to complete foreign exchange transactions with other banks. The impact of these events raised the question of the need for clarification of central bank responsibility and suggested that bank transactions with each other required a more formal framework and perhaps restrictive criteria. The latter issue was highlighted by banks reappraising their interbank lines of credit and tighter market conditions.

The closure of the Franklin National Bank in the US in October 1974 offered different but nevertheless significant lessons for the international banking system (Dean & Giddy, 1981). The combination of bad management of domestic and international activities and over-ambitious expansion led to the eventual collapse of this large bank. Concern over a period of months had increased the pressure on the Franklin Bank's operations in both domestic and international banking sectors. This was offset by continual and substantial support from the Federal Reserve Bank to prevent the problem spreading throughout the eurocurrency market. In addition to this acceptance of its responsibility to the Franklin Bank to provide support facilities, the Federal Reserve guaranteed the immediate foreign exchange commitments of the Franklin Bank following its collapse. On this occasion, in contrast to the Herstatt collapse, a central bank acknowledged its role in supporting the domestic bank and indirectly its wider role in stabilizing the international system.

These events of the early 1970s highlighted the lack of general agreement on the responsibilities of central banks and parent banks. While the response to each collapse was different perhaps the important and critical shortcoming of the international banking system at that time was the apparent lack of co-ordination and consultation between the banking authorities. The *ad hoc* and uncoordinated response by individual banking authorities demonstrated the need to establish a more open, informed and interdependent consultative procedure between national prudential authorities. This would ensure a speedier and more co-ordinated response to any subsequent crisis in the system. As well as the obvious need to establish greater co-operation in the future the essential need for the banking authorities was to discuss the lessons and precedents that emerged from their reaction to the crisis.

The main priority was to provide a framework and guidance for subsequent crises in the system which could be based on generally agreed principles. The recognition that single bank failures could affect the whole international banking system gave the need to discuss common problems a greater urgency and led to several initiatives in the system which evolved throughout the latter part of the 1970s into a set of guidelines for improving the regulation and supervision of the international banking system. In addition to the immediate problems caused by the banking crisis there was a growing acceptance that the international interdependence of banks made greater co-operation and understanding of the system very desirable.

Examination of the evolution of supervision and regulation in the system shows that the approach was one of gradualism and essentially market orientated. There were two main areas: firstly, the regulation and supervisory principles that were required for a more effective framework and secondly, the support or lender of last resort responsibilities within the international banking system.

Basle Committee

The first of these was accommodated by the Group of Ten (G10) central banks establishing the Basle Committee on Banking Regulations and Supervisory Practices in early 1975. The Committee was chaired by Peter Cooke, a senior official at the Bank of England. The 'Cooke' Committee initially attempted to establish lines of communication between banking authorities, a forum for discussion and opportunity for exchange of views and information, and early identification of potential problems within the international banking system. The Committee represents countries which undertake over 80 per cent of international bank lending.

The Committee considered and rejected the proposal for a new international institution as a means of achieving the above objectives. Problems of legal and political differences, duplication of national systems and other practical issues justified their conclusion that national authorities should provide the impetus for implementing improvements in the international banking system. This pragmatic decision allowed national supervisory authorities to initiate consultation and improve information to identify common problems within the system. Attempts were made to establish broad generally agreed principles for supervision of international banks with national banks learning from each other within this informal framework.

The Basle Concordat of December 1975 was the outcome of this approach and it summarizes the guidelines for supervising banks operating in more than one country. The main guidelines were that:

1 Supervision should be adequate and all international banks should be supervised.
2 Supervision should be appropriately divided between host and parent authorities.
3 Supervisory responsibility for liquidity be undertaken by the host country.
4 The parent bank with central bank support should be responsible for the solvency of its subsidiary banks and joint ventures in other countries.
5 Parent banks be responsible for supervision of their foreign branches and consortium banks.
6 Co-operation should be encouraged to ensure the effectiveness of the above guidelines.

The Committee has also initiated a series of important studies to facilitate greater understanding and induce harmonization of banking supervision. For example, guidelines have been produced on consolidation of accounts, capital adequacy, maturity transformation, and country risk. The Committee has also attempted to widen the discussion to non-G10 countries' supervisory authorities by the circulation of papers and information. The Committee organized conferences in London (1979) and Washington (1981) for banking supervisors to which delegates from eighty countries attended to discuss ways of improving supervisory practices on the basis of the guidelines established in the Basle Concordat and subsequent extensions. Also a number of regional supervisory authorities have been initiated by the Committee to provide a network of supervisory authorities seeking to co-operate and exchange information.

On the second issue of lender of last resort facilities and responsibilities in the system, the G10 central bankers did not attempt to formulate precise guidelines and it was only after initial concern that they announced that having discussed the issue of lender of last resort in international banking they believed it would not be practical or prudent to establish precise rules and procedures for provision of financial support. However, they claimed that adequate resources were available should the need arise in the system. This preference for retaining a vague commitment to lender of last resort facilities was thought to be sufficient and the only practical solution to potential future problems. However, it has been suggested that agreement had been reached on much firmer commitments between the central bankers which tried to establish more clearly responsibility for lender of last resort facilities between host and parent banks over branch, subsidiaries and joint ventures. Confusion over the interpretation of the G10 views on lender of last resort has led to criticism and attempts to establish in what circumstances resources would be forthcoming. However, the central banks' general statement on lender of last resort facilities is based on the view that incentives for market discipline and prudent banking would be discouraged by attempts to state precise mechanisms and rules for implementation of lender of last resort support (Dean & Giddy, 1981). Whether this fragile, loose and ill-defined framework would be sufficient in the future to prevent repercussion throughout the system arising from individual bank failures was left in doubt. Moreover, should a more widespread global international banking liquidity problem emerge, would the degree of uncertainty inhibit a co-ordinated response to provide support facilities?

The above outline of the reaction to the events of the early 1970s shows that substantial progress had been made through the G10 Committee in establishing contacts and exchange of information leading to guidelines and a more co-operative approach to international banking supervisory issues. On the other hand, concern and doubts remained on the ability of the system to react promptly and effectively to future crisis.

Management of Crisis

This final section seeks to reappraise the effectiveness of the international banking supervisory and support arrangements established during the 1970s by examining the reaction of banks to recent developments in the eurocurrency system. Firstly, an assessment is made of the implications arising from the collapse of the Banco Ambrosiano in July 1982. Secondly, an appraisal is given of the more acute general macro crisis that emerged during the second half of 1982 when several countries required refinancing of their debt repayments to eurobanks. Associated with this financing problem was the growing possibility of default being declared and several banks becoming insolvent.

Banco Ambrosiano

The collapse of Banco Ambrosiano Holdings in Luxembourg in July 1982 led to 250 banks losing $450 m with no central bank providing support facilities. The Bank of Italy accepted responsibility in Italy but refused to accept responsibility for the liabilities of the bank's subsidiary in Luxembourg (Grant, 1982).

The Luxembourg authorities also refused to support the subsidiary, arguing that it was not registered as a bank and therefore it had no responsibility for supervision or support facilities. This failure of one of the Cooke Committee's basic principles that adequate supervision was a priority, and the lack of support to provide finance for the losses incurred by liability holders of Banco Ambrosiano demonstrated the problems of having an ill-defined framework for lender of last resort facilities. While it could be argued that the Banco Ambrosiano's collapse was a special case and escaped the supervisory guidelines established by the G10 Committee, the impact on confidence in the international banking system was sufficient to induce requests for further clarification of the principles outlined in the Basle Concordat.

Problems raised by the Banco Ambrosiano's collapse and other outstanding issues in international banking in late 1982 can be summarized as follows:

1 The need for clarification and assignment of responsibility for supervision, regulation and support for subsidiary banks between the host and parent central bank.
2 The need to re-examine the case for providing more explicit guidelines on implementation of lender of last resort support.
3 The need to define what is a bank and whether to incorporate holding companies in future supervisory guidelines.
4 The need to incorporate the 1978 Cooke Committee's proposal into the Concordat Guidelines that accounts of banking groups be consolidated.
5 To examine the means of incorporating offshore centres into a more efficient supervisory framework.
6 To achieve a greater implementation of sound banking based on the Committee's studies and guidelines on consolidation of accounts, country risk assessment, capital adequacy and maturity mismatching.
7 To improve information and data on international banking operations to facilitate international comparisons and provide a more effective basis for implementing some of the above proposals.

Subsequently in June 1983 the G10 Committee published a further refinement of the guidelines for supervising international bank lending. Essentially, it presents an attempt to clarify the earlier 1975 Concordat taking into account recent developments in the international banking system. No attempt was made to clarify the problem of lender of last resort support facilities in the international banking system. The main provisions which have been accepted by seventeen offshore banking centres and are expected to be endorsed formally by the G10 members are as follows:

1 Holding companies or intermediary companies of international banks should be adequately supervised before banks be allowed to set up such business. This focuses on one important issue arising from the Banco Ambrosiano collapse.
2 No attempt was made to establish principles to overcome the repudiation of debts by foreign subsidiaries, which was the crucial issue arising from the collapse of the Banco Ambrosiano, or any comment made on the Italian authorities' handling of the repercussions of the collapse. The main responsibility for supervising the solvency of banks should be placed on the authorities of the parent bank. While liquidity matters should be the responsibility of the host country, authorities' emphasis

is placed on co-operation between banking authorities. This is essentially a restatement of the 1975 Concordat.

3 That banks should be examined on a consolidated basis to assist the supervision of complex networks of subsidiaries.

The above issues will no doubt continue to be discussed and clarified within the international banking system. Progress will continue to be made on co-operation through consultation and more effective implementation of the guidelines established in the G10 Committee. However, the above gradual and pragmatic approach to prudential supervision of the international banking system has recently been overtaken by events arising from difficulties of repayment of debt by several major sovereign borrowers from the euromarkets. The more immediate and urgent problem confronting the eurobanks has been to provide sufficient financial resources to prevent repercussions throughout the global banking system arising from default being declared by major debtor countries. The provision of financial resources to refinance repayments and maintain confidence in the banking system has become a critical priority to avoid a collapse of the international banking system.

Debt repayment crisis

We noted earlier that the central issue of concern over the viability of the international banking system emerged in the mid 1970s following the significant intermediary role adopted by the banks in recycling of oil revenues and balance-of-payment financing. We noted in particular, the rapid growth in borrowing by developing countries to finance external deficits arising from the increased price of oil imports. This concern has been heightened more recently by the dramatic events associated with the repayment problems confronting several developing countries and the possibility of defaults by one or more sovereign borrowers. This has led to a growing awareness that individual and national banks have become an integral part of the global monetary and financial system.

This macro-economic integration of banking in international finance and adjustment and the associated problems of systematic risk have widened the debate on the need for prudential supervision of the eurocurrency system. It focuses attention not only on the viability of individual banks operating in the system but on the interrelationship of the eurocurrency system within the world economic system. The implementation of agreed prudential supervision and provision of financial support facilities has now become more critical since the problem has been generalized not only for the eurocurrency system but the global economy. The problem therefore of sound banking and individual banking solvency and effective prudential supervision has become relatively less important in relation to this wider economic financial support and adjustment problem. Banks therefore have been forced to reconcile individual bank considerations with the wider macro issues of international finance and adjustment. This new dimension to international banking confronted banks with an unprecedented opportunity to demonstrate their ability to manage their operations without the need for more controls imposed by the authorities.

Emergence of crisis

It was stated previously that the Basle Committee thought that practical, legal and other constraints inhibited a more explicit statement on adopting a lender of last resort within international banking. However the growing awareness of the implications of the debt burden problem for future bank lending and exposure pointed to the need for an international lender of last resort with sufficient funds to prevent the spreading of any major country default and maintain confidence in the viability of the international banking system. Some believe that the emerging problems reflected 'distress' conditions in the banking system and supported Minsky's model of systematic fragility and inherent crisis (Kindleberger, 1978). Evidence used to support this view focused on the rapid growth in foreign debt of non-oil developing countries following their attempt to finance their external deficits in the 1970s and avoid economic adjustment which would have prevented them achieving their planned economic growth targets.

Table 11.1 *\$ bn non-oil LDCs 1973–81*

	1973	*1978*	*1981*
Current account deficit	11.6	39	99
Long term debt	96.8	276	436.9

Source: 1982 IMF Annual Report.

Banks financed \$132 billion of \$294 billion balance of payments deficits for non-OPEC LDCs between 1973 and mid 1982, equal to 45 per cent of their financing needs (Bank of International Settlements, 1983, p. 186). In particular the changing structure of foreign debt caused concern, especially the growing proportion owed to private commercial banks with a maturity pattern falling heavily in the early and mid 1980s. Bank claims in 1982 to non-oil LDCs was \$295 billion compared with \$150 billion in 1978 (Morgan Guaranty, 1983). This was equal to nearly 50 per cent of their estimated total short-term and long-term debt of \$640 billion. Moreover, almost 50 per cent of this debt was less than one year maturity. Again the increase in debt was equal to twice their growth in exports and GNP over 1973 to 1982 (Bank of International Settlements, 1983, p. 186). Mexico increased its share of short-term borrowing of less than one year maturity from 34 to 50 per cent between 1979 and mid 1982. Brazil by comparison held its share of short-term debt to around 35 per cent by mid

1982, well below the average for non-OPEC LDCs. Furthermore, the concentration of this borrowing in a small number of countries raised the important and increasing danger of bank exposure and portfolio problems. For example, the nine largest US banks' claims on Mexico, Argentina and Brazil increased at average annual rates of 35, 15 and 30 per cent between 1979 and 1982. Debt owed to banks at the end of June 1982 is summarised in Table 11.2 (Morgan Guaranty, 1983, p. 3):

Table 11.2

$ bn	*BIS Reporting Banks*	*All*	*US banks Largest*
All LDCs	347	125	77
21 major LDC borrowers	292	112	68
Argentina	25	8	5
Brazil	55	20	12
Mexico	64	25	13
Venezuela	27	10	7

Problems of capital adequacy were also being expressed in relation to these developments, some banks having more than twice their equity base in potential problem loans to debtor countries. The IMF has recently highlighted the potential insolvency situation for banks by noting that while BIS reporting banks' capital increased from $240 billion in 1978 to $330 billion in 1981, claims by the twenty largest borrowers among the non-oil LDCs increased from 50 to 70 per cent relative to this capital between 1978 and 1981 (International Monetary Fund, 1982). Profit margins were considered insufficient to reflect the risk involved in such lending patterns and bad-debt provisions were regarded as inadequate. Projections of debt payments and financing requirements into the 1980s revealed that the growth in international bank lending would need to continue to enable developing countries to repay earlier borrowing and sustain economic growth (Morgan Guaranty, 1983). Banks were becoming 'locked' into debt-financing situations with little room to change their lending policy.

In addition these debt and financing problems have been made more acute by recent trends in the world economy with depressed trade and commodity prices and reduced developing countries' export earnings. The combination of the rapid growth in short-term debt and worsening world economy trends increased the average outstanding debt of the twenty-one largest borrowers in 1982 to over 170 per cent of their exports compared with 130 per cent in the mid 1970s. Again, the debt service ratio increased from 50 to 75 per cent between 1979 and 1982. These adverse trends were significantly worse for Latin American countries, whose outstanding debt as a percentage of exports increased from 196 to 259 per cent between 1979 and 1982 and their debt service ratio increased from 76 to 125 per cent between 1979 and 1982. In addition higher inflation and interest rates increased the cost of borrowing of floating rate roll-over bank credits and have aggravated the ability of LDCs to repay earlier loans. For Mexico, Brazil and Argentina the net interest payments/export ratio increased from 31 to over 50 per cent between 1979 and 1982 (Bank of International Settlements, 1983; Morgan Guaranty, 1983).

Such a series of developments in bank lending and in the world economy led some to support the view that this represented a fragile financial situation, that crisis was inevitable and that support measures should be explicitly introduced by the authorities to provide sufficient financial resources to support banks confronting potential insolvent positions. It was argued that these measures would contain the crisis and prevent it spreading throughout the system and thus generalizing the problem. Whether through private or public, national or international support schemes such facilities were strongly advocated as a means of averting a global crisis. In the event no such support schemes were introduced and the Basle Committee framework and approach was the basis for support facilities prior to the rapid emergence of the repayment problems in late 1982. The effectiveness of this framework in resolving the refinancing crisis that emerged can be used as a basis for appraising the viability of the international system and providing lessons for future policy towards support facilities in the international banking system.

Trends in the euromarket

The market reaction to the growing concern about trends in the world economy and international bank lending implications for prudential issues is clearly evident in euromarket indicators during 1982 (Bank of England, 1983; Bank of International Settlements, 1983; Morgan Guaranty, 1983). In the period 1976–81 the growth of net international bank lending by BIS reporting banks to non-OPEC LDCs averaged over 20 per cent annually. However, this rapid expansion of bank lending was reduced substantially in 1982. Overall net international bank lending fell to an annual rate of 15 per cent to end September 1982. Also gross lending to LDCs fell from $50 billion annual rate in the first half of 1982 to $32 billion annual rate in the third quarter of 1982. This slowdown in lending was especially evident in bank lending to Latin American countries. While they borrowed $21.1 billion in the second half of 1981, this decreased to $11.8 billion in the first half of 1982 and was almost stopped in the second half of 1982. This sharp slowdown in bank lending is also seen in the medium-term bank credit. In the first half of 1982 credits for non-oil LDCs were $28 billion in each quarter, approximately 20 per cent above the average for 1981. This compares with a fall to below $9 billion by the second half of 1982. These market trends reflect the banks' caution in continuing to increase lending given worsening world economy trends and the rapidly deteriorating financial problems of many LDCs.

Mexico, the largest debtor country to banks, encountered difficulties in repaying interest and principal on its $83 billion external debt and announced in August 1982 a moratorium on repayments of principal to banks while maintaining interest payments. Mexico urgently sought to discuss the future restructuring of debt with banks. Within months Mexico's action was followed by Argentina, Brazil and a number of other small debtor countries. Together these three countries accounted for 51.9 per cent of BIS-reporting bank claims on non-oil LDCs and 40 per cent of all developing countries at end 1981. The sharp decline in undisbursed credit commitments by banks between 1979 and 1982, especially for Brazil, provides further evidence of tighter market conditions confronting major debtor countries (Bank of International Settlements, 1983, p. 125).

The immediate impact on market conditions can be seen from banks' pricing of loans. Average spread (spread above LIBOR) increased sharply in 1981. This was particularly evident in loans to Latin American countries. For example, in late 1981 public borrowers in Mexico were paying a spread of 5/8 per cent for eight year maturity borrowing whereas the spread increased to 1 per cent for three year and 1.5 per cent for seven year loans by the middle of 1982. The Bank of England, however, points out that the increase in spreads in 1982 was not as great or generalized as the earlier period of uncertainty in the market in 1974/5 following the oil price increase and failure of several banks. Non-bank borrowing costs have increased and lending curtailed rather than banks following a policy of a general increase in costs as in the 1974 period. The Bank of England also concludes that the repercussions in the inter-bank market were not as pronounced compared with 1974/5. However, some selectivity reflected in tiering of interest rates and a decrease in activity was evident in the market. For example, Brazil was seriously affected through cuts in inter-bank lines of credit amounting to over $4 billion within a few months. This hampered rescheduling arrangements and aggravated short-term liquidity problems for Brazil. Inter-bank credit restriction for Brazil subsequently were integrated into a package of arrangements to reschedule their debt repayments. Mexico also threatened to include its $7 billion inter-bank liabilities in its $80 billion of overall debt and this tended to disrupt the inter-bank market and aggravate the liquidity crisis. Bank for International Settlements figures again indicate the effects of such developments on the inter-bank business which fell from $63 billion in the last quarter of 1981 to $20 billion in the same quarter in 1982 and centred on US banks rather than between reporting banks outside the US. Such developments in the market reflect banks' changing perception of risks in their international lending operations and attempts made to improve their profitability to reflect the increased risks. Also the need for a build-up of capital through improved provisions was given a high priority by central banks in discussions with international banks. This is reflected in the bad-debt provisions of the big four UK banks which more than doubled from £381 million to £962 million between 1981 and 1982 (Financial Times, 1983).

Support measures

While these examples of the market's response to the worsening international economy and immediate debt repayment problems were expected and justified, the critical issue was the willingness and ability of banks to resolve the short-term refinancing of existing loans, and to provide additional finance to prevent a collapse of the global financial and monetary system. The primary problem was the need to maintain confidence in the international banking system and avoid a major default which could lead to the financing problem spreading throughout the system. The urgency of the problem was quickly identified and a series of speedily arranged and effectively implemented package remedies introduced. The unprecedented reaction by the banking authorities and the international monetary system provided a major rescue package by introducing a combination of measures. For example, Mexico was provided with almost $2 billion emergency bridging finance tied to subsequent IMF loans arranged by the BIS (guaranteed by central banks) and the US monetary authorities. The IMF discussed with Mexico adjustment policies combined with financing. The commercial banks established an advisory group to arrange rescheduling and financing of Mexico's debt repayments. Banks rescheduled almost $20 billion of Mexico's debt and in addition increased new lending by $5 billion (equal to a 7 per cent increase in their exposure) (Bank of England Quarterly Bulletin, 1983). This increased bank lending was in response to IMF requests to complement its $3.5 billion loan to Mexico and ensure the necessary support of their adjustment programme. A similar package was arranged for Brazil, Argentina and other countries as the widening of financing problems rapidly emerged during the second half of 1982.

While in most cases countries have continued to pay interest on loans from banks, negotiations have led to a major rescheduling of $45 billion of debt due between 1982–4. Repayment of this principal will now be made between 1986 and end of 1990 (Bank of England Quarterly Bulletin, 1983; Bank of International Settlements, 1983). This sharing of the burden of rescheduling and bridging finance together with IMF conditional financing and adjustment programmes was a significant new approach in providing remedies to debt and confidence problems. Banks have also involuntarily increased their exposure to these countries at a time when they would probably have preferred to decrease their international lending. While this may not align with attempts to implement sound banking as a basis for self-regulation, following the Cooke Committee principles, it was nevertheless a necessary prerequisite for resolving the difficulties of debtor countries and allowing them time to adjust their economies and financial requirements in the future. It demonstrates also their apparent acceptance of the need to reconcile sound banking with the wider economic issues. The co-ordinating role of the IMF and central banks and their success in persuading banks to participate in the rescue package were important aspects of the evolution of the events.

Conclusions

What lessons have been learnt from these developments within the international banking and monetary system? Firstly it could be argued that it would not have been possible to predict or effectively monitor the speed and development of the debt financing problems that emerged dramatically in the second half of 1982. Banks had continued to lend into the 1980s in the belief that the capacity of sovereign borrowers to repay earlier loans was assured by a continuation of economic growth in their economies and stability in the eurocurrency system (Bank of International Settlements, 1983, p. 118). Competition and willingness to participate in syndicated international lending continued in this growth environment. Again the insignificant losses from previous international lending did not present a threat to banks. This optimistic outlook did not anticipate the impact of the sharp deterioration in the global economy on the capacity of debtor countries to repay earlier loans without a continuation of and increased lending by commercial banks. With hindsight this may be condemned as irresponsible and evidence of mismanagement which justifies imposing controls over banks' operations in international lending. However, this fails to recognize the considerable benefits derived from international bank lending to meet the finance and adjustment needs of the global monetary system.

Again, it is unlikely that the size of the refinancing resources required to prevent actual default being declared by sovereign borrowers would have been available from any lender of last resort facilities anticipated in the preceding years, even if they had been agreed and financed. Furthermore, no individual bank or national banking system could have effectively provided sufficient finance to restore confidence. Only a prompt and concerted approach prevented a collapse of the system. The critical factor was the speed of the reaction and refinancing. It could be argued that this effective response was essentially made possible through the previously established consultation process and co-operative international approach that had been evolved by the G10 Committee during the 1970s.

Secondly, the generalized nature of the global macro-economic problem of debt finance meant that the banks, while directly confronted by the problems, could not resolve these without the solution being generalized. Thus the combination of the international banks together with the IMF and BIS became the critical factor in maintaining the system in the short term. A package solution was vital to resolve both the inherent banking problems and the wider economic problems. No one participant in the emergency measures introduced to resolve the short-term financial problems encountered by the major debtor countries could have taken effective remedies in the confidence crisis that emerged so rapidly and on such a scale as in mid 1982. On the other hand, banks could not be allowed to collapse and trigger-off a widespread financial and macro global crisis. Again, banks could not escape their responsibility in this crisis situation and assume that the IMF or national banking authorities would accept responsibility for substituting official financial support for private bank refinancing. The participation by banks, BIS, IMF and governments clearly demonstrated their ability and willingness in effectively implementing emergency measures to resolve the confidence and stability problems of the international financial system.

Some would argue that the BIS should not be expected to continue to provide emergency short-term bridging finance which should gradually become unnecessary as the system overcomes the immediate problems caused by the extreme shortage of finance by the debtor countries. It is contended that such finance when needed is best obtained through the commercial banks and national authorities establishing a system of co-operation in providing adequate short-term finance prior to agreeing on longer-term refinancing resources. However, others would stress that until such time as the current problems are resolved or the formal strengthening of the international financial system's ability to handle emergency situations is achieved, the BIS together with central banks should continue to prevent instability and lack of confidence and provide this important bridging and pivotal role in the system. The financial resources and arrangements for effective implementation of this role by the BIS should therefore be strengthened. The BIS should be the focus of provision of short-term finance to ensure a co-operative longer-term arrangement to take place between the IMF and debtor countries.

The recognition of the broader macro considerations by banks in their need to continue to participate in a co-ordinated package rescue programme and to increase their exposure to debtor countries was a significant breakthrough in assisting the arrangements to refinance the debt repayment and averting defaults being declared.

Thirdly, this pragmatic and balanced approach to solving the immediate financing problems confronting debtor countries proved effective in providing the banking system with a breathing space to reappraise future lending policy. It is doubtful that a stricter regulatory framework involving lending limits would have prevented such developments and provided a basis for dealing more effectively with the problem as it emerged in late 1982. The market-orientated approach supported by sound banking principles and general consultation and co-operation has demonstrated its flexibility and viability to react to a major problem confronting the euromarkets. The changes in market indicators such as the growth in lending, spreads, maturities and restructuring of debt reflect such an approach to resolving the disturbances in the system. While it could be argued that there were signs of 'distress' in the system, collapse of the system was avoided. Support facilities for the whole system rather than individual banks were provided speedily to sustain the system. This effective management of the problem suggests that prudential guidelines provide a sufficient framework for international bank lending rather than regulatory controls.

Fourthly, general improvements in the international economy would greatly assist the longer-term prospects of debtor countries and international lending by banks (Morgan Guaranty, 1983). Lower interest rates, growth of world trade and stable oil prices would improve the debt servicing capacity of debtor countries. Expansion of existing IMF resources including the 50 per cent increase in quotas and GAB facilities already agreed together with modifications in conditions attached to lending would assist medium-term adjustment programmes in debtor countries. In addition the prospect of moving away from unconditional to conditional finance support and the likely reduction in borrowing facilities will probably result in many LDCs reappraising their growth strategy. This will lead to the introduction of measures to adjust their economies. Such a commitment by the debtor countries would ensure continued confidence in the effectiveness of the refinancing arrangements.

Fifthly, improvements in information are important in monitoring future trends in international bank lending especially on country exposure and credit assessments. A group of private banks set up an Institute of International Finance in the autumn of 1982 to provide information for international bank lending; this is one indication of the importance attached to this aspect of international banking. The World Bank, IMF and the BIS together could also establish mechanisms and guidelines for improvements in information flows to commercial banks and national central banks. Such information could be used for highlighting the possibility and implications of delays in repayment of loans and default situations.

Sixthly, the related problem of identifying short-term borrowing changes in the inter-bank market requires a more formal exchange of information. Brazil's extensive short-term borrowing in the inter-bank market was eventually integrated into the rescheduling package and highlights the need for such countries to decrease dependence on the inter-bank market as a means of financing balance of payments and a more careful monitoring of this area of bank lending operations. The crucial liquidity role of the inter-bank market was evident at the early stages of the crisis when there existed a serious threat of the market being unable to counter the attempt by some banks to impose lower credit lines to non-bank and smaller bank borrowers. Central bank pressure to restore and maintain credit lines enabled liquidity constraints to be overcome and maintained market stability. Alternatively, central banks could intervene directly to supply liquidity to banks facing critical illiquidity positions and prevent insolvency consequences.

Another scheme proposed is that banks should provide their own pool of emergency finance for such circumstances (Dean & Giddy, 1981). Individual banks might be saved by such schemes. However, it is considered unlikely that such funds would be sufficient in cases where the liquidity constraints were generalized. In such cases central bank co-operation and more general support would be essential to prevent instability and restore confidence in the market, as recent events have clearly demonstrated. Individual banks can also reappraise their inter-bank lending policy to diminish the inherent risks involved in this area of eurocurrency banking operations. It should also be noted that the inter-bank network provides an important market mechanism in implementing a speedy reaction and liquidity flow into the eurocurrency systems.

Banks need to reflect on their new relationship with the IMF and continue to co-operate fully in achieving a better balance in their role in financing and adjustment solutions of global economic problems. A continuation of prudential and supervisory discussions and co-operation through the Basle Committee's work needs to be encouraged. Individual banks also need to be assured that the burden of financing is equitably shared amongst the banks and to continue to co-operate to maintain their lending to debtor countries and participate in refinancing arrangements. Above all, recent events are likely to change attitudes of bankers and introduce a new realism in determining future lending policy within the world economy.

Finally, the importance of the co-operative approach and the prevention of the collapse of the international banking system should not, however, be seen as completely resolving the debt repayment and inherent problems arising from international bank involvement in global finance. It merely provides an acceptable basis for the opportunity to discuss a coherent longer-term solution to the fundamental global debt, finance and adjustment problems. There are signs that implementation of the adjustment solutions in many of these debtor countries will not be without problems and inevitably will take many years to resolve. Other countries are likely to require rescheduling of their repayments to international banks. The international and financial and banking system will remain fragile for the medium term and events will have to be monitored carefully by the banking authorities.

References

Angelini, A., Eng, M. and F. A. Lees (1972), *International Lending, Risk and the Euromarkets* (London: Macmillan).

Bank of England Quarterly Bulletin (1980), 'Syndicated medium-term euro-credits', vol. 20, no. 3, (Sept.), pp. 311–18.
Bank of England Quarterly Bulletin (1981), 'Eurobanks and the inter-bank market', vol. 21, no. 3, (Sept.), pp. 351–64.
Bank of England Quarterly Bulletin (1982), 'International banking in 1980–81', vol. 22, no. 1, (March), pp. 42–55.
Bank of England Quarterly Bulletin (1983), 'International banking markets in 1982', vol. 23, no. 1, (March), pp. 43–60.
Bank of International Settlements (1983), *Annual Report* (Basle), pp. 108–31.
Brown, R. M. G. (1980), *International co-ordination and co-operation in banking supervision*, unpublished MA dissertation (Bangor: University College of North Wales).
Dean, J. W. & Giddy, I. H. (1981), *Averting international banking crisis*, Monograph (New York: Solomon Brothers).
Grant, C. (1982), 'Can the Cooke Committee stand the heat?' *Euromoney*, (Oct.), pp. 39–45.
Financial Times (1983), 'World Banking Survey', (16 May).
International Monetary Fund (1982), *International Capital Markets: Developments and Prospects*, Occasional Paper No. 14, (Washington).
Johnson, R. B. (1983), *The Economics of the Euro-markets; History Theory and Policy* (London: Macmillan).
Kindleberger, C. P. (1978), *Manias, Panics and Crashes, A History of Financial Crisis* (London: Macmillan).
Morgan Guaranty (1983), *World Financial Markets*, pp. 1–14.

PART D

Capital Adequacy

The problem of capital adequacy and the so-called capital adequacy debate have occupied an important part of the US banking literature since the Great Depression. In contrast, capital adequacy was not really an issue in UK banking until the events of the early 1970s. Since then, it has become a topic of growing supervisory concern. A bank's capital adequacy position is related to its total risk exposure, existing and planned, and the uncertain environment in which it operates. Given this accepted functional view of the problem, it is not surprising that capital adequacy considerations are a central element in supervisory systems. Part D is devoted to this problem – although, once again, it is selective. In the opening Chapter 12, Malcolm Wilcox, in his 1979 Presidential Address to the Institute of Bankers, surveys the role of capital in banking. He explores the historical development of capital adequacy considerations in UK banking. The following paper by Jack Revell considers the problems of hidden reserves and provisions in capital adequacy analysis. This is a topical problem and it serves as a reminder of the practical difficulties associated with capital adequacy analysis. Chapter 14 outlines Ted Gardener's proposals for appraising capital adequacy. It is an approach based on the simulated 'contingency testing' of banks' plans.

12 Capital in Banking: an Historical Survey*

* Reprinted with permission from the *Journal of the Institute of Bankers*, and published in June 1979, pp. 96–101

MALCOLM G. WILCOX, MBE, FIB

(This is the text of the Presidential Address to the Institute of Bankers, delivered in the Library on 16 May 1979)

I have chosen for the Presidential Address 'Capital in Banking – an Historical Survey' but, before I offer this to members of the Institute, there are two points which I should like to make:

First, when I came to contemplate the boundaries and the potential of this subject I quickly realized that it might be helpful to put on paper more than can be delivered in speech on an occasion such as this. I therefore decided to make available in print an extended version of the Address which will be published shortly and those who wish to pursue a study of the matter might like to have a copy.

Second, this is by no means a personal work. I have received great help from a number of people, both inside and outside the Institute, and I would like to place on record the value of their research and my gratitude for what they have done.

Introduction

In banking, no less than in other business enterprises, survival and growth depend on capital resources and their efficient use. In recent years the demand for capital in banking worldwide has risen to unprecedented levels, in line with the enlargement and elaboration of national financial markets and the increasing global development of banks in an inflationary setting. Banking business as such has continued to expand and the major banks have also diversified their services, embarking on a very large expansion of both their domestic and international activities.

The conjuncture of these recent radical changes with the recollections of history which the centenary of the Institute engenders, makes this an appropriate year in which to examine the role of capital in banking. This subject has, in this country, remained largely neglected and there is room for systematic study, leading perhaps to a wider understanding of its significance.

The Role of Capital in Banking

Though differences in emphasis may exist, the basic role of capital in banking does not vary from country to country. This Address concentrates for the most part on capital in the London clearing banks but it is fundamental that all banks need capital to cover and extend fixed assets and business investments, to enable trading to continue and increase, to maintain the confidence of depositors and to ensure viability in the face of loss arising from inevitable business and political fluctuation and uncertainty, particularly in an inflationary climate.

Some of the factors touching the question of capital lie within the direct control of the bank concerned – most significantly the quality of management, with its influence on the structure of the balance sheet, the maturity pattern of assets and liabilities and the quality of the asset portfolio. Other factors, which may be decisive, lie outside its control. These are essentially concerned with the environment in which the bank operates and, for an international bank, extend broadly to financial, economic and political developments in the world at large.

Defining Capital

Quite evidently, a pure definition of capital must accommodate at root those funds which are attributable to the proprietors as published in the balance sheet. In this connection the joining of paid-up capital with reserves emphasises that capital may be derived both externally from new issues or calls on existing shareholders, and also internally by, for example, the retention of profits. And as the ability to generate trading profits in a competitive climate is a significant guide to business efficiency, the terms on which new capital can be added to the old are very much related to earnings, both achieved and in prospect.

Published net worth may, in practice, also be increased from time to time by balance sheet adjustments, for instance by the transfer to reserve of provisions for loan losses no longer required, or by the revaluation of assets, such as bank properties. But the published reserves have not always told the whole story. Until 1969, the banks availed themselves of their legal right to maintain hidden reserves, though their published profits have followed the actual trend.

Over the past decade a new factor has arisen as British banks, like other major international banking groups, have strengthened their balance sheets by substantial issues of subordinated loan stock, both in sterling and in foreign currency. Such debt is obviously not available to absorb losses in the same way as equity, but it does ultimately stand between depositors and the disappearance of their funds, forming another line of defence which must be sacrificed before deposits are at risk. Loan stock may be used to finance fixed assets and within prudent limits it can provide a gearing element in relation to banking assets and liabilities.

A debate presently continues over the status of certain types of provision for loan losses. What no one disputes is that capital resources should not include specific provisions for losses on particular accounts, made on the basis of full cover for bad and doubtful debts. Nor, in their published accounts, do the banks treat general provisions for doubtful advances as part of capital, on the ground that they represent, in the light of historical experience, a prudent setting aside of earnings against latent loss. There is a very proper desire in British banking to preserve the sanctity of established capital resources, and a general provision of reasonable size plays a supporting role in this regard. How else can one prudently state that the advances' portfolio – a paramount asset – is not overvalued?

In recent months there has also been some debate over the treatment of deferred taxation. For the banks, provision for deferred tax has arisen mainly from the expansion in their leasing business and the deferment of corporation tax stemming from the related capital allowances. The extent to which it is necessary to create a provision in such circumstances – and equally the justification for recovering provisions made in past years – has to be evaluated against the chances of the taxation in question becoming payable at some later date. This is clearly a matter of judgement and it would be wrong to expect a rigid pattern to be adopted.

To summarize, therefore, it is convenient and reasonable to define capital as the net worth of the institution concerned – proprietorship funds including reserves – together with an acceptable quantity of subordinated loan stock of suitable maturity.

Capital Adequacy and the Ratios

What, then, may be said about the level of such capital resources appropriate to a particular banking business? The proportion of capital to deposits is clearly a ratio of importance, as it gives an indication of the extent to which depositors are underpinned. In any consideration of the use of funds, moreover, it is axiomatic that fixed and intangible assets – which should clearly include investments in subsidiaries, themselves needful of an appropriate capital base – should be covered by capital resources with something to spare. The balance of total capital, normally termed 'free capital', is what is thus available to support the banking business and to meet unexpected losses.

These pointers to financial strength must, however, be considered in relation to the varying degrees of risk involved in the spectrum of bank assets and in contingent liabilities off the balance sheet. Some assets may, in this, be regarded as effectively risk-free, while the assessment of others must envisage forced sale risk or credit risk, with a proportion embodying exposure under both headings.

It follows from these considerations that useful insights into the adequacy of capital may be derived from looking at the relationships between capital on the one hand and deposits or certain categories of assets on the other. It must, however, be remembered that there is no magic in numbers: fixed common yardsticks could only lead to inflexibility and would seem to be justified only on special assumptions which do not hold in the market-place. The true strength of a banking business and the amount of capital it prudently needs can only be judged by those who know the nature and quality of both assets and liabilities.

Liquidity and stability

The link between capital and the retention of confidence is provided by continuing liquidity. Before 1971, the clearing banks actively adjusted their liquidity only by changes in their asset structure – by moving money market assets or the investment portfolio. Since the introduction, in that year, of new policies and practices flowing from the Bank of England's proposals on 'Competition and Credit Control', they have, however, also been able to achieve adjustments by borrowing and lending in the wholesale market.

In conditions of strain, the existence of a lender of last resort is of course of great importance if stability is to be maintained. In the sterling markets this role is performed by the Bank of England, through the intermediation of the discount market. In the international foreign currency markets, provision of last resort facilities depends on co-operation between central banks and, in this regard, the Bank for International Settlements (BIS) has come to play a key role (McMahon, 1976).

The provision of liquidity by a central bank depends, of course, on the borrower deserving it – in other words, that the institution concerned should be solvent. Capital adequacy, present and potential, is thus crucial and these considerations were fundamental in the context of the support for some secondary banks provided jointly by the Bank of England and the clearing banks in the 'Lifeboat' operation mounted in 1973 and 1974.

Capital and the Historical Perspective

Looked at in an historical perspective the secular trend in the level of bank capital resources has generally been downwards, and this stems from a number of different causes. On the positive side, structural changes in the banking system plus technical progress, especially in communications and the supply of information for the assessment of risk, have made both for greater stability and for the more effective use of banking resources. But these overall improvements in operational efficiency have been offset by the erosion of bank capital in real terms due to the effects of inflation, which has persisted with especial seriousness in the 1970s and now constantly imperils the gains made at other times and in other ways.

The style of capitalization in British banking which has evolved against the background of these trends was a consequence largely of the failures of Overend Gurney in 1866 and the City of Glasgow Bank in 1878, and of the major crisis accompanying the outbreak of war in 1914, when foreigners, however solvent, were largely unable to make remittances to London.

Thus it can be said that the previous distrust of limited liability in respect of bank capital was finally dispelled by the failure of the unlimited City of Glasgow Bank; this left relatively few of its shareholders solvent after calls to repay depositors and led to the introduction of reserve liability for bank shareholders in the following year (under the Companies Act, 1879).

The spread of limited liability, and the growing interdependence of financial institutions, reinforced by government calls for larger banking reserves after the Baring crisis of 1890, were powerful influences behind the amalgamations in the two decades before the First World War, when it was mainly local banks or banks whose activities did not overlap geographically which were involved.

These developments had lasting effects on the level of capital in banking. The amalgamation movement enabled the larger banks thus created to exercise greater efficiency in the use of capital, and this tendency, combined with the fact that deposits were increasing, caused a general downward trend in the average published ratio of capital to deposits. In 1880 it was about 20% for joint stock banks; by 1900 it had dropped to about 13% and, as a result largely of the wartime inflation, it was no higher than 6% by 1917.

Colwyn and after

By 1918, however, the nature of amalgamations was changing and the emerging trend for the union of major joint-stock banks with extensive branch networks became a cause for concern, occasioning the setting up of a Treasury Committee under the chairmanship of Lord Colwyn. In its report (HMSO, 1918), the Committee took the view that old-style mergers should continue to be permitted but that those involving substantial territorial overlap should in future be subject to official investigation: of parallel concern was the continuing fall in the proportion of capital to deposits.

The level of bank deposits in fact rose significantly between 1914 and 1918 and, to ease the pressure on their capital, the banks substantially increased their proprietorship funds in 1920, when the average published ratio of capital resources to deposits rose from 5½% to nearly 6½%. The overall level of deposits was little changed in the 1920s but, with a fall in public sector assets, lending to the private sector rose. As 1930 approached, however, it was apparent that the banks' loan portfolios were beginning to reflect the excess capacity and non-competitiveness of the old staple industries – coal, iron and steel, shipbuilding and textiles.

Macmillan and the crisis 1931

These structural problems of industry had been greatly intensified by the onset of world depression in 1929, and formed the background to the appointment of the Macmillan Committee, which concerned itself with the supply of funds to industry. Bank capital surprisingly finds no mention in the Macmillan Committee's report (HMSO, 1931) which was published in July 1931, by unhappy chance on the very day when a major German bank failed, in the spreading financial crisis that had begun in Vienna two months before. With confidence at a low ebb, it was almost inevitable that pressures should be transmitted to London. Nevertheless, though the gold standard was finally abandoned in September 1931, the stability of the banking system did not come into public question.

Capital resources in a climate of cheap money

While the ratio of capital to deposits of the clearing banks stood at more than 7% by 1931, the ensuing cheap money period saw this ratio revert to a persistent downward path. In the 1930s, the decline was slow – to about 5¾% in 1939 – but it became more pronounced as a result of the subsequent inflation, particularly during the war years, reaching 3% by 1945, and falling as low as 2½% by 1951.

The balance sheets of the clearing banks changed dramatically during these years: their deposits trebled and their asset portfolios revealed a massive increase in holdings of public sector debt – notably gilt-edged stocks – the counterpart of which was a sharp relative decline in lending to the private sector. Advances fell from over 50% of deposits in 1931 to less than 17% in 1945. By this time the banks were accordingly excessively liquid and painfully underlent.

It must, of course, be remembered that published capital resources did not then give a true picture of the banks' financial strength since they continued to follow their traditional policy of maintaining hidden reserves. This policy, adopted in the interests of depositors, was endorsed by the Cohen report on company law amendments (HMSO, 1945) and found legal expression in the Companies Act, 1948.

The 1950s – growing pressure on capital resources

The need for these inner reserves was soon highlighted by the collapse of cheap money and the reactivation of an orthodox interest rate policy in November 1951. The basic reason was the concomitant sharp fall in the market price of gilt-edged securities which had come to form an unusually high proportion of the banks' assets. As a result, most of the banks abandoned their long-standing policy of writing down their investments by provisions from current earnings or from inner reserves. Hence, investments appeared in published accounts at a book valuation in excess of market price, 'at or under cost' but 'below redemption price', with a marginal note to the accounts giving the market valuation.

Shortly after, in 1953 and 1954, the banks' average ratio of capital to deposits reached an all-time low of under 2½%, a relationship which did not improve to any extent until the end of that decade. Not surprisingly, therefore, a clearing bank witness told the Jenkins Committee in 1960 that 'the whole history of the last fifteen years has been an effort to get the shareholders' money in the business into a proper trading relationship to the deposits' (HMSO, 1961). The banks' difficulties with their gilt-edged portfolios were compounded by the problem of generating an adequate level of earnings from advances for much of the 1950s in consequence of credit controls. Their ability to rebuild their capital resources through retentions was thus seriously inhibited.

The Radcliffe Inquiry

By the time that the Radcliffe Committee was appointed in 1957, clearing-bank capital needed bolstering, more so than at any time since the Colwyn Committee reported nearly forty years before. Despite this, the Radcliffe Committee followed the Macmillan precedent in not subjecting the banks' capital to scrutiny. The Committee recognized, however, that the banks were 'essentially commercial undertakings . . . ' whose first duty was 'to conduct their business in the interests of their owners' (HMSO, 1959, para. 127) and concluded their operations had been unduly hampered by controls. These, of course, depressed their earnings.

An officially prescribed liquidity ratio of 30% had formed part of the controls from the early 1950s. Radcliffe accepted the banks' contention that this requirement was too stringent, agreeing that a lower ratio would be compatible with prudence.

Growth, more capital and the diversification of the clearing banks

The improved economic climate of 1958, which coincided with a period of credit relaxation which was to last until 1961, provided the banks with the long-sought opportunity to reorganise their balance sheets so that they conformed more closely to the prewar pattern.

The clearing banks accordingly embarked on a programme of capital-raising which, accompanied by a welcome improvement in earnings and by asset revaluations, was reflected in substantial increases in published capital resources through the 1960s with the result that the ratio of capital to deposits more than doubled between 1957 and 1968.

The beginnings of the attempt to restore balance sheet orthodoxy coincided with the emergence of a demand for capital for a new purpose, namely diversification. The initial steps were taken in 1958 when most of the clearing banks made equity investments in finance houses, thus widening the market – both industrial and personal – in which opportunities to lend were available.

The 1960s – structural change in the banking industry

During the early 1960s, it was the growth of deposits and advances which made the greatest demand on capital resources. By mid 1961 advances had risen to nearly 49% of deposits, their highest relative level since 1932, while gilt-edged investments had fallen to less than 14%, their lowest since 1930. Bank profitability became, therefore, a more direct reflection of the general trend in interest rates, and rate levels in the 1960s were generally higher than they had been in the previous decade. Nevertheless, the clearing banks were still not at full potential, being effectively precluded by their liquidity requirements from participation in the rapid growth of the new money markets in sterling and foreign currency.

To overcome this problem, in the late 1960s all the major banks set up specialist subsidiaries which, unencumbered by the need to hold prescribed liquid assets, were able to trade effectively in these new markets. In this way, the banks gained experience of liability management which was to become a permanent characteristic of their own money market operations from 1971.

In addition, the 1960s saw the first amalgamations among the clearing banks for more than forty years. In 1962, one of the Big Five merged with a smaller clearing bank whose business was largely regional, so suggesting that more efficient use of resources in future might require bigger banks and banking groups – a possibility which received favourable comment in the report of the Prices and Incomes Board on 'Bank Charges' in 1967. In the event, two further mergers took place in 1968 and 1969, to bring the clearing banks to approximately their present form.

These structural responses in the late 1960s coincided with the decision to make full disclosure of profits and asset values in the clearing banks' annual accounts for 1969. This change had a dramatic effect on published capital ratios. In 1968, prior to disclosure, the average ratio of capital to deposits of all the parent clearing banks was about 6%; in 1969, on the new and consolidated group basis, it had risen to just over 8½%.

Before the radical changes of the 1970s, therefore, and while the clearing banks were mainly engaged in deposit banking, two long-term trends of prime importance may be identified. On the credit side, the pattern of banking developed – through integration and improved financial intermediation – in a way that promoted the more efficient use of capital. The amount of capital needed to support a given volume of deposits and assets hence declined. On the debit side, however, the effects of inflation operated to erode the real worth of the capital base, and created the need for frequent increases from whatever sources these could reasonably be obtained.

The 1970s – expansion and competition in an inflationary climate

This, then is the background to the present decade. Within these past few years the clearing banks have transformed themselves from being primarily domestic banking institutions into major international banks in the real sense of that expression, with a growing call for new capital resources. These have been needed to finance expansion, both in their mainstream business and in various related services, at home and abroad and the consequent demand for capital has been considerable. Since the extended disclosure of profits in 1969, the total capital resources of the Big Four banking groups have in fact risen fivefold, to nearly £6 billion by the end of 1978, within which rise the effect of inflation has had to be accommodated.

In domestic markets, the policies stemming from the implementation of the Bank of England paper on 'Competition and Credit Control', in the autumn of 1971, swept away many of the constraints that had formerly hampered the banks in their attempts to compete on an equal basis with other financial institutions. It is important to recognise the nature of their improved opportunities, in particular those relating to the placing of funds between banks. In any but the most adverse market conditions, major banks can now raise deposits in the wholesale markets – at various maturities – in currency as well as sterling, whenever they need, so reducing the level of uncertainty arising from the maturity structure of assets and liabilities.

Most dramatic of all has been the expansion of international business and particularly the rapid growth of foreign currency lending and deposits. Foreign currency deposits, mostly in US dollars, now amount to about one-third of clearing bank group deposits in terms of business booked in the UK. For non-dollar based banks, the valuation of such balances is sensitive to changes in the exchange rate and currency fluctuations have at times been very significant since the collapse of the fixed parity system in 1973. Hence capital ratios have been stretched and, as mentioned earlier, the banks have turned to issues of loan stock in foreign currency for reinforcement.

As is well known, the world economy in the 1970s has been characterised by instability and uncertainty and in this country these influences showed through most obviously in the secondary banking crisis, the impact of which was absorbed by the prompt action of the Bank of England and the clearing banks. In his evidence to the House of Commons Select Committee last year, the Governor of the Bank of England spoke of the 'contagion of fear' (Select Committee on Nationalized Industries, 1978) that threatened the British banking system in 1973 and 1974, so providing a reminder that the retention of confidence, in adverse market conditions, is something that may still defy rational analysis.

Over this period the story of the clearing banks is, nevertheless, one of growth and innovation. Deposits of the Big Four groups rose from some £15 billion in 1969 to over £70 billion in 1978 and capital resources over the same period increased similarly from £1.3 billion to £5.8 billion. The average ratio of capital to deposits was over 8½% in 1969 and about 8¾% last year, though during the interim period it fell to a little more than 7%. A similar trend has been shown by free capital, which fell from just over 4% of deposits in 1969 to 2½% in 1975 and had, on a comparable basis, recovered only to 3% in 1977. Last year, however, the free capital ratio rose to 4½% but accounting adjustments played a significant part in this.

In terms of current values, the pre-tax profits of the Big Four bank groups increased from £210 million in 1969 to over £1 billion in 1978 but in real terms the trend is far less positive. This suggests that pre-tax profits, at constant 1969 prices, reached a peak in 1973, dipped sharply in 1974 and 1975 and had not recovered to the level of 1973 by last year. These figures underscore the crucial difficulty of maintaining capital in real terms in an inflationary climate characterised by rising costs, price controls and unindexed taxation liabilities. The recovery in capital ratios between 1974 and 1976 was largely attributable to issues of loan stock. Last year, the further apparent improvement owed much to substantial transfers of deferred taxation to free reserves by all the banks.

Capital and Banking Supervision

In the unstable conditions of the 1970s, supervision of commercial banks by central banks, with the aim of promoting soundness, has become a dominant global theme, rendered both more necessary and more difficult by the persistence of inflation. Banking supervision has evolved informally in the UK but is in process of becoming statutory, to meet Britain's EEC commitment and in response to the growth of the financial sector. In recent years, rather more emphasis has been placed on questions of adequate capitalisation, and the regular discussions between the Bank of England

and senior management in the clearing banks have paid due regard to this consideration. In the building up of relevant global pictures, the Bank of England has played a most valuable pioneering role, taking also a leading part in the development of the concept of a 'parental responsibility' among international banks and so strengthening the forces of stability in the world's financial sector.

The Outlook for Bank Capital

To summarise: by comparison with earlier periods, the present decade has thus seen a continuing demand for capital from the banks, but one which has stemmed both from unprecedented expansion and diversification of their business and from the need to maintain their soundness in an unstable and inflationary climate.

But the basic functions of capital in banking have not changed. Capital is required to support the banking business, to permit its expansion and to cover fixed and intangible assets. To enable their businesses to survive and grow, it is essential that banks should be able to generate a level of earnings adequate to build up reserves, to make fair distributions to their shareholders and to encourage further investment.

As the Price Commission acknowledged (HMSO, 1978), clearing bank profits in the 1970s have not in themselves been adequate to maintain free capital and this has necessitated considerable efforts to raise new capital in the market. It is of unquestionable importance that a paucity of capital should not, at some future time, become a major constraint on the growth of the banks and hence on their ability to compete in the world league.

Inflation of the type experienced in the 1970s expands bank balance sheets and adds to costs in circumstances in which it is generally impossible to generate sufficient retained profits to maintain capital intact. The quest for ever increasing efficiency in domestic and international markets must, therefore, continue.

This is the more necessary because competition in all aspects of clearing bank business has increased sharply both in the sterling and in the currency markets, where other major international banks are often free to offer services in their local currencies totally unhampered by the constraints of exchange control.

Relaxation of UK exchange control could specifically assist British banks in two regards. Firstly, greater freedom to lend sterling to non-residents would enable the banks to develop international business in the same currency as their equity base and so make better use of the highly developed facilities of the London market. Secondly, authority to hold part of capital reserves in foreign currency would reduce the pressures on bank capital which can arise, as in 1976, from weakness of sterling.

The banks have tried in the 1970s to supplement their equity and to mitigate the effects of exchange rate changes on their sterling capital by issues of subordinated loan stock in appropriate foreign currencies. Such issues, as we have seen, are not the same as equity but do have their place, especially for a sterling-based bank wishing to extend its international deposits and loans and its overseas investments. Thus a series of medium-term loans with maturities carefully arranged constitutes sound support for trading.

For a major banking group, the concept of capital adequacy must relate to the totality of capital resources employed in the business. What is adequate in this respect may be judged from different viewpoints which must in practice be reconciled, namely: *first*, the bank itself has an obvious responsibility to its depositors and its shareholders to be capitalised in a prudent manner; *second*, the central bank has responsibilities for the stability of the banking sector as a whole. In discharging this task, its contact with individual banks enables it to form a unique view of the quality of their management and balance sheet structure; *third*, what the well-informed outside observer expects to see in the balance sheet may not be an irrelevant consideration.

The nature and quality of bank assets as a factor in assessing capital adequacy have been mentioned, and important in this regard must be a consideration of the implications of the growth of international business and of the diversification of banking services.

There is nothing in the present picture to suggest that British banks – parents or groups – are under-capitalised and, indeed, by world standards, they are better capitalised than their counterparts in many developed countries. But inflation and rising costs have put strong pressure on bank capital in the 1970s and are likely to continue to do so in future. This presents a fundamental challenge that bankers must meet and as we move into the second century of our Institute's history it must constitute a subject of interest and importance.

The future cannot be foreseen but there can be no doubt that we shall have a growing need for professionalism to ensure a sound banking sector as a prerequisite of a stable and well-ordered society. An understanding of the place of capital in our increasingly complex world is something which all should seek, even though final responsibility falls on the few.

References

Bank of England (1971), *Bank of England Quarterly Bulletin*, vol. 11, no. 2, June 1971, pp. 189–93 and articles in subsequent issues.

McMahon, C.W. (1976), 'Controlling the euromarkets', *Bank of England Quarterly Bulletin*, (March), vol. 16, no. 1, pp. 74–7.

HMSO (1918), *Report of the Treasury Committee on Bank Amalgamations*, Cd 9052.
HMSO (1931), *Report of the Committee on Finance and Industry*, Cmd 3897.
HMSO (1945), *Report of the Committee on Company Law Amendment*, Cmd 6659.
HMSO (1961), *Company Law Committee, Minutes of Evidence*, ninth day, (16 December 1960.
HMSO (1959), *Report of the Committee on the Working of the Monetary System*, Cmnd 827, para. 127.
Select Committee on Nationalised Industries (1978), (House of Commons) Sub-committee C. Minutes of Evidence, Session 1977–8, 18 January 1978, Bank of England Evidence, para. 3.
HMSO (1978), Price Commission, *Banks: Charges for Money Transmission Services.*

13 Capital Adequacy, Hidden Reserves and Provisions*

* Paper read at University of Modena, 20 April 1983

JACK REVELL

The debate on capital adequacy has blossomed over the past decade. It began in the US in the 1950s as the various regulatory authorities started to devise new measures of adequacy when bank portfolios were no longer dominated by government securities acquired during the war. In Europe it took the banking crisis of 1974/5 and the much more uncertain and fragile banking environment of the second half of the 1970s to arouse much interest in the subject. In Britain bank capital was not even mentioned until about 1974 or 1975, but since then there has been some debate. To some extent the debate has become an Anglo-Italian one; I have been invited to read several papers on the subject to Italian audiences, and these have been published in Italian journals.

This paper is about the old subject, the functions and level of bank capital (or own funds), as the title indicates. Much of the paper, however, will be about two topics that have only just come into prominence, provisions (particularly for possible loan losses) and hidden reserves. Both of these topics have an accounting flavour, and I must make it clear that I have no particular qualifications in that field. Accounting problems are, however, a very important part of the issue because they bring into prominence the ability of the market (meaning depositors and their advisers as well as other banks) to make an informed judgement of the soundness of any bank.

Substitutes for Capital

We are so accustomed to focus attention on bank capital as the sole measure of a bank's ability to sustain losses and to inspire public confidence that we tend to forget that this is a very recent approach. Not so many years ago the discussion would have been far more in terms of items outside the figures of published capital. Even today there are also voices, mainly of academic economists, which urge that there are means of avoiding the emphasis on bank capital and the regulation that goes with this emphasis. It is worth beginning by examining the various substitutes for capital that have existed or have been proposed.

In the early days bankers were wealthy individuals, and they published no accounts; the ability to absorb losses and to inspire confidence depended completely on the knowledge that the banker's entire private wealth could be called on if necessary, although nobody could quantify that wealth. Nowadays no new private bankers, as they are usually called, may be established in any European country, but a few banking houses of that form still linger on in some countries and even more family-owned banks with the status of joint stock companies. Another relic of the days when shareholders could all be presumed to have considerable personal wealth still remains in the form of uncalled capital, the obligation on bank shareholders to contribute further capital when called on to do so in emergency. This is an obvious legacy of the private bankers, merely formalizing and limiting the requirement on bankers to stake their personal fortunes in the venture.

Yet another legacy from the private bankers is the right of banks to have hidden reserves, which still persists in many countries and which will be only partly limited by the harmonization measures of the EEC for bank accounting. The importance that was attached to hidden reserves right up to the present day is nowhere better illustrated than in a statement by Professor Sayers (1967, p. 30) in the last edition of his classic text, *Modern Banking*:

> Nowadays, in England at least, capital has ceased to be necessary, especially as the banks are, by special dispensation under the Companies Acts, allowed to conceal their profit experience, and do in fact leave their shareholders and their customers almost completely ignorant of their trading experience.

It is somewhat ironic, in view of the crisis that came to British banks only six years later, that Sayers should have added (p. 31): 'In some other countries, where the banks are less firmly established and public confidence could be more easily shaken, the capital of banks naturally retains its original significance.'

The philosophy behind hidden reserves is that there should be something outside and in addition to the stated figures in the balance sheet to provide extra cover for risks and losses. If this extra something, unquantifiable though it be, is believed to be substantial, the published figures for the own funds of the bank become of less significance. This is exemplified by my favourite quotation (from a bank chairman's spech in 1901, quoted in Goodhart, 1972, p. 15): 'We like to feel that, not only do the figures in the balance sheet show you the true position, but that the real position is a little better still.' Hidden reserves form the subject matter of most of this paper, but it is important to realize that they are the most important and the most persistent of the substitutes for capital.

One substitute for equity capital that has come into prominence in recent years is medium-term fixed-interest finance in the form of bonds subordinated to the claims of the depositors in the event of liquidation. They have been allowed to count towards capital requirements within strict limits by the supervisory authorities of several countries. It should be recognized that they are a substitute for shareholder's capital in only one of its functions, that of providing the physical infrastructure for the operations of the bank. They are suitable for financing the acquisition of premises (real property) and computers, but they are not a substitute for equity in the loss-bearing function of bank capital.

To complete the list of substitutes for bank capital it is necessary to refer to the views of certain economists whose faith in the omniscience and omnipotence of the market is greater than mine; they are to be found particularly in the Monetarist School. These economists believe that a combination of the central bank acting as lender of last resort and deposit insurance eliminates the need for most bank regulation and supervision; by implication their views deny the overriding importance of bank capital ratios. The answer is quite simple and practical. Both the central bank and the large banks that provide the bulk of funds for deposit insurance schemes are most anxious to limit the calls on the resources of the government and insurance funds; they demand that each bank should have enough capital to cover the risks arising from anything short of a general crisis in the banking system, and they demand that banks be supervised adequately to ensure that they do not indulge in dangerous business. A short while ago an economist put to me a scheme for deposit insurance with premiums varying according to the risk involved in each bank's business as a substitute for the assessment of capital adequacy. The answer remains the same: the assessing of the premium involves what is, in effect, supervision, except that the assessor imposes a financial rather that a regulatory sanction, and for banks with low capital ratios the premium would have to be prohibitively high. Capital ratios come in through the back door as an element in assessing premiums.

Of the various substitutes for capital that have been examined in this brief survey, the private wealth of sole owners and even shareholders has largely gone the way of the world, and only hidden reserves of different kinds still play a large part in the accounting of banks. We shall begin by looking at the general question of hidden reserves and then examine in more detail the use of provisions as hidden reserves.

Hidden reserves

One very useful source of information on hidden reserves in the balance sheets of banks in EEC countries, Switzerland, the US and Japan is a survey conducted by the Frankfurt office of the international firm of accountants Peat, Marwick, Mitchell & Co. (1980) for the German Association of Public Banks. Despite its German origin, title and text, it has the very useful feature of a parallel English translation. It explains in some detail for each country the ways in which hidden reserves are created and comments on the attitudes of the various authorities to their existence.

Hidden (or inner) reserves have several different forms, but these have one feature in common; whether they are included in the balance sheet or kept completely outside it, the uninformed reader of the published accounts (and sometimes even the supervisory authorities) cannot measure their extent. There is general agreement that their main purposes are to absorb losses and to smooth the published profit figures. A dramatic example of their use for both purposes was the Chiasso affair in 1977, as a result of which the Swiss Credit Bank had to write off losses of Swiss francs 1.2 billion; by using hidden reserves it was actually able to show a profit figure in 1977 of Swiss francs 235 million, some 17 per cent higher than the 1976 figure.

The two purposes of hidden reserves necessarily go together to a large extent because unexpected losses are the main cause of adverse profits. Banking is a business exposed to several superimposed cyclical factors. The general cycle of economic activity operates on bank profits, usually with a lagged effect since interest rates and the demand for credit remain high in the first stages of a recession, and loan losses appear somewhat later. The effects of changes in interest rates depend largely on balance sheet structures through the speed with which the interest rates on assets can be adjusted relative to the speed of adjustment of liability interest rates. There are other independent cycles associated with particular industries to which banks lend. It is often the case that banks invest heavily in loans to the shipping industry and for the construction of real property during the upturn; both these industries have what might be called 'hog cycles' of their own because of the long lag between a shortage of ships or buildings becoming apparent and the completion of the construction period.

Banks have always feared that public confidence will be impaired if they show a drop in profits or an overall loss. There have been some examples in recent years of quite large banks reporting overall losses without causing a run on their deposits, but the fear remains a very real one. It is only a small step from this fear of reporting adverse results to a positive belief that banks should have the means available for manipulating their profit figures in such a way that they show a fairly steady upward trend over time. Even in those countries where hidden reserves are tolerated, the open use of hidden reserves for this purpose is coming to be frowned on or limited in some way, usually by requiring the auditor's agreement to the extent of adjustments to the actual profit figures. Switzerland is a clear exception to this statement because companies (including banks) are allowed to undervalue their assets and to create other hidden reserves 'to the extent necessary to ensure the continued prosperity of the company or to distribute as equal a dividend as possible'.

There are several ways in which hidden reserves can be classified, but possibly the most useful distinction is between 'active' reserves, which are created through the operating account, and 'passive' reserves, which arise automatically in the balance sheet as current values of assets and liabilities change from the values recorded in the balance sheet. For practical purposes a further distinction is necessary between those cases in which the size of a provision is clearcut and those in which a great deal of judgement is involved; even though the need for a provision is obvious and the amounts in aggregate are shown in the operating account, the latter cases give an opportunity for creating hidden reserves through over-provision. Hidden reserves can also be created in a passive way by failing to reverse a provision when the need for it has passed. So much for the somewhat dreary subject of taxonomy; the points can be made more easily through examples of the various ways in which hidden reserves are created.

A hidden reserve is created whenever as asset is undervalued or a liability is overvalued. Since banks are rarely required to record even longer-term assets at current market values, the scope for hidden reserves is tremendous. One favourite form of creation of hidden reserves for British banks has always been the valuation of the premises that they occupy and the real property that they may hold for investment purposes. As late as the 1960s it was common for small banks with one office to show this at a purely nominal £1 or £100 in their balance sheets, having depreciated it almost entirely in the year of purchase. Even the larger banks continued to show their branch networks at cost of acquisition even when the current values were considerably higher. During the early 1970s, however, when the acceleration of inflation made the maintenance of capital ratios more difficult, the banks reversed this process; they revalued their premises and other properties almost every year in order to transfer the hidden reserves into the published reserves shown on the balance sheet to boost their capital figures. This second process would not avail them much today because the Bank of England now operates in terms of 'free capital' for judging capital adequacy, free capital being the total of capital accounts after deduction of fixed assets such as buildings and participations.

The overvaluation of liabilities can also be illustrated from British experience. There is a list of banks which are legally exempt from the obligation to declare a true profit figure. No new names are being added to the list, but even after the larger banks had voluntarily renounced the exemption in 1969, the privilege remains of importance for discount houses and many smaller banks; it will disappear when the EEC proposals for harmonization of bank accounting practices become part of British law. The exemption works by allowing the banks to publish a profit figure after tax and after transfers have been made to and from inner reserves, the inner reserves appearing indistinguishably in the balance sheet under 'deposit and other accounts', thus overvaluing the liabilities of the bank to its customers.

Holdings of marketable securities are subject to valuation changes, but in a rather different way. Because most of those held by banks are bonds, their current values tend to decline when inflation accelerates because of the higher levels of interest rates. This may or may not affect the profit figure according to the methods of valuation followed by the banks. By far the most common method is to carry bonds at the lower of cost or market value, thus necessitating a deduction in the operating account only when a drop in market prices leads to the writing down of balance sheet values. In some Scandinavian countries bonds are reported at the market values current on the balance sheet date, and the provisions are created and written back each year as market values change. This illustrates an important point: the creation of hidden reserves has its mirror image when it depends on valuation changes. What goes up will probably come down again unless it is tied directly to inflation, and there is no guarantee that the valuation changes will always work to smooth the final profit figure. This is probably why some banks prefer to amortize the difference between cost of acquisition and eventual redemption value over the remaining life of the bond, ignoring changes in market prices.

The creation of hidden reserves through provisions has come up under the heading of marketable securities, but for most banks provisions for loan losses are considerably more important. They are so important that they must be examined in detail later on. There is also another heading of provisions that is growing in importance, provisions for future pension obligations. When the payment of pensions is considered as merely an extension of the payment of salaries, there is no problem, but increasingly auditors are demanding some recognition of the increasing burden of pension payments in inflationary times. Some banks already make partial attempts to fund their future obligations, and in others there is an independent pension fund outside the bank balance sheet, to which the bank, as employer, pays contributions and payments for deficiencies found on the actuarial valuation. In the mid 1970s, when inflation rose to record rates (25 per cent in the UK), these deficiencies were enormous. As a result banks had a useful means for smoothing profits because they could decide how far the actuarial deficiency should be covered by special payments in any one year.

Hidden reserves arise from a number of other sources, particularly from the philosophy of the accounting profession that everything must be stated on the most conservative basis possible. Thus the accountant will demand recognition of every future tax liability even when there is little possibility that the bank will be called on to pay up. British banks have been showing very large items for deferred tax on leasing transactions, although it is most unlikely that the tax will ever be paid. The same philosophy applied to other accruals. Unrealized trading gains on securities and foreign exchange are not taken into account, but all unrealized losses are.

Foreign exchange complicates the problem of smoothing profits in a further way. Large banks in the developed countries habitually make between 20 and 50 per cent of their profits on operations in foreign currencies, but they calculate their profits exclusively in the domestic currency. The profit figure in any one year thus depends greatly on the relative movements in the domestic and foreign currencies. If the domestic currency has depreciated against the currencies in which profits were earned, the profit figure in domestic currency will be boosted, and vice versa. It is possible to regard the additional reserves created when the domestic currency depreciates as hidden reserves, but it is probably more fruitful to recognize that international banking has introduced another disturbing element into the problem of reporting steady profit levels.

Provisions for Loan Losses

The question of provisions for loan losses has been prominent in the news in recent months because of the debt problems of a number of countries, such as Mexico, Argentina and Poland. At a lower level provisions for domestic loans have been necessary on a large scale. Although there has been some theoretical discussion about provisions, there are still several interesting points, and countries differ widely in the latitude they allow to banks in creating provisions for what is the largest risk in their balance sheets. Our examination will show that provisions have elements of both of the topics that have been discussed so far in this paper: they can act partly as a substitute for capital, and they can be used to create hidden reserves. They have the additional feature that the extent of accumulated provisions will remain hidden under the EEC proposals for harmonization of bank accounting.

Table 13.1 fulfils two purposes. In the first place it shows the wide disparity between the extent of provisions made by banks in different countries, measured as a percentage of average total assets during the year. In the second place it demonstrates that provisions have increased markedly in most of the countries over the three years from 1979, although the percentage has remained fairly constant in one or two. The figures are

Table 13.1 *Relative importance of provisions in various countries*

Provisions made during the year as percentages of average total assets

	1979	*1980*	*1981*	*First half 1982*
Large banks				
Austria	0.26	0.22	0.22	*
France	0.36	0.65	0.70	*
Germany	0.24	0.38	0.63	*
Italy	1.01	1.48	1.91	*
Netherlands	0.25	0.34	0.48	0.49
Norway	0.64	0.50	0.57	*
Spain	0.78	1.23	1.15	0.95
Switzerland	0.22	0.25	0.32	*
UK	0.33	0.55	0.44	*
US	0.29	0.31	0.30	0.38
All commercial banks				
Belgium	0.27	0.28	0.28	*
France	0.36	0.58	0.61	*
Italy	0.55	0.82	1.02	*
Norway	0.67	0.53	0.59	*
Spain	0.73	1.02	0.98	0.82
Switzerland	0.23	0.29	0.35	*
US	0.24	0.25	0.26	*

Source: Central banks

derived from the returns submitted by central banks as a continuation of my OECD study, *Costs and Margins in Banking* (Revell 1980); the choice of countries is thus determined by the regularity with which the central banks submitted the required statistics. The figures unfortunately include both provisions of all kinds (including those for value changes of securities) and depreciation, but provisions for loan losses are by far the largest element in most series and they account for the greater part of the increase in the percentage over the years. It is interesting to note that Italy comes out as the country with the largest provisions percentage in 1981; the rate of increase of the Italian large banks series is lower than that of several other series, but for all commercial banks Italy has the highest growth rate of all the series shown.

Provisions for loan losses are divided into two classes, specific and general.

The specific provisions are those that are specific to particular loans that have been identified as likely to lead to loss. They are thus a prudent recognition that loss is likely to occur on a particular loan, although the amount of the loss is still in doubt. They are clearly not part of the capital accounts, except to the extent that the loss would have been met out of capital (or current earnings) if the likelihood of loss had not been recognized in time through a specific provision. In most countries specific provisions may be made out of untaxed income within the limits agreed by the tax authorities; in some countries the authorities are prepared to recognize most specific provisions made by banks, and in others they are more restrictive, up to the point of requiring the debtor to become bankrupt before the provision is allowed for tax purposes. Banks may, of course, make what additional specific provisions they like out of taxed income (subject to the auditor's agreement), and they can thus create hidden reserves by a generous policy of making provisions.

General provisions are much more contentious, and they are not allowed in many countries. The rationale of a general provision, which is a provision against the loan portfolio as a whole without indentifying specific loans, is that among any group of loans there will be losses that will not be recognized at the time of granting the loan or at the date of the last balance sheet. Accounting purists argue that they are not provisions at all but a reserve forming part of the capital accounts; the Bank of England (and possibly some other supervisory authorities) takes this point by including general provisions in its capital adequacy calculations. Theoretically we could say that they are intended to deal with the uncertainty inherent in any loan portfolio, just as capital is there to cover uncertainty rather than specific risks. This argument is weakened somewhat, however, by the fact that the amount of the general provision is usually based on a formula relating it to past loan losses. In practical terms general provisions come somewhere between capital and provisions, but it is only prudent to allow for the fact that unpredictable losses will occur in any loan portfolio.

In almost all countries general provisions have to be made out of taxed income, but this again does not prevent their being used to create hidden reserves through over-generous creation of provisions; equally we must recognize that the experience of loan losses over the past five years – a common basis for the formula – will lead to the creation of too low a level of provisions when conditions deteriorate unless special measures are taken. I recently saw an ingenious scheme put forward by a reinsurance company that would, in theory, enable some general provisions to be made out of untaxed income. Recognizing the current difficulties that banks were having in maintaining capital ratios through retained earnings or by raising new capital, the scheme suggested that one-half of the loan portfolio (with some exclusions) should be insured, the risk being spread through the reinsurance market. Since the insurance premiums would be a recognized cost for the banks, this would mean that a large part of the general provisions could be made out of untaxed income – as long as the supervisory authorities were prepared to regard insurance as compensating for low capital ratios.

Accounting for Provisions

The amount of information on provisions for loan losses that is provided in the published accounts of banks varies widely, and few aggregate statistics for classes of banks give any detail. In most countries a full operating account is required, and this almost invariably contains some figure for provisions. It is rare to find this figure split down into the different types of provision; often depreciation of buildings and equipment is lumped in with provisions for securities and loans. Actual losses are rarely revealed unless they are so large that concealment is impossible. Even a single figure in the operating account serves the useful function of putting the reader on notice that the bank may have created hidden reserves when this figure is much larger than that of the year before. The key point, however, is to know a figure for accumulated provisions in order to judge whether this year's provision is adequate or excessive. All too often the level of accumulated provisions is hidden in the balance sheet by deducting it from the values of loans and securities instead of revealing it as a figure on the liabilities side.

In the past few years there has been a marked improvement among banks in revealing the full accounting for provisions. Not only have large banks in some countries begun to give figures for the differents kinds of provision and to reveal accumulated provisions under each heading, but many provide a separate provisions account showing accumulated provisions at the beginning of the year, the charge on the operating account, actual write-offs for losses, recoveries from previous provisions no longer necessary, and the accumulated provisions at the end of the year. It is therefore somewhat disturbing to find that the EEC proposals for the harmonization of bank accounting fall a long way short of this best practice and perpetuate the use of provisions as a form of hidden reserves.

The EEC Draft Directive does require the separation of 'charges for value adjustments' in respect of loans and guarantees (Article 34) from those in respect of securities and participations (Article 35), although it specifically allows charges and income under each heading to be set off against each other, leaving only a net figure in the operating account. The real trouble comes with the valuation proposals for the balance sheet. Article 37 allows loans and advances to credit institutions and customers to be shown at a value up to 5 per cent lower than their original value 'where this is necessary in view of the prudence dictated by the particular risks attaching to banking business'. It goes on to say that these lower values 'may be maintained until the credit institution drawing up the balance sheet wishes to write up the items in order to avoid undue fluctuations in value adjustment charges'. The result is a charter for the creation of hidden reserves on a vast scale, if ever there was one.

Table 13.2 uses figures from the same source as Table 13.1 to work out some examples among large banks in EEC countries (including Spain) comparing the maximum extent of accumulated provisions against loan losses permissible under the Draft Directive with the capital and reserves of the same group of banks; the percentage ratio is shown in the last column. In every case these provisions, consisting of the addition of specific and general provisions since there is no requirement that all doubtful loans should be identified, would be very large compared with the capital accounts; in the one case of the eight large French banks they would be not far short of four times as large. The previous two columns show the two factors that help to explain the diversity of figures in the last column. The accumulated provisions would be so much larger than the capital accounts in the large French banks because they have such low capital ratios and such a large part of the balance sheet total consists of loans and credits; the three large Italian banks would have a much lower ratio of accumulated provisions to capital accounts because their capital ratios are twice those of the French banks and because the proportion of loans and credits is very much lower. Through a combination of the two factors the large banks in the other countries would have ratios of accumulated provisions to capital accounts somewhere between those of the large banks in France and Italy. This particular EEC proposal takes the matter back a decade or two to the days when hidden reserves were regarded as essential for a sound banking

Table 13.2 *Comparison of capital accounts and 5% loan loss provisions; large banks in EEC countries, 1981*

Percentages

Country	*No. of banks*	*Capital accounts / total assets*	*Loans & credits / total assets*	*5% provision / capital accounts*
France	8	1.11	83.5	375.2
Germany	6	7.15	87.5	61.1
Italy	3	2.32	20.8	44.9
Spain	7	5.61	71.3	63.3
UK	30	4.81	73.3	76.1

Source: Central banks and author's calculations.

system and when it was considered necessary that there should always be some unquantifiable element of risk-bearing resources in addition to the declared capital and reserves. Homer has indeed nodded.

Provisions and Capital

In the course of the previous discussion two ways in which provisions, particularly for possible loan losses, can act as a partial substitute for capital have emerged. The first is that capital must bear losses if provisions are insufficient. The second is that provisions are a means of creating hidden reserves which can only be limited and never completely eliminated. In particular generous or niggardly provisioning can be used to smooth profit figures, and this process has been sanctified by the EEC Commission. In recent years an even stronger link between provisions and capital has been created by the need for many banks to choose between maintaining capital ratios and making adequate provisions for likely and possible loan losses.

As we noted earlier, there has been much emphasis in the past two years or so on the adequacy of the provisions made by banks. This emphasis has come particularly on the international side from the arrangements that have been necessary for the rescheduling of massive debts to certain countries in Latin America and Eastern Europe. Less prominent in the public eye has been the need for increased provisions on domestic loans as losses have piled up because of the general economic recession. In times of recession there is bound to be a tendency for bank profits to be lower than under buoyant economic conditions or in the first year of a recession, when the rest of the economy borrows heavily from the banks and when interest rates remain high as a consequence. To the extent that bank auditors and supervisors concentrate their attention on the adequacy of provisions against all doubtful loans or against the loan portfolio as a whole, banks must relax their efforts to maintain capital ratios.

The best example of this dilemma that I know of is the Spanish banking system, of which I have made a special study for several years at the invitation of a Spanish bank. In order to explain it adequately I must start by giving some brief background information.

Ever since the death of General Franco the Bank of Spain has been gradually relaxing the very rigid controls that existed over the banking system. These efforts could not have come at a worse time: it is one thing to have liberalized a banking system in the later 1960s, as many European countries did, but quite another to attempt it during the onset of a general economic recession. The result has been that since 1978 the Spanish banking system has been in a state of crisis. More than twenty banks are in the care of the Deposit Protection Fund established by the Bank of Spain; after a period of convalescence some of these unsound banks have been taken over by other banks, mostly the seven large banks. From figures provided by the Bank of Spain it is possible to calculate that the total assets of the banks under the care of the Deposit Protection Fund at the end of 1981 amounted to around 11 per cent of the total assets of the entire banking system. By way of comparison, we can estimate that the total assets of the British fringe banks that got into difficulties in 1973/4 were no more than 6 per cent of the aggregate total assets of the British banking system. Since then Banco Urquijo has been absorbed by Banco Hispano-Americano, and the Rumasa group of several banks has been taken over by the government.

Spain is one of the few remaining countries in which a minimum capital ratio applies to all banks; it is 8 per cent of deposits. In 1978 the Bank of Spain required the banks to increase their provisions considerably over a four-year period, and it has recently issued new norms for the next four years. No provision is made until a loan goes into default for the first time, and the provision is increased steadily over a period of three years while the loan remains in default. They are thus exclusively specific provisions, but the new regulation has an interesting feature: it requires that by 1986 all banks shall have accumulated provisions amounting to a minimum of 1.5 per cent of the loan portfolio. This is effectively legislating for a general provision to be created for those years in which specific provisions fall below the figure of 1.5 per cent.

Table 13.1 shows the behaviour of the aggregate provisions of both large banks and all commercial banks. For both series in Spain the ratio of total provisions to average total assets rose from 1979 to a peak in 1980 and then declined in the next two periods. The ratio of provisions by all commercial banks for loan losses alone followed the same trend at a level of around 70 per cent of total provisions in the first two periods, declining to 60 per cent in the fourth period, the first half of 1982. The provisions for loan losses by large banks are not available. This decline in the proportion of available resources devoted to provisions in the face of a deepening crisis has called forth much comment. In particular the chairman of the Banking Association has been waging a crusade to persuade banks to increase their provisions.

As we have pointed out several times in the previous discussion, figures for provisions made in a year tell us very little unless we also know the figure for accumulated provisions. A possible explanation of the decline in provisions by Spanish banks could be, after all, that the upward spurt from 1978 to 1980 had resulted in adequate provisions against the doubtful loans. The accumulated provisions can be estimated fairly accurately in this case, and they amount overall to just under 60 per cent of all loans in default. This overall percentage masks the wide difference between a 67 per cent coverage by the seven large banks and a mere 40 per cent by the small banks; since newer defaults attract only a relatively small provision, the coverage by the seven large banks may well be adequate, but it cannot possibly be for the smaller banks.

My own theory is that the banks made a conscious decision to boost their capital ratios by making provisions at a slower rate. On a few simple assumptions it is possible to calculate the difference to retained earnings available to boost capital and reserves that would have been made by continuing into 1981 and the first half of 1982 the 1980 percentage of provisions. The effect on 1981 results would have been to lower retained earnings from 0.37 per cent of average total assets to 0.32 per cent; in the first half of 1982 retained earnings would have been reduced from 0.50 per cent to 0.32 per cent. These are tiny figures in relation to total assets, but the proportion that they bear to the capital accounts is much higher. The Spanish banks seem to have been facing an extreme form of the difficult choice between maintaining capital ratios and making provisions, but it is one that has faced many other banks elsewhere.

This leaves one question unanswered: if they are faced with a clear choice between increasing capital or increasing provisions, which should banks favour? One general point is that provisions made against loan losses or losses on securities cannot readily be switched to another heading, whereas capital and reserves are protection against risks of all kinds, no matter under which balance sheet heading (or none) they may materialize. This is perhaps not a very telling point. The real choice probably depends on whether the full extent of provisions is made clear in the published accounts or whether they are a form of hidden reserve. If both accumulated provisions and capital accounts are known with precision, it probably makes little difference where the extra risk-bearing resources are placed. Even so, it requires some degree of sophistication to look for the total protection to the depositor under two quite different headings. It also makes a difference whether the provisions are for loans that are already recognized as doubtful or whether a large part of them consists of a general provision. When provisions are a hidden reserve, the choice should clearly favour boosting capital.

Conclusions

This paper has delved into only a tiny corner of the debate on bank regulation and capital adequacy, but it is a corner that contains some timely issues. It started with a look at hidden reserves in a historical perspective, but it found that the ideas used to justify hidden reserves are far from dead. The idea that the real position of a bank should be a little better than the true position as certified by the auditors still lingers on, even in such august quarters as the EEC Commission. The philosophy that depositors, potential and present, should be dependent on faith rather than fact for a significant part of their assessment of a bank's soundness does not find many active defenders these days, but it remains as a memory of banking as it used to be.

One conclusion to be drawn from the various points made in the paper is that it will never be possible entirely to eliminate hidden reserves. Those arising from changes in the values of assets and liabilities could be eliminated by requiring all items in the balance sheet to be carried at their current values on the balance sheet date. Those cases in which judgement must be exercised to arrive at the size of the necessary provision would still remain, and these are often the most important cases. Judgement can be limited by restricting provisions to loans that have been subject to a defined event, such as default on interest payment or the bankruptcy of the borrower. The price to be paid for eliminating hidden reserves of this sort is a level of provisions that recognizes only a proportion of the loans that will become losses and the creation of these provisions a relatively short time before the losses occur.

The fact that hidden reserves can never be completely eliminated does not mean, however, that no effort should be made to restrict them as far as possible. The market can never know as much as the supervisory authority about a particular bank; its information must be dated, and it can have little knowledge of that crucial element, the bank's plans for the future. The information available to the supervisory authority must largely remain confidential, and depositors are dependent on the published accounts to assess how safe it is to entrust their money to a particular bank, and other banks must use published information to decide on limits for inter-bank trading. It is therefore important that the information given in published accounts should be factually correct and complete. Within their limitations depositors and their financial advisers, as well as other banks in the system, can be useful allies to the supervisory authorities in ensuring the soundness of the financial system.

As a postscript it is worth quoting the opinion of the Peat, Marwick, Mitchell & Co. (1980) survey that the 1974 fiscal reform in Italy, with its considerable penalties for the improper creation of reserves, and the mandatory form of income statement dating from 1975 have greatly reduced the importance of hidden reserves in the Italian banking system. Many of you will know far better than I do the extent of the hidden reserves that have survived the reforms.

One particular lesson can be learned from the discussion: it is dangerous to compare the capital ratios of banks without allowing for the extent of provisions and hidden reserves. This applies more to international comparisons because each country has its own regulations governing hidden reserves and provisions, but it should also be borne in mind when comparing banks within the same country. It is difficult to allow for hidden reserves, whether they take the form of provisions deducted from the balance sheet values of assets or other forms, but it should be realized that a particular bank may well have exhausted its hidden reserves to cover losses made in previous years.

References

Goodhart, C. A. E. (1972), *The Business of Banking, 1891–1914* (London: London School of Economics and Weidenfeld and Nicolson).

Peat, Marwick, Mitchell & Co. (1980), *Stille Reserven in den Jahresabschlussen von Kreditinstituten* (Hidden Reserves in the Annual Accounts of Credit Institutions), Schriften des Verbandes offentlicher Banken (Gottingen: Verlag Otto Schwartz & Co.).

Revell, J. R. S. (1980), *Costs and Margins in Banking: an International Survey* (Paris: Organization for Economic Co-operation and Development).

Sayers, R. S. (1967), *Modern Banking* (7th edn) (Oxford: Clarendon Press).

14 Capital Adequacy and Banking Supervision – Towards a Practical System*

* Published with permission of Bank Administration Institute. The paper originally appeared in the *Journal of Bank Research*, Summer 1982 (pp. 125–36)

EDWARD P. M. GARDENER

Introduction

Much of economic theory is built on hypotheses and models that purport to provide greater understanding of how the majority of economic units are likely to behave or react under real-life conditions. In this setting, conventional economics can often provide theories and insights that enhance understanding and aid useful analysis.

Viewed in this light, the capital adequacy function is a troublesome concept when approached with the conventional tools of economic analysis. By definition, it evidences an exception to the kinds of assumptions, like systematic rationality, that often have to be incorporated into the structures of conventional theories.

The capital adequacy function is expressed ultimately in terms of helping banks to weather possible severe financial pressure or financial crises. But the latter are not the product of conventional economic theory. They are the events whose repetition banking supervision (or prudential regulation) seeks actively to avoid. Consequently, the capital adequacy problem produces a kind of logical impasse in attempts to analyse it with conventional economic tools.

Those who look for 'theoretical compartments' might place the proposals of this paper alongside the kind of methodology characterising Minsky's 'Wall Street paradigm' used to develop his theory of financial crises in developed financial systems. This kind of approach to banking problems could be termed 'institutional theoretic'. Our proposals are set up as a pragmatic resolution of the need to assess and preserve the safety of individual banking firms. Although most banks may be quite capable of looking after themselves in this regard, our proposals allow for the early detection and correction of those operators with an in-built tendency toward imprudent banking. In this paper we present strong support for our proposed system from many schools of thought.

The Proposed Supervisory System

Capital adequacy – risk and the banking firm
The operational significance of the capital cushion is that it is a potential line (or component) of defence against abnormal financial pressures that may occasion a sudden and relatively high level of realized losses. Freeman (1952) was the first to recognize explicitly this specialized function of capital adequacy. This general view was subsequently taken up in the Federal Reserve Forms ABC and is accepted nowadays by the Bank of England and UK bankers. In this sense, a bank's capital adequacy position is part of the overall prudential constraint system that should help dictate the level and kind of risk exposure a bank may safely assume throughout the period of its financial plan. The latter should be our main concern in capital adequacy appraisals; the past is done.

Although the capital adequacy function is recognized clearly, no appraisal system has yet been developed which really tackles the problem effectively in the terms defined. Rules of thumb, such as capital ratios, may suffice during periods of economic stability and low inflation. But they become less useful under conditions of threatened financial instability and upheaval, when capital adequacy is most likely to be put to the test. Such conditions may be infrequent in developed financial systems. But, as recent experiences have shown, they do occur and with significant potential repercussions. As Reed *et al.* ((1976), pp. 410–11) emphasized:

> Simplicity can be a virtue in a measure of capital adequacy, but simplicity is not an adequate guide. Bank management owes, to itself and to the depositors and the economy as a whole, a careful appraisal of all the risks facing the bank when ascertaining the adequacy of bank capital. Bank management should not be lulled into a sense of false security by good times. Devastating losses have occurred in the banking system that have shaken depositors' confidence in the financial soundness of banks: losses to depositors and stockholders, and the inability to meet the legitimate demands of borrowers.

Recent experiences in highly regulated banking systems, such as those of West Germany and the United States, have also shown that banking difficulties and failures are not prevented by myriad regulations and mandatory rules applied to all banks. Given the accepted prime function of the capital cushion, an appraisal system is needed that recognizes this function and expresses it in financial terms. This dictates an operational need to devise realistic contingency tests, express them in terms of financial variables (like deposit outflows, interest rate movements, loan losses etc.) and test these on a bank's planned financial positions.

Computer assisted banking supervision – the management system and supervisory dialog

The system proposed in this paper, therefore, requires a bank to construct a series of contingency tests in order to appraise its capital adequacy position. Having constructed formal contingency tests, the bank's plan is subjected to these tests by simulation using a suitable computer model. The purpose of these tests is to assess the simulated adequacy of a bank's prudential resources and policies devised in advance to meet possible financial pressures or emergencies. If the plan is unacceptable in these terms and does not also at the same time meet management's other aims and constraints, it may have to be reformulated accordingly and retested.

The process of the 'supervisory dialog' a key feature of our approach of 'vicarious participation' in bank management by the supervisory authorities (see Revell, 1975), entails a three-point dialog on a bank's financial plan between management, supervisors and a computer simulation model. The suggested supervisory dialog is a perodic and detailed exchange between bank management and the supervisory authorities on the appropriateness of the bank's forward contingency tests for capital adequacy purposes, and the operational reasonableness of the bank's planned reactions to the hypothesised contingencies. Supervisors may employ this computer model to validate the dynamics, or possible consequences, of a sample of some of the simulated contingency tests used by management.

The suggested supervisory dialog brings with it a new concept in banking supervision, the concept of computer assisted banking supervision (CABS). It is proposed that CABS is a logical and natural development from computer assisted planning systems (CAPS) in internal bank planning. The suggested concept of CABS is a wider approach than just the use of computers in banking supervision. It involves the direct use of a sophisticated computer simulation model by supervisors themselves to test and appraise the contingency 'survival' capabilities contained within banks' financial plans. Historical evidence with supervisory appraisal schemes and the opinions of bankers themselves suggest that this is the only realistic way to conduct capital adequacy appraisals. In this setting capital adequacy appraisal is seen to be synonymous with bank solvency assessments, a primary function of any realistic supervisory system.

A note on vicarious participation

Under the proposed system, the authorities would also have to consider, at least in broad terms, the possible circumstances under which they would be required to step in and support the banking system. In this connection, they would have to be the final arbiters on the rigor and nature of the contingency tests simulated by banks in their plans. The objective of this exercise would be to avoid banks duplicating significant elements of the central bank support function into their own internal risk-cushioning resources. This should help to reduce the social cost of intermediation, even though the latter may not be wholly measurable in practical, quantitative terms.

Some might argue, of course, that this vicarious role of the supervisory authorities could detract from the private-enterprise character of banking. But if the central bank support function is not an abrogation of private-enterprise banking, vicarious participation is but a short remove from similar treatment. Banks must recognize that it is in their own interests to emphasize the role that adequate capital plays in a private-enterprise banking system. The proposed methodology for appraising capital adequacy seeks to draw out the importance of these policies. Such a system would also ensure that over-capitalized banks be given more encouragement to expand their operations, besides mitigating the dangers to overall banking confidence of imprudent operators.

Not every student would agree that even the lender of last resort function is necessarily desirable. Many would argue that the market unaided is the most efficient control mechanism. However, the lender of last resort function and the need for effective banking supervision are facts of banking life: they have evolved out of the practice and needs of the market rather than the mind of the economist. The dangers of unsupervised banking and ineffective lender of last resort action have been demonstrated clearly on several occasions; this same point was emphasized by Kindleberger (1978). The Bank of England (1978, p. 233) also stated in this regard:

> As a result of their experiences with the Overend Gurney crash of 1866, the Baring crisis of 1890 and the prolonged international crisis of 1929–33, the Bank – and the world at large – had come to regard the taking of prompt and decisive action to prevent a spreading loss of confidence as one of the essential roles of a central bank.

The fact is that banking firms are a special case compared to other firms in terms of both the key economic functions they perform and the possible 'spillover effects' precipitated by the failure of even a single bank, especially a large one. In his detailed historical survey of financial crises, Kindleberger (1978) concluded that although the lender of last resort function should exist, its presence should be doubted. His argument is that if the market is sure it is going to be saved, its self-reliance may be weakened. In a system of vicarious participation, a similar broad desideratum clearly applies: the authorities should not make public the conditions under which they feel their support function would come into effect. By similar reasoning the authorities must have clearly defined and effective powers of redress against recalcitrant and imprudent banks.

Managing Banking Risks: a Starting Point

To fulfil the main bank functions of extending credit and operating the payments mechanism, risk is unavoidable in banking activities. As long ago as 1888, Edgeworth (1888, p. 1) pointed out: 'Probability is the foundation of banking. The solvency and profits of the banker depend upon the probability that he will not be called upon to meet at once more than a certain amount of his liabilities.' A banker who seeks to avoid all legitimate risks would not survive in the market-place for long. The efficient banker seeks to strike a judicious balance between potential profitability and risk exposure.

For capital adequacy purposes, this study is directed primarily toward non-insurable risks. Insurable risks, on the other hand, may best be handled within the developed corpus of conventional business risk management and will, as a result, lie outside the strict terms of reference of this investigation.

With these points in mind, a logical first step might be to identify the main categories of risk a bank may face in its operations. These risk categories (such as liquidity and credit risk) have been identified in some detail by students like Crosse (1972) and Revell (1975). The step from listing potential sources of risk to the construction of a quantitative expression of overall risk exposure, however, is a major and problematical one. A fundamental difficulty in this area is that the possibility of realizing many banking risks is often linked to other variables and events, both internal and external to a bank.

Capital adequacy appraisal is concerned with all the risks to which a bank is exposed. It is bound up with the possibility that these risk events may be of a much more severe and/or different order than that covered within a bank's original planning estimates and hedging strategies. At an operational level, capital adequacy is concerned with the capital cushion's potential contribution to a bank's overall ability to meet sudden and unforeseen financial pressures of significant magnitude. These latter pressures may themselves precipitate marked increases in several risk exposures, such as credit and market risk. In this setting, the capital adequacy function is seen clearly as being concerned essentially with the problem of uncertainty.

What are the risks?

Let us look more closely at banking liquidity risk in order to develop a general practical aspect of risk appraisal that lends support to our proposed methodology. For expository purposes, liquidity demands may be regarded as having potential primary (or impact) effects and secondary (or incidence) effects on a bank's overall risk exposure in the financial plan. In these terms, one may refer to corresponding primary risk exposures and secondary risk exposures. The primary risk effect in this case is the liquidity demand materializing, which has to be met when it occurs. The secondary effects comprise all the financial adjustments and other possible risks that may be occasioned through this demand, particularly if it is relatively heavy and unexpected.

For instance, liquidity demands (a primary risk in the terms defined above) may precipitate bonds having to be sold at a loss to realize market risk (a secondary risk), and financial risk (another secondary risk) may also be realized if these losses adversely affect the market's rating of a bank's net worth or earnings position. Many other possible financial disturbances flowing from a primary risk realization could also be identified and chains of resultant risk realizations (secondary effects) envisaged stretching over the bank's planning period.

All other banking risks have this primary and potential secondary risk dimension. Although banks may often be able to make some quantitative evaluation of at least the range of a possible primary risk (such as liquidity and credit risk) occurring in the plan, potential secondary risk effects are not captured in this measurement alone. As a result, a bank's real (or economic) risk exposure, the sum of primary and potential secondary risk exposure, is underrated. Most conventional attempts at measuring a bank's risk exposure are guilty of this sub-system view that directs attention only to the possible primary effects of potential risk realizations.

What is really required in this area is a dynamic framework of analysis, a forward-looking and comprehensive financial 'test bed', in which the full risk implications flowing from a bank's likely primary risk exposure, other events and bank policies may be evaluated. In this kind of setting, the possible prudential consequences of financial policies in areas such as maturity unmatching in the balance sheet and maturity spacing in the bonds portfolio are exposed in an explicit fashion. The significance of such policies is that their risk potential is not realized until other events, such as relatively heavy and unexpected liquidity demands, occur. This is not to imply, however, that it is possible to measure a bank's secondary risk exposure in the same way that a bank's primary risk exposure may be measured.

The specific secondary consequences of a single primary risk realization are invariably entangled with many other variables and events in the plan. An important factor in this connection is how the bank could and would meet the risk demands in practice. Nevertheless, a suitable framework of analysis based on a bank's simulated financial plan may be used to assess the broad consequences of particular policies and their associated primary risk exposures. By simulation tests, a bank can decide whether it can safely support the financial consequences of alternative primary risk exposures. For example, in this approach a bank may evaluate whether other financial objectives and desired constraints are liable to be threatened if certain primary risk exposures are assumed alongside particular financial policies.

In practice, of course, many competitive banks already undertake (albeit often informally) similar simulation exercises or sensitivity tests, though not in the context of appraising their capital adequacy positions. For supervisory purposes, however, these operational desiderata do expose the fallacy of attempting to equate a bank's primary risk exposure with the bank's respective real risk exposure. Supervisory appraisal schemes that only list assets and assign respective percentage capital covers to reflect corresponding 'riskiness', for example, are guilty of this fallacious equation. Even the Federal Reserve Form ABC does not tackle this aspect in a satisfactory fashion, although it is the only supervisory tool that attempts to recognize the problem. Realistic supervision requires that supervisors 'go behind the balance sheet' and adopt a more comprehensive and dynamic systems view in a forward-looking setting. In short, a suitable computer simulation model is required, together with a complementary and realistic testing methodology.

Although this approach means that neat and precise measures of a bank's real risk exposure may not be practical (or needed), one should be able to assess the most significant 'solvency consequences' of the primary risk exposures and financial policies assumed by management. Attention may now be directed towards an explanation of how the proposed system is both a supervisory aid and an additional tool to handle the uncertainty dimension in banking risk management. It will be recalled that a bank's capital cushion is essentially a kind of internal insurance fund against the possible financial uncertainties faced by a bank.

Contingency testing to handle uncertainty – a systems view

Contingency testing for capital adequacy is concerned with a specific aspect of banking risk management – the problem of uncertainty and a bank's corresponding ability to respond effectively to severe financial pressures that may be realized during the time spanned by the financial plan. A marked advantage of contingency tests is that they expose the financial consequences of a bank's planned risk exposure in a dynamic setting. This planned risk exposure includes the influence of such elements as balance sheet matching policies, access to liquidity liabilities and maturity-spacing positions in the bonds portfolio on a bank's ability to meet sudden financial strains. In short, capital adequacy appraisal is a systems problem and cannot realistically be divorced from all the other key areas of bank balance-sheet management. A dynamic setting implies the need for a suitable computer model in which a bank's reaction strategies to possible financial pressures may be simulated and appraised.

The proposed system is, therefore, both a new approach to the supervision of bank prudential adequacy (of which capital adequacy is an important and interdependent component) and a tool to help handle the uncertainty problem in banking financial management. This system, however, might not be a feasible possibility were it not for two recent important developments. First, the evolution of formal planning in banks has opened up the practical potentials of contingency testing planned positions and policies. Secondly, the development of suitable computer simulation models has brought with it the possibility of more realistic contingency tests in a dynamic and systems setting. In this approach, the intervening prudential strategies open to a bank may be identified and appraised, thereby bringing in the important flow dimension to prudential appraisals.

Contingency Testing for Capital Adequacy

Background to contingency testing

Contingency tests are essentially a collection of 'financial shocks' applied to a bank's planned financial positions. The advantage of using a computer simulation model is that the dynamics of such tests on a bank's plans may be explored fully, together with the feasibility of simulated reactions. With this kind of testing program the role of the capital cushion may be seen more clearly and its adequacy appraised realistically. Randall (1965, pp. 123, 124) observed:

> Actually, both the design of a relative measure of capital adequacy and the setting of capital standards must be done in terms of some particular form and degree of economic stress, which could occur in the future, although greater precision is required in the latter undertaking. Banks require capital to meet contingencies of individual, regional and national scope. The greatest demands on the capital of individual banks are likely to occur when a national economic crisis is superimposed on a local problem.

Randall's thesis, however, did not develop this particular approach any further.

Until recently, the data requirements of a realistic contingency testing program militated against its development as a supervisory and managerial aid. In the absence of an efficient simulation model, for example, contingency testing was confined either to selected planning variables or to a balance sheet at a particular point in time, usually historical. The Federal Reserve Forms ABC are a good example of the latter 'stocks-orientated' methodology. Such schemes are clearly sub-system analyses because they do not approach the problem simultaneously within the context of the total bank plan and over the time spanned by a bank's detailed planning horizon. As a result, the important flow dimension of realistic contingency testing is neglected.

The theory and practice of contingency analysis

Some contingency tests and test variables within other contingency tests involve varying degrees of subjectivity. For example, the simulated level of loan losses in many contingency tests may often be amenable to relatively high levels of exactitude, given the assumed economic conditions underlying the test. Nevertheless, the most rigorous contingency tests must by definition be characterized by a comparatively high level of subjectivity. After all, their basic purpose is to test the resiliency of the bank plan to abnormal and unexpected pressures.

One of the closest decision problems in the contemporary management literature to these latter 'disaster tests' is in a project analysis that involves attempting to assess the likelihood of a disastrous event occurring, e.g. in deciding on the height of a sea-wall defence to prevent flooding. Although some statistical work has been done in this area (e.g. see Van Dantzig, 1956) it would appear that decision-makers cannot avoid in practice heavy reliance on their own subjectivity. No statistical approach can replace this needed element in such decision problems (see Massé, 1962). Management and supervisors, therefore, have to face up to the unavoidable fact that contingency testing for capital adequacy is essentially a subjective process.

Much can be done to harness subjectivity, but it cannot be avoided in the final analysis. Nevertheless, a structured approach for constructing realistic contingency tests is both possible and desirable. This approach implicitly separates out unforeseeable and unforeseen events in banks' plans. A structured contingency test programme seeks to bring previously unforeseen events into the planning system. On the other hand, the unforeseeables refer to that collection of events that cannot really be detected in advance by normal planning methods. The important disaster tests within the overall contingency test programme are addressed to such events. Some would argue that if no real objective level of exactitude is possible in constructing disaster tests, they should be ignored.

Clearly, this paper disputes the above argument. Practitioners themselves state that the primary function of the capital cushion is to help protect the bank's solvency against this kind of adversity. Even though disaster tests cannot avoid high levels of subjectivity in many instances, they can be used as useful tools to probe for and detect developing prudential weaknesses. Such information is of obvious value to both supervisors and management. Nevertheless, this kind of test programme does require a final arbiter. There has to be some authority exercising a general 'guardian eye' over the character and possible implications of such tests. We have already emphasized that the supervisory authorities cannot avoid this function and this is a prime feature of the suggested CABS approach.

Given the reasonable assumption that banks may face periods of severe financial stress some time in the future, is there an alternative to the kind of contingency testing program proposed in this study? As suggested earlier, one alternative would be to ignore such possibilities in the plan on the grounds that they cannot be estimated in a precise and objective fashion. In the light of recent banking experiences and the current economic climate, this approach is naïve at best and may be exceedingly dangerous to continuing bank solvency at worst.

Another alternative would be to set up a completely arbitrary programme of disaster tests of varying character and severity, and subject the plan to 'destructive testing', i.e. the formal identification of the kind of contingency events that would be liable to precipitate severe solvency problems for the enterprise. Bankers and supervisors would then have to ask themselves if they were prepared to allow the plan to carry the potential of such possibilities. This approach would certainly be an improvement on the first. It comes very close at one level to the kind of methodology proposed in this study. Nevertheless, a structured approach to the generation of disaster test data is possible that can avoid to some extent the complete arbitrariness of simulated disaster tests. A recommendation to generate a completely arbitrary set of disaster tests might also be unacceptable to practitioners.

Contingency analysis in corporate planning

The author's (1979) doctoral investigation (a condensed version of this study has now been published in book form by Gardener, 1981) found that some UK bank planners tend to regard contingency analysis as a similar exercise to the kind of informal sensitivity analysis they already conduct on key strategic planning variables. Bank corporate planning texts, like ILTAM (1974) and Handscombe (1976), also appear to reflect this view. In the general management literature, the formal process of contingency analysis and planning has also been neglected until recently. For example, Steiner (1969) does not really develop this function in any depth. As will be explained in the next section, however, the work by Donaldson during the 1960s is a marked exception to this general pattern. Nevertheless, it would appear that a more formal approach towards contingency planning is now beginning to emerge. Haner (1976) for example, discussed (albeit briefly) the concept of contingency planning in both short-range operational planning and long-range planning.

Recent attention has been focused on developing a contingency model of organizational design, see for example Shetty & Carlisle (1972) and Khandwalla (1977). The premise underlying this so-called contingency theory is that there is no one best organizational structure for an enterprise. This theory seeks to recognize explicitly the conditional dependence of the appropriate organizational structure on the dynamic interaction between such forces as environmental factors, the characteristics of organizational tasks and the composition of the management team. The contingency analysis proposed in this study, however, is not really the same concept as this specific contingency theory of organizational composition. Donaldson's work is much closer to the kind of scheme recommended by this investigation.

Donaldson's concept of 'financial mobility'

The most significant work to date in the corporate and financial management literature on formal contingency planning is undoubtedly that of Professor Donaldson of the Harvard Business School. Donaldson developed his contingency planning approach in the context of companies devising strategies for what he termed 'financial mobility'. He defined (1969, p. 57) this concept as follows:

> The capacity to influence the rate of change of economic resources from one form into another and hence to determine the mix of resources at a point in time will be referred to in this study as financial mobility. The ultimate aim of financial mobility is to achieve a state of equilibrium in funds flow consistent with essential corporate objectives.

Donaldson emphasized that it was uncertainty that gave rise to this need for financial mobility and he added (1969, p. 57):

> Thus the observation of the impact of and response to the unexpected event provides not only the best opportunity for identifying what the strategy of mobility may be but also the chance to observe financial policy in the form of a constraint on that strategy. It may be said that the economic function served by a strategy of financial mobility is the opportunity to reduce unproductive resources to a minimum without violating the company's financial policies or risk posture.

Donaldson stressed the need not only to test corporate financial mobility in the plan, but also to devise appropriate response policies in advance where indicated by these tests. He saw the latter as the major break with contemporary business forecasting and planning approaches which tend to concentrate on 'most-likely' outcomes. He made the important point that a simulated inability to meet severe financial pressures may itself increase the likelihood of a company having to face similar pressures in the future.

Contingency analysis and simulation v. forecasting and conventional sensitivity analysis

Contingency analysis and simulation are not being proposed as alternatives to bank forecasting and conventional sensitivity analysis. Indeed, a bank's plans, framed in the light of its forecasts, are the essential starting point for conducting contingency tests. Bank forecasting, however, is directed primarily towards locating the most probable band of outcomes on key forecast variables. Thus the purposes of contingency analysis and forecasting differ, even though some contingency events and test variables may sometimes be derived from the bank's forecasting base.

Because the aims of contingency analysis and forecasting differ, so do their respective information requirements and tools. For example, econometric models are important forecasting tools in some banks. Such models, however, are not appropriate techniques for contingency analysis because they are invariably constructed with the purpose of locating most-probable trends and relationships. Of course, some econometric models (see Behravesh, 1975) can be adapted to handle a crude form of contingency analysis by introducing 'random shocks' into the model's structure. Despite this possibility, econometric models are not the best tools for contingency analysis. Unlike econometric modelling, contingency analysis is much more 'micro oriented'. Realistic contingency analysis also requires the full participation and interaction of management and supervisors in the process. Contingency analysis and forecasting, therefore, are not the same process: each has its own clearly defined purposes. The most efficient tool for contingency analysis is an advanced computer simulation model of the financial position of an organization.

The kind of sensitivity analysis conventionally conducted by banks on key forecast variables is also not the same as the contingency methodology advocated by this study. In bank planning, conventional sensitivity analysis is invariably an informal process and it is usually directed at strategic variables, i.e. key planning variables beyond one year forward. The proposed contingency analysis is a more formal process and it is directed primarily toward variables within the one-year financial plan. Nevertheless, it will become clear that the general technique of sensitivity analysis does have a useful role to play in the recommended appraisal system.

Early warning research and contingency analysis

Contingency analysis is developed in this study as an early warning tool to aid both supervisors and management. The purpose of contingency testing is to identify in advance possible prudential gaps and weaknesses in bank strategies that may expose an inadequate capital cushion. Conventional research to date on constructing early warning systems in banking, however, has tended to concentrate on the use of statistical techniques, like multivariate discriminant analysis (MDA).

These statistical methodologies aim to complement and support the bank examiner's (or supervisor's) job. Such techniques have been suggested to direct the examiner towards potential problem banks as revealed by the statistical screening. These early-warning systems seek to select the smallest set of variables, usually ratios and trend relationships from the balance sheet and income statement, and derive a single discriminating score based on these same variables. On the evidence of this score, the techniques purport to give useful advance information on possible deteriorating financial positions in banks. The bulk of the research to date in this area has been done in the United States, e.g. Sinkey (1975) and Korobow, Stuhr & Martin (1977).

The first point to be made here is that contingency analysis and conventional early warning research techniques (like MDA) are clearly not the same process, although their broad aims may be construed as being similar. The second point is that significant methodological problems still have to be surmounted in devising and implementing practical early warning systems based on statistical techniques. For this reason contingency analysis may be a more efficient and acceptable tool for capital adequacy appraisal with the present state of the art. As will be demonstrated, other students also now appear to be leaning towards this view.

Many of these statistical techniques are based on deriving a discriminant score from a sample of failed and non-failed banks. This immediately raises a potential methodological difficulty: the population of failed banks in most developed banking systems is extremely thin compared to the population of non-failed banks (see Guttentag, reprinted in Altman & Sametz, 1977). Recent years have also witnessed the phenomenon of the large bank failure. The population of large bank failures is even smaller than the population of small bank failures compared to non-failed banks. Similar methodological problems also emerge in statistical attempts to compare larger banks to a derived 'peer' group of banks. How can one locate statistically a peer group for large banks when each large bank is different? Even if this were possible, how could one go about using these data in a predictive fashion? What kind of updating procedure should be used to alter peer group characteristics as economic conditions and banks' asset, liability and capital mixes change? To date, these fundamental questions have not been resolved satisfactorily.

Another problem in such research is that many of the US systems have been based on attempts to replicate or forecast the ratings assigned to banks by examiners. Such approaches start off by making the implicit assumption that examiners' ratings are themselves accurate, even though the facts have not always supported this underlying hypothesis. It is not even clear that any early warning systems developed to date can forecast examiners' ratings in a meaningful way. Again, in recent years, fraud and embezzlement have proved to be major causes of bank failures. Under these latter conditions, statistical techniques based primarily on sometimes suspect balance sheet and income statement data are liable to be inaccurate.

A useful and up-to-date collection of papers by leading students on statistical early warning research in banking was published recently in Altman & Sametz (1977). Most of the potential defects outlined above in this section are expanded upon and substantiated further in this text by a panel of experts. It will prove germane for the purposes of this study to extract some of their quotations. On large banks, Guttentag, reprinted in Altman & Sametz (1977, p. 58):

> The high social costs of large-bank failure and the weakness of statistical approaches to monitoring large banks call for a fundamentally different approach to early warning systems. What is needed is to develop a hand-tailored model for each large bank. The model would be used to simulate changes in the bank's balance sheet – especially its net worth position – under a variety of assumed economic scenarios. The bank's soundness rating would be based on the least favourable set of conditions it could survive.

Eisenbeis, reprinted in Altman & Sametz (1977, p. 65), stated in a more general context, 'Today's models focusing on today's problems may not capture tomorrow's problems very well.' He added, 'Monetary policy, inflation, the level of and changes in interest rates, and the general state of the economy are all factors beyond an individual bank or savings and loan association's control, which can impact different portfolios differently and can affect our assessment of risk.' He concluded, 'Additionally, I am sure that Guttentag would argue that the agencies should attempt, via simulation, to determine the ability of certain types of portfolio compositions to sustain various types of shocks.'

All of the aforementioned experts expressed concern at the current methodological foundations of the statistical schemes developed to date. As much of this concern was directed at the problem of detecting even small 'problem banks' in a banking system such as that of the United States, the efficacy of similar early warning systems in a UK-type system must be open to much graver doubts. The US banking system comprises more than 14,000 individual banks, and the number of bank failures and problem banks to date has been much higher than in the United Kingdom.

Against this background the door is now open for the CABS approach advocated by this study. This proposed system is also not the same as the National Bank Surveillance System (NBSS) set up by the US Comptroller in September, 1975 (see Comptroller of the Currency, 1976 and Mullin reprinted in Altman & Sametz, 1977). Although the NBSS is a computer-based monitoring system, it does not involve the kind of simulated contingency testing and analysis programme proposed by this study. The evidence and opinions to date support clearly the practical potential of the suggested CABS approach in this study.

The simulation model

Given the systems character of the capital adequacy appraisal problem and the practical desirability of a contingency testing approach, a simulation model is needed that can efficiently run such tests on banks' plans. The simulation approach in capital adequacy appraisal has already been proposed by Vojta (1973), although he did not use the kind of contingency testing approach recommended in this paper. Our approach seeks to develop the kind of methodology first suggested by Freeman (1952) and exploited in the 1956 and 1972 US Federal Reserve Forms ABC. The difference is that our proposals allow for much more realistic and comprehensive contingency tests. These tests may also be conducted quickly through the use of computer power.

A model is required which can simultaneously exploit managerial and supervisory experience, and also the computational speed and other advantages of computer power. A simulation testing framework for capital adequacy may dictate a rapid and extensive sequence of 'What if . . . ?' questions. High response speed to data inputs is needed because answers to certain 'What if . . . ?' questions may themselves dictate the requirement to set up resultant tests in order to probe further into the prudential characteristics of a bank strategy. The proposed supervisory dialog dictates an interactive computer simulation model. The delays characteristic of batch mode operations, on the other hand, would militate against the practical acceptability of the suggested supervisory dialog in CABS.

The computer model must also be easily usable and understandable by non-technical persons. Model users should not be confined necessarily to functional specialists such as operations researchers. Efficient exploitation of the proposed CABS concept and the associated contingency testing for capital adequacy requires that top management and supervisors be able to use the full potentials of the model without extensive learning. A mathematical or computer background should not be a prerequisite for direct use of the model. Experience to date has shown that model acceptability to practitioners is often very much dependent on whether they can use the model, fully appreciate what it does and relate it directly to their own activities.

A deterministic model is best suited to meet these needs. These requirements also suggest that the model should be of a financial nature. After all, the appraisal of a bank's capital adequacy and other associated prudential capabilities is a problem of financial management. Formal planning systems in banks also invariably require planning variables to be expressed ultimately in financial terms.

The model's inputs and outputs, therefore, should be in financial terms and in such a presentation format as accords closely with existing accounting and financial systems. Presentation of the simulated financial position of an enterprise is facilitated, for example, through the employment of conventional accounting formats, such as balance sheets and income statements. It is also desirable that all model outputs should be capable of being easily validated (if required) by model users using their own financial and management backgrounds. A deterministic, accounting-type model is best suited to meet these requirements.

Although the model should be simple to use and its functions easily comprehended by managerial and supervisory users, a simple model would be of limited use for the problem at hand. Capital adequacy appraisal is a system problem and, as such, is best tackled within the overall financial planning framework. This means that the model itself needs to be internally sophisticated because it will be required to perform a great many tasks on demand by the user. For example, it must be capable of producing on request a relatively comprehensive financial picture of a bank as it progresses through a simulated contingency test. A sophisticated model is required to fulfil these functions on demand for the user but, at the same time, he must be able to work easily with the model, evaluate clearly its outputs and manage the bank's financial position with these data as the simulation exercise progresses.

Finally, the proposed model should preferably be of a top-down nature. The model is designed to be used by many parties and, as a result, it should not be specific to any particular kind of banking organization. This is not to deny that data from an existing CAPS may be used in the model, but its potentials should not necessarily rest on whether a bank has already installed a CAPS in its own internal planning function. The proposed model may even form a useful starting point for a CAPS in some banks with current limited computer facilities in their planning. The model should be accessible to and capable of being used by any kind of bank. In a wider context, the supervisory authorities may eventually need to use the model in the supervisory process on other financial institutions, such as finance companies and building societies. The Bangor Simulation of Financial Institutions (SOFI) model meets all the basic specifications outlined in this section.

Building on similar work already undertaken in the United States, for example the BANKMOD model described by Robinson (1973), SOFI was constructed within the Institute of European Finance at the University College of North Wales, Bangor. The SOFI model, developed under government research funding, is under the ultimate authority of the British Technology Group. In 1979 SOFI became available generally on a time-sharing basis to users in the US and Western Europe through the services of INFONET (CSI-UK-Computer Sciences Corporation (CSC)). The available published evidence in this field suggests that SOFI will be one of the most advanced and flexible models of its kind currently available on the open market.

How the system might work

The first point to be considered relates to the composition of a bank's contingency test programme, its series of contingency tests set up to appraise its capital adequacy position by computer simulation. For supervisory purposes, the proposed system seeks to make relative capital adequacy appraisals more meaningful. By definition, one cannot appraise capital adequacy in an absolute sense. This need might suggest that, for comparative purposes, all banks be subjected to exactly the same contingency test programme. Although this may be a viable proposition for certain kinds of bank with a limited range of business, it becomes difficult to envisage this as practical for larger banks and those engaged in many different lines of business. As explained earlier, many statistical appraisal schemes have already encountered the problem of identifying practical peer groups in banking. With these points in mind, it is unrealistic that banks should be subjected to exactly the same contingency tests. Nevertheless, the authorities should dictate the composition of at least some of the contingency tests simulated.

Contingency testing for capital adequacy requires a new kind of information system for effecting prudential appraisals. In contrast to contemporary supervisory systems, it is essentially forward-looking. For some banks with limited planning capabilities it may precipitate the need to develop a more formal planning system. Indeed, a significant benefit from these proposals is that many banks may find themselves forced to plan in a more positive and structured manner. We need to recognize from the start, however, that the potential volume of data capable of being generated in a large contingency test program might make the system impractical.

In his doctoral research, the author (1979) concluded that contingency testing for capital adequacy be confined initially to the one-year plan. It was also recommended that contingency test programs be concentrated on the first two quarters of the bank plan, each quarter's planned position being subjected to six separate contingency tests. Of course, a contingency test initiated at the end of quarter one or quarter two of the plan is simulated up to the end of the one-year plan in order to appraise fully a bank's 'contingency response' to the respective test. These recommendations were shaped by a survey amongst UK banks conducted by the author and with the objective of reducing the data needs of the system. Even with the aid of computer power, one must be careful not to launch an unnecessary 'data explosion'.

Needless to say, individual banks and the supervisory authorities can always conduct more detailed sensitivity tests with the model if required. For example, having submitted its contingency test results to the authorities, a bank may be required during the ensuing supervisory dialog to undertake simulation tests in order to probe further into the prudential capabilities of the bank plan. It is proposed that a contingency test program comprise a series of 'supervisory tests' and a collection of contingency tests devised by bank management itself. The supervisory tests were recommended against the background of recent financial crises and associated research in both the US and UK.

Minsky (1975) was an early and important student of financial crises; the main thrust of his argument is that financial crises are the result of the normal functioning of a mature economy, such as that of the United States. In this respect he emphasized the inevitability of crises, or 'systematic fragility', in the financial system. He developed his 'Wall Street paradigm', an institutional approach, to help explain the kind of speculative pressures leading up to modern financial crises. Minsky's model attempts an explanation of financial crises based on observable practical events in the market, rather than abstract theories.

Other students, however, believe that the likelihood of future financial crises is reduced by economic units learning through the experience of past financial crises. For example, Kaufman (in Altman & Sametz, 1977) suggested that a certain level of financial crisis (such as the 1974/5 US experience) is sufficient to ensure that economic units adopt more prudent policies in the future. For present purposes, it is germane to note the following proposal by Kaufman (in Altman & Sametz, 1977, p. 159):

> In the current and prospective environment, where constraints are diminishing and where many structural changes in the market-place have occurred, monetary policy, to be effective, may have to engineer mini crises or at least have the market perceive the actual risk of such events if financial crises of increasing intensity are to be avoided.

The book by Altman & Sametz (1977) contains several papers on recent US financial crises. The discussants on these papers demonstrated a preference for an eclectic crises theory, and they stressed the problem of unanticipated inflation and risky corporate financial policies in fuelling financial crises. Altman (1977, p. 137) concluded:

> My own impression of these papers is that a consensus is developed that the concept of 'crisis inevitability' has few supporters either in theory or in practice. In contrast to the Minsky approach, the other papers stress the 'therapeutic' effects of learning by experience the development of 'conservative' financial policies in the *private* sector, and the evolution toward 'correct' *public* monetary and fiscal policies.

An important point drawn out by many students of financial crises is that the ultimate safety of the banking system may be preserved through bankers learning from the experience of past financial crises. Recent banking history has also shown that unwise financial policies within the banking system can themselves help precipitate a financial crisis arising from a period of financial stress and instability. The latter then provides the 'trigger mechanism' that exposes the financial dangers of policies like excessive maturity and interest rate intermediation.

Fortunately, periods of severe financial stress and financial crises are comparatively rare events in today's developed financial systems. As the most recent financial crisis fades into banking history, however, so its significance diminishes in the policies adopted by many bankers. As the more adventurous begin to move into new areas of finance, others may soon follow suit. Even the more conservative may begin to forget the lessons of the past. A kind of 'Gresham's law' in financing policies begins to operate: more risky financing begins to assume greater importance over safer and proven prudential forms of financing.

In the UK, Barclay, Gardener & Revell (1978) suggested that a cyclical pattern in bank risk assumption can be observed in modern financial systems. The process is started off by certain operators, the 'fringe institutions', moving into newer and apparently more profitable lines of business. When things are going well, these institutions are seen to be more profitable than the prudent operators who tend to hold back from such activities. This tempts more prudent banks to follow suit. Then when events take a turn for the worse, the downturn produces the phenomenon of 'loss bunching' and the penalties for over-committed banks may be severe.

As noted above, Kaufman went so far as to suggest that the authorities could minimize these potential cyclical tendencies by engineering periodically 'mini crises' in order to expose the possible risk consequences of current financial positions. This proposal seems an extreme and relatively costly undertaking, even if it were a practical possibility. Kaufman's proposals, however, clearly contain the kernel of the practical supervisory philosophy propounded by this study. As Wojnilower (in Altman & Sametz, 1977, p. 235) observed, 'Unless financial institutions are compelled to build shelters, periodic total destruction is assumed. Banking history, I believe, bears out this conclusion.'

A supervisory system of simulated disaster testing for capital adequacy is designed to encourage the building of such shelters without the kind of real world costs that may be involved in Kaufman's proposals. Against this background, the proposed supervisory tests are designed to replicate recent financial crises on the bank plan. The authorities may also conduct sensitivity analyses within these tests.

Conclusions

Sound and efficient bank managements have nothing to fear, indeed a great deal to gain, from the proposed system. The potential spillover risks of reckless and unsound banks in developed financial systems have been demonstrated on several occasions recently. By implementing our proposals, imprudent banking operators may be detected earlier, monitored more effectively and, if necessary, corrected well before they get to the stage where they may precipitate wider spillover dangers for the system. The methodology (see Gardener, 1981) is proposed as an aid to the encouragement of sound banking.

References

Altman, E. I. & A. W. Sametz (eds) (1977), *Financial Crises: Institutions and Markets in a Fragile Environment* (New York: Wiley-Interscience).

Bank of England (1978), 'The secondary banking crisis and the Bank of England's support operations', *Bank of England Quarterly Bulletin*, (June), vol. 18, no. 2, pp. 230–9.

Barclay, C., Gardener E. P. M. & Revell, J. (1978), *Competition and Regulation of Banks*, Bangor Occasional Papers in Economics, No. 14 (Cardiff: University of Wales Press).

Behravesh, N. (1975), 'Forecasting the economy with mathematical models: is it worth the effort?', *Business Review*, Federal Reserve Bank of Philadelphia, (July/Aug.), pp. 15–25.

Comptroller of the Currency (1976), *1976 Annual Report* (Washington, DC)

Crosse, H. D. (1972), *Management Policies for Commercial Banks* (Englewood-Cliffs: Prentice-Hall) 7th edn.

Donaldson, G. (1979), *Strategy for Financial Mobility*, Division of Research, Graduate School of Business Administration, Harvard University.

Edgeworth, F. Y. (1888), 'The mathematical theory of banking', *The Journal of the Royal Statistical Society*, vol. 51, part 1, (March), pp. 113–127.

Freeman, G. A. (1952), *The Problems of Adequate Bank Capital* (Illinois: Illinois Bankers' Association).

Galitz, L. C. (1977), *SOFI (Simulation of Financial Institutions): General Description and Operating Manual*, SOFI version 2A (Bangor: Institute of European Finance).

Gardener, E. P. M. (1978), 'Capital adequacy and bank prudential regulation', *Journal of Bank Research* vol. 9, no. 3 (Autumn), pp. 173–80.

Gardener, E. P. M. (1979), *A Study on Capital Adequacy Criteria for Commercial Banks*, PhD thesis (Bangor: University of Wales).

Gardener, E. P. M. (1981), *Capital Adequacy and Banking Supervision*, Bangor Occasional Papers in Economics No. 19 (Cardiff: University of Wales Press).

Handscombe, R. (ed.) (1976), *Bankers' Management Handbook* (Maidenhead: McGraw-Hill).

Haner, F. T. (1976), *Business Policy, Planning and Strategy* (Cambridge, Mass.: Winthrop Publishers).

ILTAM Corp. for Planning and Research (1974), (The Bank of Israel & The Association of Banks in Israel), *International Seminar on Systems and Planning in Banking and Finance 1974: Proceedings*.

Khandwalla, P. M. (1977), *Design of Organisations* (London: Harcourt Brace Jovanovich International).

Kindleberger, C. P. (1978), *Manias, Panics and Crashes: A History of Financial Crises* (London: Macmillan).

Korobow, L., Stuhr, D. P. and D. Martin (1977), 'A nationwide test of early warning research in banking', *Federal Reserve Bank of New York Quarterly Review*, (Autumn), pp. 37–52.

Massé, P. (1962), *Optimal Investment Decisions*, (Englewood Cliffs: Prentice-Hall).

Minsky, H. (1975), 'Financial resources in a fragile financial environment', *Challenge*, (August), pp. 6–13.

Randall, R. E. (1965), *High-Cost Deposits and Capital Adequacy*, Thesis submitted in partial fulfilment of the requirements of The Stonier Graduate School of Banking conducted by The American Bankers Association at Rutgers (New Brunswick: The State University).

Reed, E. W., Cotter, R. V., Gill, E. K. & Smith, R. K. (1976), *Commercial Banking* (Englewood Cliffs: Prentice-Hall).

Revell, J. R. S. (1975), *Solvency and Regulation of Banks*, Bangor Occasional Papers in Economics, No. 5 (Cardiff: University of Wales Press).

Robinson, R. S. (1973), 'BANKMOD: An interactive simulation aid for bank financial planning', *Journal of Bank Research*, (Autumn), pp. 212–224.

Shetty, Y. K. & Carlisle, H. M. (1972), 'A contingency model of organisational design', *California Management Review* (Fall), vol. 15, part 1, pp. 38–45.

Sinkey, J. F., Jr (1975), 'A multivariate statistical analysis of the characteristics of problem banks', *The Journal of Finance*, vol. XXX, no. 1, (March), pp. 21–36.

Steiner, G. A. (1969), *Top Management Planning* (London: Macmillan).

Van Dantzig, D. (1956), 'Economic decision problems for flood prevention', *Econometrica*, (July), pp. 276–287.

Vojta, G. J. (1973), *Bank Capital Adequacy* (New York; First National City Bank).

Vojta, G. J. (1973), 'Capital adequacy: a look at the issues', *The Magazine of Bank Administration*, vol. 49, part 9, (September), pp. 22–5.

PART E
Deposit Insurance

Part E closes the book with a more detailed consideration of bank deposit insurance. The UK deposit insurance scheme provoked considerable debate at the time it was first proposed. Many bankers were hostile towards it. A further examination of the economics of deposit insurance would now be useful. One problem that we have noted earlier is that deposit insurance is often partly (sometimes almost wholly) motivated by non-economic factors, like political and social philosophies currently in vogue. Nevertheless, there are undeniable economic issues associated with deposit insurance, and the following papers address some of these. Deposit insurance is an important supervisory issue in the United States, and it has provoked considerable discussion and analysis. The deregulation debate has prompted renewed interest in the concept of risk-related deposit insurance premiums. A considerable academic literature has developed and many of the issues may apply generally to other developed banking systems. Against this background and the apparent paucity of UK academic concern with these issues, three US papers were invited to close this collection of papers in Part E. Mark Flannery opens with an examination of why bank regulation may be needed with a deposit insurance scheme. Restrictive bank regulations are seen as an attempt to limit the alleged distortive impact of deposit insurance on bank decisions. In the following Chapter 16, Paul Horvitz argues the case against risk-related deposit insurance premiums (RRP). Many economists have advocated that RRP would be more efficient and equitable than flat-rate premiums. The final contribution in this book is from Paul Peterson, and this article was written whilst he was a consultant for the Federal Home Loan Bank Board (FHLBB). Paul Peterson tackles some of the problems with RRP raised in Paul Horvitz's paper. His thesis is that further work should be directed towards adopting a RRP system.

15 Deposit Insurance Creates a Need for Bank Regulation*

* Reprinted with permission from the Federal Reserve Bank of Philadelphia, *Business Review*, Jan./Feb. 1982 (pp. 17–27)
The author, an Assistant Professor of Finance at the University of Pennsylvania, is affiliated with the Philadelphia Finance Research Department.

MARK J. FLANNERY

Many bank managers and owners have long complained that they are over-regulated by a plethora of government agencies. The thrust of their complaint is that they could do a better job – i.e. become more profitable or increase their bank's market value – if left unencumbered by regulations limiting portfolio choice, capital adequacy, holding company formations, deposit rates, and so forth. They are doubtless correct. Yet banking in the US possesses institutional characteristics that require at least some of the regulations currently in place. In particular, Federal deposit insurance gives insured bankers an artificial incentive to undertake more risk than they would in an unregulated and uninsured free market. Bankers insured by the Federal Deposit Insurance Corporation (FDIC) can benefit *privately* by undertaking risks that the *society* as a whole consider excessive.

Restrictive bank regulations can thus be viewed as an effort to undo (or at least to limit) the distortive impact of deposit insurance on bank decisions. This view of bank regulation is certainly not all-encompassing, since numerous regulations pre-date FDIC and others are not directly related to bank risk-taking. Nonetheless, considering the impact of FDIC insurance on bank behavior can often provide a useful framework for evaluating bank regulations and regulatory reform.

The Federal Deposit Insurance System

Congress introduced nationwide bank deposit insurance by creating the FDIC in the Banking Act of 1933.[1] By year end 1980, 98.2 per cent of all commercial banks in the US were insured by FDIC. If an insured bank fails, FDIC promises to repay its depositors' losses, up to a maximum of $100,000 per account. Today, coverage extends to 79.9 per cent of all bank deposit balances in the US. In return for this insurance coverage, each insured bank pays FDIC an annual premium set by statute at 0.083 per cent of total deposit balances.[2] The FDIC uses this income to pay its expenses (including any insurance claims from failed banks' depositors) and to maintain an adequate insurance reserve fund. After providing for operating expenses, losses, and necessary additions to its reserve fund, FDIC is required to refund 60 per cent of its remaining premium income to insured banks. In recent years, such refunds have lowered the net cost of FDIC deposit insurance to 0.03 per cent or 0.04 per cent of a bank's total deposits – less than half the statutory rate.

As with any insurance operation, FDIC's reserve fund is its first line of defence in the event of bank failures. At year end 1980, this fund amounted to $11 billion, or 1.16 per cent of total insured deposits. Unlike private insurers, FDIC also possesses a unique second line of defence behind its reserve fund – a $3 billion credit line from the US Treasury. Although the government's formal commitment to support FDIC ends here, many economists and regulators believe that the Federal Reserve and the Treasury would continue to provide almost limitless support to FDIC in the event of serious bank failures. This gives the taxpaying public a substantial indirect interest in the FDIC insurance fund's viability.[3]

Despite the fact that FDIC closely resembles private insurance companies in many regards, FDIC's fixed-rate premium structure is unusual, and this constitutes the *raison d'être* for other banking regulations. Private insurers use a variety of methods to calculate the level of premiums they charge, but all have the same goal: providing adequate funds to cover future losses. Setting adequate premium levels requires an accurate asessment of the likely losses associated with each contract.

Insurance companies that cover automobiles, homes, and personal property generally charge a premium that varies with the perceived risk of the activity being underwritten. A seventeen-year-old urban male driver with three recorded accidents pays more for auto insurance than the elderly couple who live in a rural area and drive only on Sundays. Why? Because the insurance company anticipates that the teenager is more likely to have an accident and file an insurance claim. Greater perceived risk requires higher auto insurance premiums if the company is to stay in business.

Life insurance companies assess premiums in a slightly more complicated fashion. Take the case of term insurance, which pays off only if the insured dies during the policy's term. Term insurance premiums increase with an individual's age because, according to the annuity tables, older people are more likely to die during the contract period, exposing the insurance company to a loss. Like the automobile insurer, life insurance companies charge their higher-risk customers more. At the same time, however, most insurance companies try to avoid the highest risk applicants in each age-group by requiring applicants to undergo a physical examination. People in relatively poor health are denied coverage.

These examinations protect the insurance company against a phenomenon known as adverse selection. A person in poor health knows he is more likely to die than the average person his age in the general population. If all people the same age could purchase insurance for the same premium, those in worse health would be more likely to buy a policy. The average policy-holder would therefore be more likely to die than the average person in the population, and the life insurance company would find itself paying for greater death benefits than it had expected from its annuity tables.[4]

The FDIC's premium structure is like the life insurance company's in one way: each bank must initially demonstrate an acceptable level of financial health in order to qualify for FDIC coverage. But FDIC also requires frequent check-ups (bank examinations) as a condition of continued coverage. This need constantly to re-examine insured banks arises because the provision of deposit insurance itself encourages the bank to become riskier than it was before becoming insured.

Distortions Caused by FDIC Insurance

Consider first a bank with no deposit insurance. If it goes bankrupt, the shareholders will lose their entire investment and depositors will be less than fully repaid. Knowing this, each potential depositor should assess the riskiness of a bank's operations.[5] While a riskier loan portfolio is likely to mean higher returns for the bank, it also raises the prospects for bankruptcy. Depositors and stockholders will require compensation for bearing that risk in the form of a higher return on their funds. Thus the willingness of bank managers to make risky loans is held in check by the concern of depositors and stockholders for the safety of their funds. Indeed, free-market advocates contend that the ability of people to shift funds from one bank to another ensures that banks will undertake a socially correct amount of risk.

Now consider the impact of fixed-premium deposit insurance on the bank's risk-taking decision. It is easiest to begin with an assumption that 100 per cent of all bank deposits are covered and banks have no stockholders.[6] If the bank fails, FDIC stands ready to repay depositors in full, so depositors no longer care how risky the bank's asset portfolio really is. So long as people retain faith in FDIC's ability to make payments, the bank's borrowing (deposit) costs are the same no matter how risky its asset portfolio. One natural check on bank risk taking has thus been eliminated. Since riskier assets offer higher expected returns and since deposit costs don't vary with the bank's perceived risk, the bank maximizes expected profits by purchasing the riskiest available assets. This decision becomes perfectly rational from the bank's private perspective once deposit insurance has been procured. In other words, *banks have a clear incentive to become more risky when FDIC begins promising to absorb their default losses* (see Appendix to this paper).

This example overstates the argument by ignoring two important considerations. First, the bank's deposits and other liabilities are not fully (100 per cent) insured by FDIC. Some depositors will therefore demand higher interest rates when the bank's underlying portfolio risk rises, making the banker's ability to profit by undertaking socially excessive risks smaller than it would be with 100 per cent insurance coverage. Second, banks do have stockholders, and these owners are concerned about their risk exposure. Their aversion to risk will provide some limit to the manager's willingness to make ever riskier loans. FDIC insurance will still distort the private incentive to bear risk, however, by reducing the increase in deposit costs that would normally accompany greater bank portfolio risk.

Economists refer to distortions such as those resulting from FDIC deposit insurance as externalities, since one individual's actions affect the well-being of other people. An externality can be either good or bad. Picking up litter in a public park, for example, constitutes a good externality: the clean view is enjoyed by people *other than* the do-gooder. A factory whose chimney dumps soot onto nearby residents' drying laundry is a bad externality. The factory could burn cleaner fuel or install stack scrubbers, but these actions would mean lower profits.[7] The outcome – air pollution – illustrates how government regulation – pollution control – can improve overall social welfare even though it imposes a real burden on private parties such as factory owners.

Just as factories would ignore their polluting effects in the absence of regulation, banks will ignore the extra risk they impose on society as a result of not having to be concerned about the safety of depositors' funds. In response, bank regulators have taken steps to limit the risk that insured bankers are allowed to undertake. Effective regulations will reduce bank profits relative to what they would be without regulations (though with deposit insurance), but society should be made better off because of the diminished amount of bank risk-taking.

Bank Regulations as a Response to Deposit Insurance

Many types of banking regulations can be interpreted as efforts to counteract the distortive effects of fixed-premium deposit insurance. With the introduction of one distortion (the insurance), others are required to prevent too great a departure from the socially ideal result that an unregulated market mechanism would yield. (The fact that FDIC received extensive regulatory powers in conjunction with its insurance responsibilities is consistent with this view.) Not all regulations and portfolio restrictions arise because of deposit insurance, but it often provides a useful framework for evaluating new or existing regulations.

Asset limitations

Banks are subject to a large number of restrictions on the type or quality of assets they may hold in their portfolios. Banks may not own stocks or significant amounts of real estate; unsecured loans may not exceed 10 per cent of a national bank's net worth (the lending limit); equipment leases must be conservatively valued; the quality of bank loans is evaluated carefully by bank examiners (see Bank examinations, p. 263). Recently, the Federal regulators promulgated far-reaching restrictions on bank activities in the financial futures markets that many industry observers contend limit banks' ability to profit in these markets.[8] In each instance, the regulations limit bank expansion into areas that are presumed to be relatively risky. Would bankers be better off (more profitable) without such restrictions? Almost certainly the answer is yes. Eliminating regulations won't make banks worse off, because they could choose the same portfolios if they wanted.

If banks choose new portfolios, it must be because expected profits are higher. Risk may also be increased, though, and the intent of these asset restrictions is to prevent insured banks from undertaking too much risk from society's point of view.

Capital adequacy

A bank whose acquisition of risky assets is blocked by regulations could increase its shareholders' expected returns by lowering its equity cushion. Earnings from the same volume of assets would then accrue to a smaller number of shareholders, raising the expected return to each one. Since bank equity serves as a buffer to absorb losses, lowering the equity cushion also exposes the FDIC to greater risk. A smaller proportional loss on assets would more readily bring on bankruptcy, raising the probability of an FDIC payout. Bank regulations try to prevent this by imposing minimum capital (net worth) ratios that all banks must meet to be considered sound.

The issue of adequate bank capitalization has been hotly debated and is the subject of often bitter dispute between bankers and regulators.[9] It should be. If capital regulations did not constrain bankers (that is lower their expected return on equity), they wouldn't complain, but neither would the regulation be successfully counteracting the distortive effects of FDIC insurance.

Bank holding company permissible activities

In some other countries, banks are closely affiliated with a myriad of financial and non-financial firms via holding companies or overlapping ownership and management. In the US, Congress has limited bank holding companies to activities 'so closely related to banking as to be a proper incident thereto' (Bank Holding Company Act, 1970 Amendments). While there may be other reasons for these limitations, bank safety is a prime concern. To allow banks to become closely affiliated with firms in non-banking lines of commerce, the regulators fear, would expose the banking subsidiary to unacceptable risks of at least two sorts. First, the public might confuse a troubled holding company or non-bank subsidiary firm with the bank itself and then withdraw deposits and cause a liquidity crisis. Second, the bank may extend unsound loans to other holding company subsidiary firms in an effort to forestall disaster in the non-banking firms.

Interest rate ceilings

Bank competition for selected types of deposit funds has also been limited by regulation over the years. Congress prohibited the payment of interest on demand deposit (checking) accounts in 1933, and it empowered the Federal Reserve to set maximum permissible rates payable on time and savings deposits (Regulation Q). The initial intent of both these rules was to limit bank risk-taking. Banks were viewed as bidding against one another for deposit funds, then being forced to invest in risky assets in order to earn enough to cover their deposit costs.

Over the past ten or fifteen years, financial markets have developed an impressive array of devices aimed at circumventing Regulation Q. Faced with this new, unregulated competition, banks often become unable to acquire deposits in sufficient quantity at the regulated rates. While deposit rate regulation was introduced as a means of limiting bank risk exposure, it has instead become a threat to bank stability. This development was recognized by Congress when it voted in March 1980 to eliminate Regulation Q ceilings by 1986. (This process has already begun, under the control of the Federal Depository Institution Deregulation Committee.)

It is impossible to identify precisely how much these various regulations reduce the additional risks banks take in response to their deposit insurance. The key point, however, is that insurance and regulation are *linked* activities. If one side is subjected to reforms – take deregulation as an example – then unless something is done with the present insurance scheme society will be left to bear more risk (see Reforming deposit insurance, p. 264).

Conclusion

Bankers benefit substantially from fixed-rate FDIC insurance, which allows them to procure a large supply of funds at a low (that is, riskless) interest rate regardless of their assets' riskiness. Severing the connection between portfolio risk and deposit costs leads banks to undertake risks they otherwise wouldn't, secure in the knowledge that they get all the benefits of a good outcome while suffering less than all of any losses that may occur. To counteract this distortion, regulators impose portfolio restrictions, capital standards, and so forth on insured banks as a means of limiting the risk FDIC is forced to insure against. These regulations limit bankers' freedom and may reduce bank profits. Yet neither of these observations implies that the attendant regulations are socially bad, only that they are effective. If bankers felt no pain from regulators' actions, the regulations could not be affecting bank behavior!

Is there too much corrective regulation? This is a very difficult question to answer. It requires a careful comparison of society's losses (in terms of lower output) from the restrictions placed on bank decision-making versus the social benefits of a safer financial environment. To date, no one has made much of an attempt to grapple with this big issue. Until some answers are generated, it will be quite difficult to say how much regulation (or deregulation) is ideal from society's point of view.

ANNEX

Bank Examinations and Capital Adequacy

On-site FDIC bank examinations play an important part in identifying bank behavior that is considered overly risky. An examination evaluates many dimensions of bank operations, including liquidity, earnings, and the quality of management. In addition, asset quality and capital adequacy receive considerable attention:

> One of the most important aspects of the examination process is the evaluation of loans for, in large measure, it is the quality of a bank's loans which determines the risk to depositors. (*FDIC Manual of Examination Policy*, Section H, p. 1.)

> Some qualifications are necessary, but in general the degree of protection afforded depositors is closely related to the strength of a bank's capital position. For this reason many important phases of the bank examination procedure have as their purpose the determination and analysis of a bank's capital. (*FDIC Manual of Examination Policy*, Section D, p. 1.)

Examiners' loan quality evaluations can heavily influence the level of capital considered adequate for a particular bank.

Loan losses are a routine, if unpleasant, aspect of any bank's operations. In recognition of this, bankers carry a Loan Loss Reserve in the capital account. This reserve represents the banker's best guess of the loans on her books that will not be repaid. If this evaluation is accurate, the bank's balance sheet fairly reflects the value of its assets. (In particular, bank capital – the residual difference between assets and liabilities – is correctly recorded on the balance sheet.) If the Loan Loss Reserve understates likely future losses, however, the bank's books tend to overvalue loan assets and hence overstate the true capital position.

The loan examination process constitutes an effort to verify the adequacy of the Loan Loss Reserve account. The loan examiner generally selects a subset of the bank's loan population for scrutiny emphasizing relatively large loans and those with recent payment problems. Some examined loans will (usually) be criticized by the examiner, reflecting her opinion that the loan is somewhat unlikely to be repaid in full. In other words, the examiner does not consider the asset to be of bankable quality. The examiners take the bank's reported (book) capital position and *subtract out* a portion of the loans that have been criticized. If the bank's Loan Loss Reserve was at least sufficient to cover the examiner's estimated likely loan losses, there is no change in the bank's reported capital position. Otherwise, the bank's balance sheet overstated the true degree of protection afforded the depositors (and the FDIC). Examiners may require that some loans be written off, or that the Loan Loss Reserve account be increased through retained earnings. In any case, the regulator's determination of bank capital adequacy will be based on the reported book capital *adjusted for* the examiner's estimate of likely loan and security losses.

This connection between loan evaluation and capital adequacy can sometimes make the bank examination process acrimonious. Examiners have the primary power to criticize a bank's activities as too risky, and this criticism affects the bank's need for additional capital. Since more capital reduces the expected rate of return to equity holders, bank management views this process as intrusive. It is. Banks and FDIC hold differing views on the issue of bank risk-taking. On-site examinations constitute a prime tool by which FDIC monitors and controls its insured banks' activities.

Reforming Deposit Insurance

If the existing deposit insurance system requires such a myriad of restrictive bank regulations, why not change the system and remove the regulatory burden? Either of two significant reforms would eliminate some of the current system's distortions, but each would be difficult to implement in practice.

First, Federal deposit insurance could be eliminated entirely. Eliminating FDIC would strengthen the impact of market forces on bank risk-taking decisions, allowing at least some bank regulations to be removed. At the same time, however, depositors would find themselves exposed to more risk, and they would have to evaluate their investment decisions more carefully. Imposing this burden on small depositors seems to contradict the initial spirit of the Federal insurance programme. A middle course here would reduce the extent of FDIC coverage, e.g. from $100,000 back down to $20,000 or $10,000. Deposit costs would then reflect bankers' asset decisions more closely, while small savers, for whom investment and information evaluation costs are presumably most burdensome, would still benefit from insurance protection.

A second possible reform would be to make the insurance premium paid by banks vary according to the riskiness of their portfolios. (The Federal Savings and Loan Insurance Corporation has recently announced its intention to pursue a policy of this sort.) Just as automobile insurance companies charge more to insure unsafe drivers, riskier banks would pay a higher price for insurance than safe banks. With a perfectly accurate method of assessing the risk of a bank's portfolio, a variable premium system would mimic the private market. It would give bankers the socially correct incentives to undertake risks while extending the benefits of Federal deposit insurance to bank depositors. The problem here is that any practical system for measuring risk would be imperfect, overestimating the risk of some activities while underestimating others. (This is also true of other existing types of insurance.) If bankers and their customers felt a particular activity was really less risky than FDIC did, the bankers would find it unprofitable to undertake these investments because the expected return would not cover deposit costs plus the variable insurance premium. Alternatively, an FDIC premium that bankers considered too low for some particular type of risk would generate too much risk-taking of this sort.

Distortions to bank asset portfolios would not disappear under a variable rate system, but they probably would be smaller. Some existing bank regulations could be modified accordingly or eliminated. Offsetting these gains, however, would be the increased complexity of determining an appropriate FDIC premium rate for each bank. Accurately comparing the effects of a risk-related FDIC premium v. the current system is a formidable task but one that bears further study.

APPENDIX 15.1

A Simple Example of How FDIC Insurance can Distort Bank Risk-Bearing Incentives

This example is set in a highly simplified world. The bank finances its asset acquisitions by issuing a single type of deposit liability, and it has no net worth. Uncertainty is limited to the fact that either of two possible states of the world may occur in the future. Bank assets return their higher value in the good state, and their lower value in the bad state. At the time investments are made, each future state of the world is considered equally likely to occur. (That is, each has a probability equal to ½.)

Example 15.1: Determining the deposit rate and equity market value
This first example serves to illustrate the basic components of bank valuation. Assume the bank buys a one-period asset today for $900. If state number 1 occurs, the bank's asset will be worth $1,000, while in the second possible state the asset's value will be $2,000. The bank finances itself by issuing a deposit liability of $900, giving it an initial balance sheet:

Assets	Liabilities
900	900
	....
	0 net worth

At the end of one time period the bank will collect on its assets, pay off the depositors, and go out of business. The riskless market rate of interest is 6 per cent per year.

The value of the firm's equity can be calculated from the expected value of its future profits assuming *risk neutrality* on the part of the owners and depositors.[10] First consider the depositors. Even in the bad future state of the world the bank will be able to pay off depositors their principal plus interest at the riskless rate ($954). The deposit rate will therefore be 6 per cent. Risk-neutral owners will value the bank's equity at the net present value of expected future earnings after interest payments. Ignoring the discount rate:

$$\text{Value of equity} = \tfrac{1}{2}\,(\text{profit in state 1}) + \tfrac{1}{2}\,(\text{profit in state 2})$$

$$= \tfrac{1}{2}\,(1{,}000 - 900(1.06)) + \tfrac{1}{2}\,(2{,}000 - 900(1.06))$$

$$= \$546$$

In other words, the right to receive this bank's (uncertain) end-of-period profits would be worth $546.

Example 15.2: Risk-bearing with deposit insurance
Now consider the situation where the firm has the opportunity to buy an additional asset for $300. The firm will have to borrow $300 to acquire the asset, resulting in the balance sheet:

Assets	Liabilities
900	900
+300	+300
	....
	0 net worth

The new asset will be worth \$100 in state number 1 and \$500 in state number 2, giving it an expected return of 0 per cent (½ (100) + ½ (500) = 300, the asset's purchase price). No one should wish to purchase such an asset when the riskless market rate is 6 per cent. Nonetheless, it will be shown that a bank whose deposits are insured at a fixed premium would be willing to buy this asset.

At the end of the period, the firm's total assets will be worth \$1,100 (\$1,000 for the initial asset plus \$100 for the new one) in state number 1 and \$2,500 (the initial \$2,000 plus \$500) in state number 2. Bankruptcy will result if state number 1 occurs: depositors will not be paid interest (or even repaid all the principal). FDIC insurance is now valuable to the bank's owners. Suppose FDIC promises to repay the bank's depositors in full (including interest) in return for a \$1.00 premium (0.083 per cent of the \$1,200 deposits). Insured depositors will lend to the bank at the riskless rate of 6 per cent, making the value of equity:

$$= \tfrac{1}{2}(1{,}100 - 1{,}200(1.06) - 1) + \tfrac{1}{2}(2{,}500 - 1{,}200(1.06) - 1)$$

$$= \tfrac{1}{2}(1{,}100 - 1{,}273) + \tfrac{1}{2}(2{,}500 - 1{,}273)$$

Since expenses in the first state of the world are greater than earnings, the owners expect to receive no return for this period and will default on their obligations – that is, the firm will be declared bankrupt. (Because of deposit insurance, however, all deposits will still be paid off.) Even though the firm is worth nothing if state number 1 occurs, owners will bid a positive price for the firm's equity because profits will be positive if state number 2 occurs:

$$\text{Value of equity} = \tfrac{1}{2}(0) + \tfrac{1}{2}(2{,}500 - 1{,}273)$$

$$= \$613.50$$

With deposits insured by FDIC, the owners of the bank will undertake to buy the new asset because the value of their equity rises from \$546 (without the new asset) to \$613.50. Why does this occur? Because the owners receive *all the profits* in the good state of the world but *have only limited liability* in the bad state of the world.

Example 15.3: Risk-bearing without deposit insurance
Now suppose the bank's deposits are not insured. If the bad state of the world occurs, the firm goes bankrupt and the depositors as a group receive only $1,100 for their $1,200 of deposits. To compensate for this possible loss, the depositors must be offered a rate of return (R) in the good state of the world high enough to make their *expected* return on deposits equal to or greater than the risk-free rate. That is, for deposits of $1,200, depositors must be promised a rate R such that:

$$\tfrac{1}{2}\,(1{,}100) + (1{,}200\,(1 + R)) \geq 1{,}200\,(1 + 0.06)$$

$$R \geq 20.3 \text{ per cent}$$

Risk-neutral depositors would accept a promised return of 20.3 per cent; risk-averse depositors would demand more.

With this higher promised deposit rate, the value of the bank's equity after it purchases the $300 asset will be:

$$= \tfrac{1}{2}\,(0) + \tfrac{1}{2}\,(2{,}500 - 1{,}200\,(1 + 0.203))$$

$$= \$528.02$$

Undertaking this new investment without deposit insurance therefore would make the firm's value drop below its initial value ($546). The bank would not invest in the asset, which is the socially correct decision.

These examples could be made considerably more realistic by increasing the number of possible future states, introducing positive net worth and several classes of depositors, allowing risk-averse depositors or bank owners, and so forth. None of these changes would alter the basic conclusions. The important implication of this example is that a bank *will undertake risky projects with a fixed-premium insurance program that it would not normally undertake*. The bank has an incentive to take on greater risks because it does not pay FDIC a premium that fully reflects the *social* cost of the bank's risk taking.

Suggested Readings

The notion that FDIC insurance distorts bank risk-taking decisions has been developed by John H. Kareken and Neil Wallace (1978), 'Deposit insurance and bank regulation: a partial-equilibrium exposition', *Journal of Business*, (July) pp. 413–38; Robert C. Merton (1978), 'On the cost of deposit insurance when there are surveillance costs', *Journal of Business*, (July) pp. 439–52; and William F. Sharpe (1978), 'Bank capital adequacy, deposit insurance and security values', *Journal of Financial and Quantitative Analysis*, (Nov.), pp. 701–18.

Reasons for Federal provision of deposit insurance and alternative ways of setting premiums for that insurance are discussed in Kenneth E. Scott and

Thomas Mayer (1971), 'Risk and regulation in banking: some proposals for Federal deposit insurance reform', *Stanford Law Review*, (May), pp. 857–902.

Notes

1 Although this article explicitly discusses only commercial banks, the same arguments apply to savings and loan associations, mutual savings banks, and credit unions.

2 Note that banks with some accounts in excess of $100,000 are paying for insurance coverage their depositors won't receive. Since larger banks more often have large customers, the effective cost of their deposit insurance (per insured deposit dollar) appears higher than it is for small banks.

3 An example of this connection between FDIC and the general public occurred in 1974. During that spring and summer, Franklin National Bank was in serious danger of failing. Rather than close the bank and pay off its insured depositors, FDIC wanted to find another bank to acquire Franklin National. To keep the troubled bank afloat while FDIC sought a suitable merger partner, the Federal Reserve Bank of New York extended sizeable loans at a below-market interest rate. This action cost the Federal Reserve Bank an estimated $25 million. Since Federal Reserve operating surpluses are returned to the Treasury, US taxpayers ultimately paid this cost. See Joseph F. Sinkey (1976), 'The collapse of Franklin National Bank of New York', *Journal of Bank Research*, (Summer), pp. 113–22.

4 Some insurance companies write policies for people without requiring a physical. This insurance is more expensive (has a higher premium) because the company knows it will suffer adverse selection. Healthy people are more likely to purchase lower-cost policies that require a physical.

5 Whether depositors do or can evaluate bank risk is an entirely different issue, related to the initial reasons for Federal government provision of deposit insurance. See Ian McCarthy (1980), 'Deposit insurance: theory and practice', IMF *Staff Papers* (Sept.) pp. 578–600.

6 A large school of thought contends that FDIC in fact has extended insurance coverage to all bank liability holders by its decisions to arrange mergers (technically called a 'purchase and assumption') rather than closing failed institutions outright. See David B. Humphrey (1976), '100% deposit insurance: what would it cost?', *Journal of Bank Research*, (Autumn), pp. 192–8; or Gary Leff (1976), 'Should Federal deposit insurance be 100 per cent?', *Bankers Magazine*, (Summer) pp. 23–30.

7 From the factory owner's own (selfish) perspective, spewing soot is the optimal decision. It maximizes her profits. Suppose, however, it would cost $10 per year to eliminate the soot, which would make the neighbours feel $15 better off. The *socially* optimal decision would be to eliminate the soot. Pollution control laws are intended to bring about the desired result. Since the factory owner finds it privately more profitable to pollute, her profits will decline as a result of enforcing these regulations. (If profits do not decline, either the regulations are ineffective or the factory owner was operating inefficently to begin with.) Despite the factory owner's loss, the society as a whole – factory plus neighbours – will be made better off under a proper set of pollution restrictions.

8 Not surprisingly, some of the futures exchanges are most critical of these regulations.

9 For more on this subject, see Ronald Watson (1974), 'Insuring some progress in the bank capital hassle', *Business Review*, Federal Reserve Bank of Philadelphia, (July), pp. 3–17; or Robert Taggart (1977), 'Regulatory Influences on Bank Capital', *New England Economic Review* (Sept.) pp. 37–46.

10 A person is risk neutral if she will take a fair bet. For example, consider a game where the dealer flips a coin, promising to pay the player $1.00 if heads come up, but nothing in the event of tails. A risk-neutral person would pay up to 50c to play this game – the expected (mean) value of the winnings. A risk-averse person would pay less than 50c; a risk-loving person would pay (a maximum of) more than 50c.

16 The Case Against Risk-Related Deposit Insurance Premiums*

* Reprinted with permission from *Housing Finance Review*, July 1983, vol. 2, no. 3, (pp. 253–63)

PAUL M. HORVITZ

Horvitz holds the Judge James A. Elkins Chair of Banking and Finance at the University of Houston. This paper has benefited from discussions with George Kaufman, Edward Kane, Fischer Black, Tim Campbell, and Stanley Silverberg. Preliminary versions of part of this paper appeared in the *American Banker*, May 26, 1983, and as testimony before the Committee on Banking, Housing, and Urban Affairs, US Senate, 21 June, 1983. The views expressed in this paper are those of the author and are not intended to reflect the views or policy of the Federal Home Loan Bank Board.

Economic theorists have long argued that a system whereby insured institutions pay deposit insurance premiums based on their riskiness would be more efficient and equitable. This view neglects the fact that risk to the deposit insurance system is more a function of the amount of loss suffered in a failure than of the chance of failure. If insured institutions are closed before their net worth is totally depleted, losses to the insurance system are small, regardless of the riskiness of individual institutions.

Relating insurance premiums to risk requires a means of measuring risk, which does not now exist. The present system, while not ideal, is difficult to improve upon.

Introduction

All savings and loans insured by the Federal Savings and Loan Insurance Corporation (FSLIC) pay deposit insurance premiums at the same percentage of their total deposits (1/12 of 1%). All institutions insured by the Federal Deposit Insurance Corporation (FDIC) pay insurance premiums at the same rate (1/12 of 1% of assessable deposits). Economists have long criticized this system as failing to measure up to two basic economic criteria: equity and efficiency. The equity argument is rather obvious. Some institutions operate in a manner that makes it very unlikely they will ever generate loss to the insurance agency. Yet these safe and sound institutions must pay for deposit insurance at the same rate as institutions that take much greater risks and that have accumulated a portfolio of high-risk assets. It is unfair that the former institutions should have to pay for the losses to be caused by the latter.

The argument against the present flat-rate premium system on efficiency grounds is somewhat more subtle, but is more important to the ultimate soundness of the deposit insurance system. It is easiest to see the argument by considering the manner in which competitive deposit markets would operate in a world without deposit insurance. Since depositors clearly prefer safety, they would choose among competing institutions on the basis of their soundness.

Riskier institutions would be able to attract deposits only by paying higher interest rates. The increased cost of funds to risky institutions would be a market discipline that would reduce incentives toward excessive risk-taking.

Federal deposit insurance reduces or eliminates that market discipline. Depositors no longer care about the soundness of their bank or thrift – in case of adversity they look to the deposit insurance system and not to the resources of their particular institution. The institutions can now raise funds at a rate commensurate with their riskless status, and they face no market penalty for investing in risky assets or engaging in risky activities.[1]

Deposit insurance actually provides an incentive for increased risk-taking. Since the insured institution does not pay increased deposit insurance premiums or increased interest costs if it adopts a risky posture, the owners keep all the increased returns that may be associated with increased risk. On the other hand, if the risks turn out badly and the institution fails, the costs are largely borne by the insurance agency (though the owners would lose the amount of their equity investment in the institution).

These considerations have led some to argue for the elimination of federal deposit insurance. That argument may have validity in a world of perfect information, competitive markets, zero transaction costs, and complete confidence in the wisdom of government economic policy, but it is not satisfactory as a real-world policy solution. Deposit insurance was instituted to deal with instability in the financial system, specifically runs on banks and a resulting decline in the money supply. During the 1920s and early 1930s it was possible for a sound financial institution to suffer a sudden withdrawal of deposits in response to rumors or doubts about its financial condition. This could result from the failure of a nearby or related institution, coupled with an important asymmetry in the costs of participating in a run: it costs very little to withdraw funds from a bank on the basis of a rumor that turns out to be false; but, without deposit insurance, the cost of not withdrawing funds quickly from a bank truly about to fail is very large. Even the informed depositor who knows that his bank is sound may be well advised to participate in the run before the actions of other depositors bring down the bank. Given the relative costs and returns involved, participating in a run is not irrational.

Federal deposit insurance has worked, and this problem has been resolved. Runs on financial institutions are rare events even when substantial financial problems are known to exist. Thrift institutions have been able to continue operating in a stable manner despite general knowledge of the erosion of their net worth.

The federal deposit insurance agencies have traditionally dealt with these efficiency and perverse incentives problems by means of supervision of institutions and a comprehensive set of regulations designed to limit risk. Through the early years of deposit insurance, bankers were generally a conservative group of businessmen, with recent memories of the Great Depression. As tendencies toward risk-taking developed over time, the insurance system was protected by increased regulatory powers. Although its importance was not fully recognized at the time, deposit interest-rate ceilings represented a substantial protection to the insurance system. Interest-rate ceilings limited the ability of risky institutions to attract funds. Such institutions were generally limited to the funds they could obtain locally, though there were some instances of uses of money brokers to obtain non-local funds.[2]

The end of interest rate ceilings means increased risk for the deposit insurance systems. This is not because any significant number of institutions will be irresponsible in setting their rates (the traditional argument in favor of interest rate ceilings as a safety device). Rather, the end of interest rate ceilings means that an institution that is inclined to take greater than normal risks can obtain all the funds it wants by simply paying a modest premium over going market rates (perhaps by use of brokers who can easily sell insured deposits on a national basis).

A trend toward deregulation means that the deposit insurance system must protect itself by other than the traditional supervisory and regulatory means. It is in this context that consideration of risk-related deposit insurance premiums, long relegated to discussion in academic journals, has become a matter of serious policy debate. Economists have argued that the tendency of deposit insurance to remove market discipline could be prevented by pricing deposit insurance so that risky institutions pay higher premiums than conservative ones. It is important to note that risk-related premiums not only resolve the 'equity' problem (it seems fair that risky institutions should be charged more for deposit insurance), but deal with the efficiency problem because an institution has less incentive to engage in risky activities if those activities result in higher insurance premiums.

It has generally been accepted that risk-related premiums represent an ideal solution to the problem in principle, and most of the discussion has focused on the question of feasibility or implementation. Proponents of risk-related premiums argue that a good system for measuring risk can be developed, or, as in the Federal Home Loan Bank Board (FHLBB) report, *Agenda for Reform*, stress that 'a perfect measurement system is not necessary for risk-sensitive premiums to be useful' (Federal Home Loan Bank Board, 1983, p. 99). While admitting the considerable attraction of such a system, and recognizing that the trend toward deregulation may conflict with the soundness of deposit insurance, this paper argues that there are problems in the theory, as well as in implementation of a system of risk-related insurance premiums. This paper is not intended to represent a balanced evaluation of the advantages and disadvantages of risk-related premiums – it focuses on the case against risk-related premiums because the case in favor has been well presented in a number of articles.[3]

Risk of Failures Distinguished from Insurance Risk

Before we get to the problem of measuring risk for a risk-related insurance premium system, we must define risk. Most advocates of risk-related premiums have been imprecise as to the meaning of risk in this context, usually assuming an identity between risk of bank failure and risk to the insurance system. That definition would be valid if deposit insurance were like life insurance. For a life insurance company, risk of death of the insured and risk of loss to the insurance company are identical – when the insured dies, the insurer must pay the contractual amount of the insurance policy. But that analogy is not a valid one. If we must use analogies with other forms of insurance (and in discussing deposit insurance such analogies are more often misleading than helpful), it is more apt to consider fire insurance. Risk to the insurer is not the same as the risk of fire. Other variables, such as how quickly the fire is detected, whether there are sprinklers, and how quickly the fire department responds, affect the extent of the damage and the cost to the insurer. Small fires quickly extinguished that do less damage than the deductible in the policy may be very disturbing and expensive to the insured, but represent no loss to the insurance company.

Advocates of risk-related premiums point out that variables of this type are measurable, and insurance companies use available information to set premiums in accord with risk. Life insurance companies charge different premiums based on age and (up to now, at least) sex; auto insurance companies charge higher premiums to young men and to drivers with poor records; and fire insurance companies charge premiums related to the combustibility of the property insured and the quality and availability of fire protection. But deposit insurance is different from these other types of insurance in a fundamental way. The deposit insurance agencies have control over the extent of their losses when an insured event (a failure) is imminent. The losses of the deposit insurance system are not closely related to the riskiness of insured institutions. Losses are more a function of the timing of the closing of a failed bank or savings institution.

Most bank failures do not occur instantaneously, but rather result from losses over time. If the FDIC is able to monitor a bank's condition and closes it when its capital gets to zero (or slightly before), the FDIC suffers no loss regardless of how risky the bank was. The life insurance company cannot cancel the policy when the insured is on his death bed.

The key point in this analysis is that if insured institutions are operating with positive real net worth, and the insurance agency is able to monitor their condition, then the risk of loss to the insurance agency is low, *regardless of the riskiness of individual institutions*. The records of the FDIC and FSLIC (Federal Savings and Loan Insurance Corporation) show large losses only when these conditions are not met – i.e. when institutions are allowed to operate without capital or where fraud prevents the detection of insolvency.

Over its fifty-year history the FDIC has lost very little except under these circumstances. The largest loss suffered by the FDIC in insurance of commercial banks was probably incurred in the failure of United States National Bank of San Diego, though the Penn Square of recent Tennessee cases may turn out to be more costly. There have been allegations of massive fraud in all these cases. The banks had substantially negative net worth at the time they were closed. It should be noted that fraud is not the major cause of bank failures, but it may be the major source of FDIC commercial bank losses.[4]

The failure of Franklin National Bank is an interesting contrast with these cases. Franklin took great risks in its lending policy, branch expansion, and foreign exchange transactions. Mismanagement of the bank led to failure, but fraud was not involved. The condition of the bank was followed closely by the Comptroller, and as its financial position deteriorated, the regulatory agencies worked out plans for handling the situation. Solving the problem took time, during which the condition of the bank worsened. Nevertheless, the bank was closed close enough to the point of zero capital that the FDIC losses in that case will be near zero.

One factor that helped keep down the FDIC losses in Franklin is that Franklin had a very large retail branch structure throughout Long Island that represented an attractive franchise to be acquired by the bank that took over the assets and liabilities of the failed bank. Because of that, several potential merger partners offered substantial premiums to gain that franchise. Other failed banks might have operated with less risk than Franklin but ended up costing the FDIC more because their location was less attractive to potential bidders. This is an important factor in the risk to the insurer. It is not clear that advocates of risk-related premiums would endorse higher insurance premiums for banks in less desirable markets. Yet an actuarially sound system of risk-related premiums must take this factor into consideration.

The experience of the FDIC with mutual savings bank failures, and the FSLIC with savings and loans, illustrates a different aspect of the determinants of risk to the insurance system. Until very recently, the FDIC and FSLIC incurred very little loss from failures of thrift institutions. Very large losses have been recognized in 1981–3. Nearly all the thrift institution failures of recent years have been due to interest-rate risk – an increase in interest rates damaging to institutions with long-maturity assets and short-term liabilities.

The recent thrift institution problems were not due to a sudden and permanent increase in interest rates in 1981. Interest rates have shown a rising trend since the mid 1940s. As distinct from other business firms, depository institutions have been allowed to carry assets (and liabilities) on their balance sheets at values that may be substantially higher than their true economic value or their market value. The upward trend in interest rates had made many thrifts insolvent on a market-value basis by 1966. If thrift institutions had been closed by the FSLIC and the FDIC in 1966, 1969 or 1973, as their economic net worth disappeared, the losses to the insurance system would have been negligible.

This comment is not intended as a criticism of the policy followed in the 1960s and 1970s, nor as a recommendation as to what policy should be today; but a policy of merging or liquidating thrift institutions as rising interest rates eroded their net worth would have minimized the losses of the insurance agencies. There were good reasons to avoid large-scale closings of thrift institutions in the 1960s: concern over disruption of the mortgage market, fear of the effect on depositor and market confidence, fear of adverse macro economic effects, and the perceived benefits of delay in facing up to the problem (interest rates might come down and the problem would go away, or even if the problem got worse in future years, at least it would be a different set of agency heads who would have to wrestle with it). The decision to temporize in the 1960s, with principal reliance on interest-rate ceilings, may have been correct or incorrect, but that is not relevant for the present discussion. What is important to recognize is that the outcome of policy decisions to allow insolvent institutions to continue operating, with the possibility of their becoming more and more insolvent, cannot be factored into an analysis of the riskiness of individual institutions in the setting of insurance premiums.

Consider two thrift institutions with equal probability of becoming insolvent. One will be liquidated promptly as its net worth reaches zero, so that loss to the insurer will be zero. The other will be allowed to continue in operation even though net worth is zero or negative (perhaps because of a policy determination or because the accounting system in use does not force recognition of the losses that have occurred). If the second institution suffers additional losses before it is liquidated, the ultimate loss to the insurer may be large.[5] Would it be reasonable to charge the second institution a higher insurance premium than the first, since it poses a greater risk to the insurer?

These considerations lead me to conclude that the case for risk-related premiums is flawed on theoretical grounds. But even if risk-related premiums are desirable in principle, it would not be possible to implement such a system in a way that would be actuarially sound. While the FHLBB report argues that risk-related premiums can promote economic efficiency even if the system is not actuarially perfect, it is possible that such a system could result in a greater distortion of the allocation of resources than the present system.

Implementation Problems

The key problem with risk-related premiums, of course, is the difficulty of measuring risks *ex ante*, i.e. before they result in losses. If we were designing a risk-related premium structure five years ago, it is unlikely that we would have recognized loans to Mexico as particularly risky assets. It is unlikely we would have recognized the risk inherent in many loans secured by drilling rigs or proven oil reserves. We might not even have recognized the enormous risk in buying energy loans from experienced and active originators of such loans. More important, if the system was designed ten years ago we might have failed to recognize the risk inherent in the asset-liability mismatches of commercial banks. There were bank management textbooks published in the mid 1970s that made no reference to interest-rate risk.[6]

If the riskiness of certain activities or assets is recognized by the premium system only *after* they have resulted in loss, then the premium structure has not served its purposes of inhibiting risk-taking. If high premiums were assessed on Mexican loans today, no such lending would be inhibited, because no such new loans are being made. No bank is buying loans from Penn Square today, so imposing higher deposit insurance premiums on banks that did buy them in the past can only represent a punishment for a wrong decision and not a contribution to a more efficient allocation of resources.

These difficulties are particularly severe when we attempt to measure credit risk. It is admittedly easier to measure exposure to interest-rate risk, and it is generally believed that interest-rate risk is the most serious threat to survival of thrift institutions. The FHLBB report defines interest-rate risk in terms of the average duration of the institution's assets and liabilities: 'When the durations of an S & L's assets and liabilities of equal market value are not equal, fluctuations in interest rates will cause fluctuations in the market value of the institution . . . The greater the mismatch, the greater the risk exposure' (Federal Home Loan Bank Board, 1983, p. 91). This is a valid definition in concept, and the FHLBB report makes a good case for a means of approximating a measurement of duration mismatch in practice, though many will find the methodology impractical for many savings institutions.

There are a number of problems in the application of duration mismatch as the basis for a risk-related premium structure. Perhaps these problems can be resolved, as advocates claim, but so far no one has worked out the details of how these problems can be overcome in a manner that will promote efficiency. Consider, for example, two thrifts with differing capital ratios and different duration mismatches. For a given increase in interest rates, the institution with the greater mismatch and greater capital may appear stronger, i.e. a higher resulting ratio of capital to assets. However, if a greater increase in interest rates is assumed, that institution may pose a greater risk of loss to the insurance system. How do we determine which should pay the higher insurance premium?

Another problem with the duration approach is that portfolio duration does not change in a constant manner with the passage of time. Consider the thrift with assets and liabilities of equal average duration. If that institution does nothing to change its portfolio, it is likely that after, say, six months it will no longer have a matched position. Maintaining a matched duration takes constant management (unless the portfolio consists entirely of zero coupon instruments). An appropriate premium structure would penalize the portfolio that will have a greater tendency to move away from the matched position or that will require greater management.

Use of maturity rather than duration would be operationally much simpler, particularly for smaller institutions. But such an approach is not only conceptually less sound, it may promote perverse actions. An institution that wants to take some interest-rate risk, and faces a premium structure that penalizes *maturity* mismatch, can achieve whatever degree of interest-rate risk it wishes by moving toward assets with shorter maturities but longer duration.

The latter consideration suggests a problem with any system that covers only part of the risk faced by depository institutions. Interest-rate risk may indeed by the principal risk to be faced by thrift institutions in the future. It may be possible, despite the implementation problems discussed here, to design a premium structure that appropriately accounts for interest-rate risk. But the risk-prone management that faces a premium structure that inhibits taking interest-rate risk may simply shift towards greater credit risk. A risk-related deposit insurance premium that covers only some of the types of risk is vulnerable on this score. After all, finance theory tells us that there is a trade-off between risk and return, and institutions choose where they want to be on that risk-return frontier. If the problem is that financial institutions choose a position without recognizing the risk they are taking, then risk-related premiums are not necessary to push them toward a lower-risk position – they can simply be told about the risk.[7]

Implementation of risk-related premiums requires a decision as to the information base to be used for determining premiums. The supervisory agencies believe that the examination process is the best means of obtaining information on the financial condition of depository institutions (otherwise they would not undertake this very expensive effort). But there are problems in the use of examination data in setting premiums. Examinations are conducted at different dates and differing frequencies for each bank. Banks are examined, in some cases, at intervals as great as three years, so that premiums could be based on data that are significantly out of date. Because of the different times at which institutions are examined, economic conditions may be different. The institution examined at a trough in the economy will appear to be in worse condition than if it were examined in a period of prosperity. Moreover, the examination process necessarily involves subjective judgements. This poses no problem when the purpose is a general supervisory one of reviewing the condition of the institution, and when there is opportunity for examiner and management to negotiate on the actions to be taken in the future. That is less satisfactory when the judgement of the examiner directly results in increased costs of insurance.

This last point suggests the major disadvantage of using the examination process as the source of information for setting risk-related premiums. The examination process is now a more-or-less co-operative one, with a free exchange of information between management and examiner. The FDIC report recognizes this problem (Federal Deposit Insurance Corporation, 1983, p. II–9):

> Most bankers are willing to discuss their problems at an early stage with examiners but there are few, if any, monetary costs involved. They might be less open about potential problems in order to minimize insurance costs. If bankers became less free with their information, the examination process would have to be expanded significantly in order to remain effective. The costs of doing this would be very substantial.

In view of these problems, the FDIC recommends that any risk-related premium be based on information not collected during the examination process. The reasons for that conclusion are persuasive, but it seems paradoxical to refuse to use the information that the agency believes is actually the best for appraising the condition of insured institutions.

Any plan for risk-related premiums must confront the question of how great the variation in insurance premiums should be between institutions viewed as low-risk and those deemed to involve high risk to the insurance fund. This is a crucial matter, because a small differential is not likely to have a significant effect on management behavior, while too large a differential represents an implicit form of regulation.

The recommendations of both the FHLBB and FDIC for risk-related premiums involve relatively small differentials. The FHLBB proposal concerns the amount of rebate to be given from an additional insurance premium of 12½ basis points, while the FDIC proposal involves the rebate of 60% of the excess of premium income over FDIC expenses and losses. For FSLIC-insured institutions the amount at stake is a maximum of 12½ basis points, while under the FDIC plan the maximum is 4 or 5 basis points. It is not at all clear that differentials of this magnitude will have a significant effect in inhibiting risk-taking by a management so inclined. Yet it is also not clear that there is an actuarially sound basis for an *ex ante* differential larger than those numbers.[8]

Of course, if the insurance premium associated with a risky activity is large enough, it can clearly be effective in inhibiting such risk-taking. But that does not necessarily bring about a market-determined or efficient level of risk in the system. Risk-related insurance premiums can be a perfect substitute for all existing direct regulation. Suppose, for example, that all deposit interest-rate ceilings were eliminated, but that institutions paying over 5½% on passbook savings accounts were required to pay an additional insurance premium of 500 basis points on such deposits paying interest over 5½%. No institution could afford to offer more than 5½% on such accounts, and the effect would be no different from a continuation of a regulatory ceiling.

This would not be a problem if an actuarially correct system could be devised, but no one has really claimed that that is a realistic possibility. The real issue in instituting a risk-related insurance premium system, even if we accept the idea that such a scheme has merit in principle, is whether the sort of imperfect system that might be implemented will do more good than harm.

Conclusions

The logic behind relating insurance premiums to risk of loss is clearly compelling. Applying that concept to deposit insurance faces difficulties both in principle and in implementation. Risk of loss to the deposit insurance system is not the same as risk of failure of an insured institution. It is very difficult to measure risk of failure by a depository institution, let alone measure the implications of such failure for loss by the insurer.

Much of the literature on risk-related premiums consists of suggestions for conceptual approaches to resolving the problem that do not wrestle with the empirical problems of applying the concept to thousands of institutions.

Interest-rate risk is clearly more measurable than credit risk, but even there it is easier to determine that one institution faces greater risk than another, than it is to determine how great that risk is. Interest-rate risk has not been the major cause of commercial bank failures, so a system limited to interest-rate risk would not be useful for those institutions. Moreover, any risk-related system that covers only part of the risks faced by insured institutions will have effects that may be perverse as institutions tend to move toward greater assumption of risks not covered by the system. The broader powers now available to savings and loans suggest that credit risk may become a more important source of problems in the future than in the past.

A significant source of losses to the FDIC has been fraud (out of proportion to its importance as a cause of bank failures). Fraud is difficult to factor into a risk-related premium system since the perpetrator of the fraud has every incentive to prevent its discovery.[9]

It is impossible to conclude that risk-related insurance premiums are undesirable. A fair conclusion, however, is that no implementable system has yet been designed that promises to provide greater benefits than costs. More research on the implementation problem is clearly necessary before any system is adopted, but I am skeptical that this research will be fruitful.

References

Federal Deposit Insurance Corporation (1983), *Deposit Insurance in a Changing Environment. A report on deposit insurance to the Congress from the Federal Deposit Insurance Corporation* (Washington, DC).

Federal Home Loan Bank Board (1983), *Agenda for Reform. A report on deposit insurance to the Congress from the Federal Home Loan Bank Board* (Washington, DC).

Maisel, Sherman J. (ed.) (1981), *Risk and Capital Adequacy in Commercial Banks* (Chicago: University of Chicago Press for the National Bureau of Economic Research).

Mayer, Thomas (1965), 'A graduated deposit insurance plan', *Review of Economics and Statistics*, (Feb.), pp. 114–16.

Merton, Robert C. (1977), 'An analytic derivation of the cost of deposit insurance and loan guarantees: an application of modern option pricing theory', *Journal of Banking and Finance*, (June), pp. 3–11.

Notes

1 Some market pressure toward conservatism may emanate from other suppliers of funds. Stockholders may have a preference for conservative operations, and uninsured creditors clearly have such a preference. For an analysis of the effectiveness of market discipline from these sources, see Federal Home Loan Bank Board (1983, Section II).

2 It is interesting to note that interest-rate ceilings, though on the books since 1933, first

became binding in the mid 1960s at the time that banks and thrifts showed increasing proclivity to take risks.

3 Good examples of this literature are the following: Thomas Mayer (1965), Robert C. Merton (1977), Sherman J. Maisel (1981). For a useful survey of this literature and a bibliography see Federal Deposit Insurance Corporation (1983, Appendix A).

4 It would be economically sound, therefore, to charge a higher rate of insurance premium to banks that will engage in fraud and put out financial reports that do not represent the true condition of the bank. Such a system would prove hard to implement.

5 Additional loss is likely, since an institution operating with zero or negative net worth has every incentive to take excessive risks – if successful, the owners reap the benefits, if unsuccessful the insurance agency bears the loss.

6 There is a traditional banking nostrum about the dangers of 'borrowing short and lending long', but that warning concerned liquidity risk – the danger of not being able to sell long-term assets at the time of a run-off of deposits. The nineteenth-century banker who coined that phrase was not thinking of the effect of rising interest rates on the earnings of a liability-sensitive institution.

7 In a structure consisting of thousands of depository institutions, many of them quite small, it is likely that some management decisions are made in ignorance of information concerning risk that may be known to the regulatory agencies. A small difference in insurance costs may convey this information more effectively than a policy statement or a newsletter.

8 The insurance agencies have a bureaucratic motive to maintain a rather small differential. Since the amount of insurance premiums that different institutions pay is likely to be based on factors that are somewhat subjective or somewhat arbitrary, an institution faced with a very costly premium can be expected to argue or sue. To the extent that the penalty imposed on institutions deemed to be unusually risky is small, they may be inclined to pay rather than fight. It is not unreasonable for a supervisory agency to prefer to minimize conflict with the institutions it supervises, but that preference may conflict with the intent to develop a risk-related premium system that will be effective in inhibiting risk-taking.

9 One side-effect of a risk-related insurance system is that institutions would have incentive to conceal the extent of their risk-taking. Additional accounting and disclosure requirements will be necessary to overcome this tendency.

17 The Case Against Risk-related Deposit Insurance Premiums: a Contrary View*

* Reproduced with permission from *Housing Finance Review* July 1983, vol. 2, no. 3 (pp. 265–68)

PAUL T. PETERSON

This article was written while Peterson was a consultant for the Federal Home Loan Bank Board. He is now Chairman of the Twin Pine Federal Savings Association, Berkeley, California. The views expressed in this paper are those of the author, and are not intended to reflect the views or policy of the Federal Home Loan Bank Board.

The deregulation of financial institutions has created a renewed interest in the use of risk-related deposit insurance premiums, as a means of creating a market-like discipline to help control the insurer's risk. The preceding paper argues against the use of risk-related premiums. This paper responds to some of the arguments in that paper and concludes that the problems are not as serious as stated and recommends further analysis and movement toward the adoption of a risk-related premium system.

Introduction

In the preceding article, Professor Horvitz presents the emerging view of the case against risk-related insurance premiums (RRPs). His arguments are characteristic of those who oppose the recommendations of the studies conducted by the Federal Home Loan Bank Board (FHLBB) and the Federal Deposit Insurance Corporation (FDIC) recommending RRPs. The purpose of this paper is to argue that a good case does exist in favor of RRPs. This paper is not intended to represent the definitive debate but rather to serve as a counterbalance and a stimulus to policy debate and further analysis.

Horvitz cites problems with both the theory and the prospective implementation of an RRP system. As a result of these problems he concludes that 'the present system, while not ideal, is difficult to improve upon' (Horvitz, 1983, p. 253). This paper argues that the problems with both the theory and the prospective implementation of an RRP system are not as serious as presented. Furthermore, even if one accepts all of his arguments, it is not necessary to accept his conclusion.

Theory

In his theory section Horvitz centers his arguments around the distinction between the risk of failure and insurance risk. He concludes that 'if insured institutions are operating with positive real net worth, and the insurance agency is able to monitor their condition, then the risk of loss to the insurance agency is low, *regardless of the riskiness of individual institutions*' (Horvitz, 1983, p. 257). If the insurance agency is not able to monitor on a timely basis the real net worth of insured associations, however, then the risk of loss to the insurance agency is not low, and the risk of failure becomes the important consideration.

Arguments can be made suggesting that it is unfeasible for the insurance agency to monitor the real net worth of insured associations on a timely basis. First, it is necessary to understand what is meant by real net worth. Real net worth is obtained by adjusting book net worth for unrealized gains and losses determined from the market value of assets and liabilities, and by including intangibles that are not already represented on the balance sheet. Both of these adjustments cause problems in monitoring real net worth. Given the current financial structure at thrifts and some banks in periods of volatile interest rates, the real net worth of an association can change dramatically in a month or even a week. It would be very difficult to monitor and time closings in such a way to eliminate the loss to the insurance fund. Moreover, it may be inappropriate to close an association whose real net worth is temporarily negative due to an interest-rate spike that may soon abate, returning the association to solvency.

Intangible assets pose another problem to the determination of real net worth. Real net worth should include such intrinsic values as the desirability of a franchise and other measures of goodwill. Intangible assets are very difficult to quantify and thus make it difficult to determine real net worth.

Historically, net worth of financial institutions has been measured on a book value basis. However, an association that has a zero or slightly negative book net worth may have a substantial negative real net worth and can be very costly to the insurance fund. This has been especially true during the recent period of high interest rates. Thus given the apparent inability to measure and monitor real net worth, the probability of insolvency (risk of failure) becomes an important consideration. Furthermore, given that it is a legitimate function of federal deposit insurance to promote confidence by stepping in when failures occur, the risk of failure is an appropriate basis for an RRP system.

Implementation

As Horvitz states, it is impossible to design an RRP system that incorporates all of the risks associated with a financial institution. However, a system that addresses the major risks can do a lot to protect the insurer. Many proposals to date have suggested that an RRP system should be designed around three types of risk: credit risk, interest-rate risk, and capital. Horvitz has described some of the problems with measuring the various types of risk. He indicates that it is difficult to measure risks *ex ante* and that *ex post* measures of risk do not provide the proper incentives (Horvitz, 1983, p. 259). To the contrary, it is possible to create the desired incentives with an *ex post* measure of credit risk. If management had sufficient warning that premiums would vary at some point in the future depending upon the association's number of slow loans, an incentive effect would be created even though slow loans are an *ex post* measure of credit risk.

Interest-rate risk can also be measured in such a way to eliminate many of the problems posed in the paper. Horvitz indicates that potential discrepancies in risk-rating can result when measuring interest-rate risk at two different interest-rate levels. Though this is true, certain interest-rate levels pose greater risk than others. Generally higher interest rates pose a greater risk to the insurer. However, the low probability of certain rate scenarios allows the insurer to disregard such interest-rate levels. For example, the insurer would not need to insure against interest rates of, say, 100% because of the small probability of their occurrence. By comparing the associated risk and the expected probability of a particular level of interest rates, it would be possible to estimate the highest level against which the insurer desires protection. This interest-rate level is the one that would be used to estimate premiums. Alternatively, the insurer could decide some arbitrary extreme interest-rate scenario against which it wanted protection. A candidate for this scenario would be market rates at the peak of the last interest-rate cycle. Give an interest-rate scenario from one of the indicated methods, the insurer could develop an RRP system by using either duration analyses or perhaps the more easily understood current value calculations. In either event, associations would be given credit for capital.

If it was deemed an appropriate policy goal to protect solely against the largest immediate risk to the FSLIC, interest-rate risk, this would not necessarily result in a perverse allocation of resources as Horvitz supposes. The question is whether or not associations have made a conscious choice along the risk-return frontier. But as Horvitz suggests as a possibility, financial institutions have chosen their position without recognizing the risk they are taking. The evidence rests in the fact that, historically, very few associations have made any effort to measure or analyze their degree of interest-rate risk. The absence of such measures or analysis is analogous to making a loan without doing a credit check or without verifying the prospective borrower's income. Only with the aid of such analysis or appropriate procedures can an association choose its point on the risk-return frontier.

Even if the preceding argument is rejected, a shift from one risk to another may be desirable to the insurer. Interest-rate risk is systematic in that the effects of it hit all associations at the same time. If associations shifted risk as the result of a premium structure that penalized interest-rate risk, the result could be a dispersion of the risk in such a way that it would no longer be systematic. That is, one association may move into high-risk consumer lending, another into high-risk commercial lending, and so on. Such an outcome could clearly reduce the probability of coincident insolvencies, which have been a major problem for federal deposit insurers during the recent recession.

In his final arguments, Horvitz indicates that current RRP proposals will not create the desired incentive effect because of the small size of the differential. The current proposals do not pose a large enough differential to create the incentives that will impose the desired market discipline. However, this may be one of the greatest advantages of the current proposals. *Not only won't they create the desired incentives, but they also won't create any of the feared perverse incentives.* The current proposals serve two purposes. First, they represent what may be the very best means of 'telling' associations about their risk. Both managers and directors would be forced to face the interest-rate problem and make a conscious decision about risk and return. Second, they would serve as a test of the feasibility and desirability of an RRP that would have a large enough differential to provide the desired incentives.

Summary and Conclusion

There are strong theoretical arguments in favor of the development and implementation of an RRP system. Ideally, such a system would provide incentives similar to those provided by free-market discipline. Though there is disagreement about the ease of implementation and about the real effect of an implementable system, it is important that research and experimentation continue in this area. The real concern is what will happen in the absence of any attempt to develop a rational insurance system built around RRPs. As Horvitz states, 'a trend toward deregulation means that the deposit insurance system must protect itself by other than the traditional supervisory and regulatory means', and 'the end of interest-rate ceilings means increased risk for the deposit insurance systems' (Horvitz, 1983, p. 255).

To reject the viability of advisability of an RRP system without offering alternatives for providing a market discipline to control the insurer's risk, is to support by default a return to supervisory or regulatory control. Given the lack of apparent alternatives, an RRP system appears to be the best means of avoiding an otherwise inevitable and undesirable move towards re-regulation.

Reference

Horvitz, Paul M. (1983), 'The case against risk-related deposit insurance systems', *Housing Finance Review*, (July) vol. 2, no. 3, pp. 253–63.

Index

For Product Safety Concerns and Information please contact our EU representative GPSR@taylorandfrancis.com Taylor & Francis Verlag GmbH, Kaufingerstraße 24, 80331 München, Germany